LIFE, LIBERTY

AND THE PURSUIT OF

HAPPINESS,

VERSION 4.0

To Bill

With warm personal regards,

Gordan L Anderson

9/22/2009

PARAGON ISSUES IN PHILOSOPHY

PARAGON ISSUES IN PHILOSOPHY

THE PARAGON ISSUES
IN PHILOSOPHY SERIES

At colleges and universities, interest in the traditional areas of philosophy remains strong. Many new currents flow within them, too, but until recently many of these went largely unnoticed in undergraduate philosophy courses. The Paragon Issues in Philosophy Series responds to both perennial and newly influential concerns by bringing together a team of able philosophers to address the fundamental issues in philosophy today and to outline the state of contemporary discussion about them.

More than twenty volumes have been published; they are organized into three major categories. The first covers the standard topics—metaphysics, theory of knowledge, ethics, and political philosophy—stressing innovative developments in those disciplines. The second focuses on more specialized but still perennial concerns in the philosophies of science, religion, history, sport, and other areas. The third category explores work that relates philosophy to specialized fields such as feminist criticism, medicine, economics, technology, and literature.

The level of writing is aimed at undergraduate students who have little previous experience studying philosophy. The books provide brief but accurate introductions that appraise the state of the art in their fields and show how the history of thought about their topics has developed. Each volume is complete in itself but also complements others in the series.

Traumatic change characterizes recent decades. All of our pivotal issues involve philosophical questions. We are grateful for the work of Professor Frederick Sontag, now retired, for helping to design this series. It has now secured a place among philosophy departments throughout the English-speaking world. As we continue to locate and update new texts for this series, we hope that it will encourage the understanding needed to address a future that will be as complicated and problematic as it is promising.

John K. Roth
Claremont McKenna College

Gordon L. Anderson
Paragon House

Praise for the book:

"Smart, balanced, and wonderfully readable, *Life Liberty and the Pursuit of Happiness Version 4.0* is the perfect antidote to the malaise encompassing vast segments of American society. Gordon Anderson brings much needed balance to the debate over the changes that must occur if the United States is to regain its footing. No axe to grind—just a world-class researcher providing insights into some of the most vexing issues of the day."

—Robert Looney, Professor, Naval Postgraduate School

"This book does a wonderful job explaining how our evolving political-economic system has moved in a direction not intended by the framers of the U.S. Constitution."

—Gary Quinlivan, Dean, Alex G. McKenna School of Business, Economics, and Government, St. Vincent College

"Gordon Anderson continues his penetrating analysis of the American constitutional system, of the 'worms' that have infected it, and of a restored structure that will enable it to fill the noble mission the Founders intended."

—Morton A. Kaplan, Professor of Political Science Emeritus, University of Chicago

"Anderson advances bold strategies that emphasize personal responsibility, the common good, and realistic hope for the American future. Cogent, constructive, controversial—this significant book should be widely read."

—John K. Roth, Edward J. Sexton Professor Emeritus of Philosophy, Claremont McKenna College

"In his clearly articulated "report card" on the status of America's national "mission statement," Gordon Anderson seeks to accomplish through peaceful, critical, and surgical analysis the objectives advocated by Thomas Jefferson in his suggestion for the rewriting of the Constitution every couple of decades. Its lucid contents and writing style make it a most appropriate supplemental reader for university courses about government, public policy and political economy."

—Nicholas N. Kittrie, University Professor in Law, American University

GORDON L. ANDERSON

LIFE, LIBERTY

AND THE PURSUIT OF

HAPPINESS,

VERSION 4.0

PARAGON HOUSE ✦ ST. PAUL

PARAGON
ISSUES IN
PHILOSOPHY

First Edition 2009

Published in the United States by
Paragon House
1925 Oakcrest Avenue
St. Paul, MN 55113

Library of Congress Cataloging-in-Publication Data

Anderson, Gordon L. (Gordon Louis), 1947-
  Life, liberty, and the pursuit of happiness, version 4.0 / Gordon L. Anderson. -- 1st ed.
     p. cm. -- (Paragon issues in philsophy)
  Includes bibliographical references.
  Summary: "This book advocates upgrading the U.S. government from the 'Version 3.0' the Founding Fathers put in place to 'Version 4.0' that enables citizens to pursue life, liberty, and happiness in a complex post-industrial and global world. Core political principles, and reforms of Congress, taxes, and welfare policy are covered"--Provided by publisher.
  ISBN 978-1-55778-886-3 (pbk. : alk. paper)
  1. United States--Politics and government--Philosophy, 2. Political culture--United States. 3. Social values--United States. I. Title.
  JK31.A534 2009
  320.973--dc22
                                2009018993

The paper used in this publication meets the minimum requirements of American National Standard for Information Sciences—Permanence of Paper for Printed Library Materials, ANSI Z39.48-1984.

Manufactured in the United States of America
10 9 8 7 6 5 4 3 2 1

For current information about all releases from Paragon House,
visit the web site at http://www.paragonhouse.com

For those who would build societies where life, liberty, and happiness are pursued by all.

Acknowledgements

The history of great societies and the thoughts of a number of great philosophers helped define the fundamental political principles of the United States founding. We are indebted particularly to Aristotle, Livy, Thomas Hobbes, Charles de Secondat Montesquieu, Benjamin Franklin, Thomas Jefferson, and James Madison. For further understanding of basic political principles, I am indebted to St. Augustine for his division of society into cultural and temporal spheres, to Immanuel Kant for his vision of *Perpetual Peace*, to Alexis de Tocqueville for his understanding of *Democracy in America*, and to Forrest McDonald for his work on the intellectual origins of the Constitution. Friedrich Hayek and Professors Timothy Taylor and Robert Whaples sharpened my understanding of economic principles, and the late Kenneth R. Gray should be thanked for his summary of agency theory.

There are also a number of contemporary writers who, from various philosophical perspectives, have illuminated the problems of the present system of government, including Robert Reich, Ron Chernow, David C. Korten, Thom Hartmann, Walter E. Williams, Harold Holzer, Hernando de Soto, and Dennis Gottfried. I would like to thank Professors Morton A. Kaplan and the late Edward Shils who guided me in organizing a major international conference, "Liberal Democratic Societies: Their Present State and Future Prospects," for the Professors World Peace Academy in London in 1989, and the relationships that developed with the 90 scholars that attended. I would also like to thank Professor John Roth for his supervision of the Paragon Issues in Philosophy Series, and colleagues on the board of the Minnesota Legislative Evaluation Assembly for many years of work in evaluating state-level legislative processes.

Finally, I thank my wife Mary Jane for her continual support and feedback, and Rosemary Yokoi and Jayna Anderson at Paragon House for their work on the production of the book.

Contents

Part I: Basic Principles

   Human Motivation, 4; A Political Immune System is Essential, 6; Political Operating Systems Version 1.0, 2.0, and 3.0, 7; A Peaceful Federation of States, 12; Government, Culture, and the Economy, 15; Life, Liberty, and the Pursuit of Happiness Version 4.0, 16

   The Desire for Protection, 19; The Right to Life, 20; Thomas Hobbes, 22; The Founding of the United States, 23; The Right to Life in International Law, 25; Pressing the Boundaries of Life, 26; Protection of Property, 28; Promotion of Good, 30; Preventing Good, 34; Promoting Harm, 37; Conflicts of Interest, 39; The Control of Information, 41; Conclusion, 42; Questions for Review and Reflection, 42

   Natural Subsidiarity, 45; Social Subsidiarity, 46; Use of the Term Subsidiarity, 49; Freedom and the Principle of Subsidiarity, 50; The Late Middle Ages, 50; The Pyramid as a Symbol for Subsidiarity, 52; The Family at the Base of the Pyramid, 53; The Organization of Families into Tribes and Communities, 55; The Conditions for Democracy in America, 57; Observations of Alexis de Tocqueville in Early America, 58; Cities and Social Complexity, 60; Bureaucracy and Abuse of Power, 62; Corporations, States, and Federations, 64; The Problem of Centralized Power, 66; Realism and Centralized Power, 69; The United States and the Inversion of Subsidiarity, 72; Subsidiarity in Culture and Economy, 74; Stronger Societies Practice Subsidiarity, 77; Questions for Review and Reflection, 79

   Specialized Components in the Social Organism, 84; Separation of Church and State, 87; The "Wall of Separation", 91;

Preface

Americans increasingly complain that the U.S. government is not working well, and politicians campaign on platforms promising reform or change. The U.S. society is a system of interrelated parts and, for any system to operate smoothly, all the parts must be coordinated in such a way that the system as a whole functions according to its purpose. I have come to realize that the primary reason for government dysfunction and breakdown is the erosion of the Constitution and the laws designed to safeguard the original purpose, coupled with the passage of new laws that the undermined system is unable to support. The purpose of this book is to provide an understanding of this situation and explain how it can be remedied.

Modern society is a system with three major sectors: culture, government, and the economy. The U.S. founders were primarily concerned with the operation of government. The Founders created organs of government designed to thwart the consolidation of political power. They did not create cultural or economic institutions. While separating church and state, they emphasized that the state would not be able to survive without a culture that raised citizens capable of self-governance.

New economic power based on the development and growth of American industry, especially the railroads, began exercising political power by the middle of the nineteenth century. Industries funded the Republican Party and backed the Civil War. Up until the Sherman Anti-Trust Act was passed in 1890 the consolidation of economic power continued unabated. The rise of Communist ideology and its influence in the early 20th century created a backlash in which governments tried to centrally control business. The Soviet Union eventually collapsed for this very reason. The United States experimented with aspects of socialism beginning in the 1920s, prolonging the Great Depression. Since then we have witnessed bouts when government attempts to run the economy or industry in the name of justice. There are other periods when industries attempt to shape public policy in the name of economic growth. Both approaches are viruses that have been introduced into the legal system. Both approaches redirect public funds for narrow interests and weaken the entire system.

Any system must operate in good health to fulfill its purpose. The human body is a system that must be healthy if it is to serve the person who wants to accomplish a task—like running, lifting, or drawing. The nervous system is the "operating system" that regulates the interaction among the organs to keep the body healthy. When the basic system is functioning, an individual can make a conscious decision to perform a task and the body will be able to carry out the brain's instructions to do so.

Likewise, a computer is a system made up of various organs: a central processing unit (CPU), a power supply, a disk drive for storage, a keyboard for input, and a monitor and printer for output. The operating system provides the information that coordinates the interaction of the organs so a user can use the computer for various purposes. These specialized purposes could include word processing, maintaining a database, or browsing the Internet. Additional software applications are written to enable users to perform each of these tasks. Viruses, like viruses in the human body, live as parasites on the computer, capturing data or remotely hijacking operations, slowing down the computer or causing it to crash.

We must begin to see society in the same way. Society is a system that requires a good basic operating system that coordinates all of the social organs so that it can perform its specified purpose. In the United States, that purpose was spelled out in the Declaration of Independence: Life, Liberty, and the Pursuit of Happiness. One might argue that a nation should have a different mission statement. A communist might say it should be to take care of the people. A capitalist might say it should be to buttress growth of industry. However, I haven't found a better mission statement for a nation. It was implicit in Hammurabi's Code in Ancient Babylon, and the establishment of the Ancient Roman Republic. Only in freedom do people work hard and prosper, causing the rise of great civilizations. Other societies tend to die with the tyrants who rule them by force.

In 1789, after the American Revolution, the United States installed a "clean" operating system with its Constitution. I call it "Life, Liberty, and the Pursuit of Happiness, Version 3.0." When installed, it served its purpose well. However, like the Microsoft Windows 3.1 operating system that could not serve to regulate all of the new computer hardware that was invented after 1985, the U.S. Constitution was not designed for modern post-industrial society. Worse, the Congress that was supposed to write the additional code (laws) that would govern these new developments often introduced "viruses" instead of writing anti-virus code. And, the Supreme Court that was designed to prevent Congress from introducing such viruses remained silent, and often introduced its own worms. These viruses have now weakened the system and threaten its survival.

Anything human beings design must follow the laws necessary for its function. When engineers design a bridge, they do so with an understanding of the strength of materials used and the traffic load it will bear. I live in Minnesota, and my office is only a few miles from where we had a major bridge collapse on Interstate 35 on August 1, 2007. The bridge was designed and built with new materials in 1967. While the design was not perfect, it was not intended for the volume of traffic, the increased size of trucks, frequent application of salt to melt ice that corroded the steel, or extra layers of pavement and piles of sand that were heaped upon it when it collapsed. Many people simply used the bridge and treated it in a way that served their immediate purpose without concern to maintain its structural integrity.

Similarly, Americans take our system of government for granted, thinking they can use it for their own purposes without vigilantly weeding out the viruses that have crept in—some in incremental legislation and others in the form of Constitutional Amendments and interpretations that undermined the original integrity of the Constitution. In the chapters that follow I explain the structural principles required for a sound government and how they can be implemented to upgrade the government to an operating system that functions in our modern post-industrial society.

Legislators write the laws. They are the programmers of our society's operating system. They must weed out and guard against viruses rather than capitulating to the interest groups with the most lobbying dollars. We must charge them with the task of upgrading the operating system to "Life, Liberty, and the Pursuit of Happiness, Version 4.0." A blueprint follows.

Part I:
Basic Principles

The six chapters in this part of the book explain five basic principles that should be honored in overcoming the shortcomings in the Constitution of the United States and the various viruses and parasites that have come to use it as a host, weakening it to the point of collapse. These principles are (1) protection of life, liberty, and property, (2) the principle of subsidiarity, (3) the principle of separation of powers or functions, (4) the principle of transparency, and (5) the right to secede.

1

Government as an Operating System

In *Philosophy of the United States: Life, Liberty, and the Pursuit of Happiness* I explained how the founders of the United States attempted to create a constitution in which all citizens could pursue life, liberty, and happiness. The Constitution was not perfect, but it enabled the United States to prosper and retain a continuous government for 220 years. But, by the onset of the twenty-first century, the United States had become more like an oligarchy or a traditional empire than a free republic. The pursuit of life, liberty, and happiness has been hamstrung by high taxation, cumbersome bureaucracy, corruption, inept leadership, and bankruptcy.

The U.S. Constitution was based on study of previous societies and was a state-of-the-art document in 1787. It was a document aimed at providing the defense of liberty. But that document only provided defense against known sources of attack on liberty at the time, and in Thomas Jefferson's opinion, did not cover every base then. As he wrote to James Madison in 1789,

> [If] a positive declaration of some essential rights could not be obtained in the requisite latitude, [the] answer [is], half a loaf is better than no bread. If we cannot secure all our rights, let us secure what we can.[1]

Jefferson knew that people would change over time and that the founding generation needed to guard against what they might become. He also knew institutions change and bend rules, and he compared the problem to the attack of gangrene on the body.

> Time indeed changes manners and notions, and so far we must expect institutions to bend to them. But time produces also corruption of principles, and against this it is the duty of good citizens to be ever on the watch, and if the gangrene is to prevail at last, let the day be kept off as long as possible.[2]

Thomas Jefferson lived long before the invention of the modern computer and the continual software upgrades required to prevent attacks from computer viruses, but his comparison to disease is apt. The process of upgrading government against abuse and corruption can be much like the process of upgrading software defenses against malicious attacks. Viruses constantly seek to exploit weaknesses in the human body, and the immune system identifies new forms of viruses and develops defenses against them. The process in government should be similar. In the United States, a healthy body was created with the constitution, but the immune system was weak. It has not kept up with the attacks that have assailed it, and it is in the process of succumbing to disease without an "inoculation" or "critical updates."

Human Motivation

Understanding human motivation is a key to good government. Modern economics sees all human beings as rational maximizers. People implicitly or explicitly weigh the costs and benefits of decisions. Incentives that allow people to pursue life, liberty, and happiness lead to economic productivity and growth. When that pursuit is thwarted, economic decline and eventual social collapse follows.

Public choice theorists Kenneth Arrow, James M. Buchanan, and Gordon Tullock developed economic principles for the analysis of behavior in politics, specifically the behavior of voters, bureaucrats, and politicians. As one might expect, all people, whether they are in private business or work for the government follow economic principles of maximizing benefits. In business, this is accomplished by producing more for less, so that profit is increased. However, in government it involves ways of taking more from the taxpayer or reducing payments to recipients in order to maximize one's position. Economists call this "rent-seeking behavior."

Economic improvement is a natural objective for human beings. It is part of the pursuit of happiness. The pursuit of happiness and economic improvement is not, by itself, evil. Evil occurs when one's gain comes at someone else's expense. The problem for government is to referee a system in which people are protected from the harm other people's pursuits might cause, while allowing the free pursuit of good and productive behavior that will create a better society.

Understanding human motivation is a key to good government. Modern economics sees all human beings as rational maximizers.

The accumulation of power that occurs with centralization, whether it be political or economic, creates temptations for abuse. It is a social weakness, not strength, even though many historical monuments have been built to those who accumulated greater power or wealth through centralization. Bank robbers seek banks that have lots of money, not those with little. Lawyers are motivated to sue large companies because settlements might be large. Similarly, centralized political power attracts those people who desire to control others. The strongest and healthiest systems, those that are most likely to resist such theft or conquest, are those in which power and wealth are not consolidated. If a state had only one bank, and that bank was mismanaged or robbed, the entire state might suffer financial collapse and many citizens lose their savings and starve. However, if there were hundreds of community banks, and one were robbed, the state would hardly be affected, and insurance might be able to cover the loss without difficulty.

A Political Immune System is Essential

Political and economic viruses are most likely to appear where economic and political power is concentrated. This is where a society's immune system must be strong. Unless defenses to protect against such attacks can be mounted or inoculations applied to ward them off, they will eventually kill the host. This is why empires rise and fall. The United States was created with checks on such accumulations of power, but over time laws were passed that conflicted with the founding philosophy; the courts did not object, and new concentrations of power became entrenched, undermining the basic purposes the founders enshrined in the Constitution.

> **Political and economic viruses are most likely to appear where economic and political power is concentrated. This is where a society's immune system must be strong.**

This should not be surprising to most parents who understand this process as they watch their children constantly testing the rules and limits they create, rules designed to protect them and help them grow to become responsible adults. Governments are organized by citizens to protect them from the violence and robbery that occurs in what Thomas Hobbes described as "the state of nature." The Constitution and laws of a state are foremost for this purpose of security.

The rule of law of a state can be compared to the operating system of a computer. The United States Constitution, like the Microsoft Windows operating system, is designed as the basic platform upon which people can perform their tasks. Both of these systems have been subjected to viruses and unnecessary overhead that infect or impede the operation of the system. The corruption of power can be viewed as analogous to the countless viruses seeking a host where they can thrive and expand colonies.

Computer viruses, like political and economic corruption, do the most damage when they can infect a centralized system. The decentralization of computer processors among millions of personal computer users (rather than having everyone connected to one main processor) provides much more protection. If a hacker takes over one person's computer, there is little danger the entire internet would go down. But, if the entire internet were tied to one huge computer, the danger of it going down and causing everyone potential disaster would be significantly increased. When an individual dies, a family business folds, or a personal computer malfunctions, the life of the world proceeds normally and peacefully. However, when a big centralized system goes down, as with the collapse of the Roman Empire, or the burning of the library of Alexandria, or the collapse of Wall Street, it can create human disaster of apocalyptic proportions.

Political Operating Systems Version 1.0, 2.0, and 3.0

As human civilization has developed, it has needed appropriate political systems for citizens to pursue life, liberty, and happiness. There have been many types of political systems designed to impose the will of the rulers. They have been the norm. Systems designed for the freedom of citizens to pursue their own happiness have been the exception. However, those exceptional systems are the ones that have given birth to the great and durable societies that have thrust civilization forward. A brief recap of the political systems that I call Versions 1.0, 2.0, and 3.0 is in order.

Babylon: The Code of Hammurabi

Western culture and language come from the cradle of civilization developed along the Tigris and Euphrates rivers. Emerging on the foundations of the Akkadian Empire, the Babylonian Empire was based on the rule of law that provided greater freedom and decentralization. The law code of Hammurabi (c. 1760 B.C.) can be seen today on an ancient stele on display in the Louvre in

Paris. Under this code Babylonians prospered and the Babylonian language became the *lingua franca,* or universal language of the entire Near East and Mediterranean areas. Enforcement of the law code was exceptional in that Babylonian leaders were held to a higher standard and treated with harsher penalties than regular citizens, promoting the concept that with greater power comes greater responsibility. The code was simple enough so that it could be memorized by all citizens, who, if they remained within its boundaries, were free to pursue life, liberty, and happiness. In software terms, we might view the Akkadian Empire as Beta 0.9 and Hammurabi's rule as Life, Liberty, and Happiness, V. 1.0.

Aristotle considered a King to be a leader installed by people on the basis of his virtue, sacrifice, and leadership skills. A tyrant, on the other hand, arises from a mob.[3] Both are single leaders who have little check on their power. This power is often abused as leaders put their own interests above those of the citizens they serve. They often create family dynasties rather than leadership based on ability; often spoiled and incompetent children inherit the throne and destroy the governments they inherit. Kings often obtain their power through some form of military conquest. Such power is held tenuously, reflects the King's personal character, and often does not survive long after the King's death.

Rome: The Twelve Tables

The Roman Republic was the first major political system based upon rule of law in which common people have representation. Rome was originally ruled by wealthy land-owning families. After the plebeian class went on a general strike, a new government was created based on the study of previous political systems. The "Twelve Tables" of Law (509 B.C.) that were approved by both the aristocratic class and the plebeians were a social contract. Like ancient Babylon, the laws applied equally to rich and poor, giving the government legitimacy. One reason the Roman Republic initially expanded is that neighboring peoples admired the freedom and prosperity they witnessed. They often helped Roman armies to overthrow their own tyrants so that they could live under Roman law and be more free and happy. In software terms, we might view the Twelve Tables as "Life, Liberty, and the Pursuit of Happiness, V. 2.0."

With the passage of time a commercial class arose, and the old class distinctions began to disappear. The Roman Republic suffered internal decline based on selfishness and corruption when people found ways to circumvent or change the law or attain political favors. Sexual licentiousness and moral laxity led to a decline in good political leadership. Eventually power was seized by Julius Caesar (c. 100-44 B.C.) who promoted marriage and family as a way to strengthen society and create citizens of good character. The Empire, like the Republic before it, eventually saw greater corruption of power. The laws promulgated by the emperors, often for personal reasons, turned the justice of the original Twelve Tables into a relic. Cicero (106-43 B.C.) lamented the loss of rule of law under the Twelve Tables and was the first known to use the saying paraphrased by Lord Acton as "power corrupts, and absolute power corrupts absolutely."[4]

The Roman Empire eventually adopted Christianity as an official religion in an effort to create a culture that would produce people of the necessary character and vision to guide the ailing empire. However, the system fell into stagnation and a period of Dark Ages after the Church, modeling itself after the hierarchical system of political rulers, and also suffered from corruption and abuse of power. The rise of independent city-states, the Renaissance, and the Reformation gave birth to a new culture in which science, humanism, and personal responsibility all played a greater role.

Nicolo Machiavelli laid the foundation of modern political philosophy with the analysis, use, and control of power from his study of the history of Rome. Thomas Hobbes also contributed to modern political philosophy with his discussions of sovereignty and social contract. Practical checks on power had begun earlier in England with the Magna Carta and the creation of the House of Lords. Power was further devolved followed a rising commercial class and the formation of the House of Commons. Following the Treaty of Westphalia that concluded the Eighty Years' War in 1648, the idea of the modern sovereign nation-state with religious liberties and greater human rights was first adopted in the Netherlands.

The United States Constitution

In 1787, building on the Western tradition, British law, and the more recent political writings of Montesquieu, Blackstone, Hume and Adam Smith, the founders of the United States sought to create a "more perfect" government. They focused on creating checks and balances on power and a Bill of Rights designed to protect the rights of all citizens to pursue life, liberty, and happiness. In software terms, we might view the U.S. Constitution as "Life, Liberty, and the Pursuit of Happiness, V. 3.0."

Like Babylon and Rome, the United States became the preeminently admired society in its time, a haven for refugees from tyranny, and a place of opportunity. People flooded to the United States to start a new and better life. But the United States was not perfect. Among the problems posed by the Constitution was acceptance of slavery, which contradicted the idea in the Declaration of Independence "that all men are created equal." The issues of slavery and tariffs led to a Civil War that cast a pall on the American Experiment leaving 560,300 dead. The Civil War also accelerated the consolidation of federal power. The post-War Supreme Court allowed the further consolidation of economic and federal political power. Except in the South, this consolidation and growth of federal power did not set off serious alarms until it became oppressive with taxes and adventurous in waging foreign wars. By then, it was difficult to reverse its course.

Centralization of federal power in the United States led to increased abuses of that power. New legislation, presidential orders, and Supreme Court decisions often ignored the core principles and the checks and balances on power that shaped the framing of the original Constitution. The Constitution became termed a "living document," reinterpreted by justices in their own time in ways not unlike theologians who reinterpreted the Bible. In its later incarnations, the Constitution reflected much less of its original purposes—from imposing high taxes and unfunded mandates on citizens, to conscripting youths for foreign wars the citizens never approved.

Like the Roman Empire, the American Empire became not a "government based on the people," but based on "the people in the government." In the United States, large corporations and special interest groups that bought political votes created much of the legislation. Clear votes on single issues that citizens could hold their representatives accountable for disappeared. "Pork," or the policy of adding funds for special local projects, was used to buy the votes necessary for special interests whose bills would not pass on their own merits. This created large and confused bills at great expense. Often, not even the representatives who passed the bills or the agencies charged with enforcing them, fully understood them.

In 1787, building on the Western tradition, British law, and the more recent political writings of Montesquieu, Blackstone, Hume and Adam Smith, the founders of the United States sought to create a "more perfect" government.

After 9/11 the federal government implemented many special powers, like the PATRIOT Act and FISA, in direct opposition to protections guaranteed by the Bill of Rights. These developments are like viruses that were not kept in check by a healthy immune system to protect the American Republic.

The present U.S. government has become very sick, and the need for change has become obvious. Both presidential candidates in the 2008 election repeatedly stated, "Washington is broken." Many Americans lament the loss of a "golden age" where the Constitution was revered and people voluntarily followed it, pursuing life, liberty, and happiness without any sign of government in their daily lives. These sound like Cicero's laments about Rome. Examples can be found in two 2008 books, *The Revolution: A Manifesto*[5] by U.S. Representative Ron Paul and *Don't Start the Revolution Without Me!*[6] by former Minnesota Governor Jesse Ventura.

A simple return to the original Constitution is not possible; the world has changed too much, and many "viruses" have developed. Rather, an upgrade to "Life, Liberty, and the Pursuit of Happiness, Version 4.0" is required. Without reforms that reinstitute or create new checks and balances on power, the United States will no longer be a society of free people, but will revert to some type of authoritarianism or oligopoly comparable to that which the Revolutionary War was fought to overthrow.

A Peaceful Federation of States

Life, liberty, and the pursuit of happiness is not simply an Enlightenment goal, even if the phrase was popularized by Thomas Jefferson in the U.S. Declaration of Independence. It is a concept essential for national peace as well as global peace. Any government that does not allow its citizens to freely pursue their goals is a system that forces them to pursue the goals of others. Systems based on force not only deprive people of liberty, but also cause frustration and resentment, the seeds of violence and revolution. Peace is not inherent in any system based on force.

Since the end of the Cold War in 1989, the primary problems of violence in the world are found in systems where government force is used by one group in control of a government to oppress other people within their borders. Such political systems sometimes carry out acts of genocide. State sovereignty as an inviolable principle is claimed by rulers who shield themselves with this doctrine while they oppress citizens and perpetrate atrocities.

The doctrine of state sovereignty has roots in the Peace of Westphalia. It reached its height in the philosophy of G.W.F. Hegel and his idea that the state is the final end of the march of the Absolute through history. The establishment of the League of

Nations after World War I and the United Nations after World War II were efforts by victorious powers to prevent wars among states, and the doctrine of state sovereignty was considered sacrosanct. The U.N. Universal Declaration of Human Rights, drafted in 1948, serves as an articulation of rights that are due to individual people, but its acceptance and fulfillment by states is voluntary. In the present world order, the sovereignty of the state thus trumps the sovereignty of the person.

This situation is the reverse of the philosophy of the founders of the United States and the idea that the fundamental unit of sovereignty is the individual person, not "states" or "peoples." The Bill of Rights was designed as a form of protection from governments that limited government actions. When the fundamental social unit in a philosophy of society is larger than the individual, the end result will inevitably be some form of un-peace, or "structural violence."

The philosophy of the founders of the United States was that the fundamental unit of sovereignty is the individual person, not "states" or "peoples." The Bill of Rights was designed as a form of protection from governments.

One fundamental thesis in this book is that global peace must be built from the bottom up, upon the voluntary association of individuals into marriages and communities, communities into cities and counties, the voluntary membership of cities and counties into states, and the voluntary membership of states in a federation of states. The idea of voluntary association also includes the conditional right of individuals or units of government to secede from higher bodies.

A similar theory was elaborated by Immanuel Kant in his famous 1795 treatise, *Perpetual Peace.* Kant argued that states would be forced by the cunning of nature and history to join into a federation of states, realizing it was to their advantage, in order to escape the natural state of war that interrupts normal life. Kant distinguished between a "league of peace" *(foedus pacificum)* and a "treaty of peace" *(pactum pacis)*. A treaty of peace is an imposition by powers and ends a particular war without ending the natural state of war. It is an arrangement of force. However, a league of peace, voluntarily joined for mutual security, is the path to end all wars.[7] Hence, although Kant's writing heavily influenced the idea of a League of Nations *(foedus pacificum)*, in practice what got implemented in the United Nations was a system imposed by the ruling powers, a *pactum pacis*.

Kant argued that ultimately there are only two types of governments, republican and despotic. Simple democracies are despotic, he said, because they do not guarantee the right of minority members equal protection under the law, but rather impose a tyranny of the majority over all. The United States was founded as a republican government, but by Kant's definition, it ceased to be one when the North imposed its will on the South by force during the Civil War.

The United States was founded as a republican government, but by Kant's definition, it ceased to be one when the North imposed its will on the South by force during the Civil War.

Global peace, like national peace, requires the voluntary association of social groups with their peers at each level for their protection. Only republican forms of government in Kant's sense of "republican" are not held together by force. Admission of a despotic society into a league of peace promotes the acceptance of un-peace, and such a society should not be considered a legitimate member of the league.

Any league of peace should be mutually beneficial, and commitment should not be casual. A member must be willing to give something to the common cause and should not casually drop out. A marriage between two spouses is an example of this type of commitment. If each spouse does their part, both are enriched. Divorce is much discouraged because of the interdependence created and the effects on the children. Yet, the right to divorce in the case where one spouse is causing great harm to another should be respected, or the abused spouse might get beaten to death. Similarly, the right to secede from a federation of states should be seen as a measure of last resort if other members of the league, or the league itself, is causing more harm than benefit to the member state.

Government, Culture, and the Economy

Some type of imposed order is necessary where people are irresponsible, immature, or selfish. One cannot assume that simple voluntary association is adequate or that, if it is held up as a model, it will be followed. As David Hume observed,

> In contriving any system of government, and fixing the several checks and balances, every man ought to be supposed a knave…[having] no other end…than private interest.[8]

The main purpose of a Constitution and the rule of law is to protect against any legal actions that would harm the public good, or any citizen. On the other hand, the Constitution and rule of law ought to allow and encourage all voluntary responsible behavior, good citizenship, and economic productivity. In short, government should prevent all harm and allow all good.

This is not an easy task. It has been considered by many to be an impossible task unless the people being governed are sufficiently educated, moral, and economically productive. As James Madison said,

> To suppose that any form of government will secure liberty or happiness without any virtue in the people is a chimerical idea.[9]

This leads to the conclusion that even the most perfect government requires perfect cultural, educational, and economic institutions for its success. The corollaries of this conclusion are that perfect culture would require appropriate legal and economic institutions, and a perfect economy would require perfect legal and moral institutions.

This tripartite division of society into culture, economy, and government was not clearly developed at the time of the founding of the United States. The word "economy" had only been recently coined, and whether the world's economic resources were a pie to be divided or economies that could grow or expand was only beginning to be debated. Today, economic laws are better understood, and there exists a significant history of economics that better understands the laws of banking, credit bubbles, and market behavior.

Life, Liberty, and the Pursuit of Happiness Version 4.0

This book focuses primarily on upgrading the government of the United States from what we have called "Life, Liberty, and the Pursuit of Happiness Version 3.0" to Version 4.0. However, it does not preclude the possibility that a "clean installation" of Version 4.0 might be successful in some countries. The basic political principles we discuss apply to all governments. The United States prospered on the basis of its original Constitution and therefore has a cultural memory of the type of self-reliant and responsible character of a people required of such a government. Because of this, reforms (rather than an entirely new installation) could revert the United States from an empire of force to a republican force for peace in our global age. This would enable the United States to perform its desired role of a world leader and model for other governments.

> The tripartite division of society into culture, economy, and government was not clearly developed at the time of the founding of the United States. The word "economy" had only been recently coined.

Part I of this book discusses five fundamental principles

that should be honored in overcoming the shortcomings in the Constitution of the United States and restricting the various viruses and parasites that have come to use it as a host, weakening it to the point of collapse. These principles are (1) protection of life, liberty, and property, (2) the principle of subsidiarity, (3) the principle of separation of powers or functions, (4) transparency, and (5) the right to secede.

Part II discusses specific problems that have to be addressed in order to allow the basic principles to work smoothly. This includes the structure of Congress, taxation, and welfare. These areas are where the "viruses" that are draining the economy and people of prosperity have taken root. Reforms to control greed, abuse of power, centralization of power, and economic dependency upon government are essential for the long-term health of the nation.

We conclude with an optimistic assessment for the future as these principles and the types of reforms suggested are applied. It will not be an easy task, but the first task is knowledge and understanding of what exists and what is required. The best choice is not always the first, as human beings inevitably want to believe in short-cuts. However, "Life, Liberty, and the Pursuit of Happiness, Version 4.0" is an upgrade that most people will be happy to see.

2

Protection of Life, Liberty, and Property

The sole object and only legitimate end of government is to protect the citizen in the enjoyment of life, liberty, and property, and when the government assumes other functions it is usurpation and oppression.

—Alabama Constitution (Art. 1, Sec. 35)

The Desire for Protection

Thomas Hobbes called "the state of nature" a condition in which human beings have to defend themselves, relying on natural instincts, brute strength, personal tools, and skill. The state of nature is a state of anarchy. One's life is protected only by one's own power. Therefore, people band together not only for raising children, but also for protection from other human beings and other sources of harm. For the same reason, animals travel in herds and packs to create safety in numbers.

In simple societies, people often form bands or gangs around a leader who is strong and capable of defending himself and protecting others. The unwritten law in such simple societies is that the leader will protect you if you do what he asks. The leader does not necessarily view other members of the gang as sovereign individuals, but as useful for his purposes. Members of such gangs are not viewed as having an inherent right to life, a right to promote ideas opposed to the leader, or the right to pursue their own independent liberty and happiness. Those rights are forfeited to the leader upon joining the group in exchange for the leader's protection.

Larger human societies and political systems are also formed around the need for protection. As groups get larger, a gang leader or warlord may become a king or emperor with subordinates in charge of different groups that have been conquered by force. The top leader has superior power and issues the final commands. He is the law, the center of power, and the sovereign. He typically treats his people as if they were his personal property. The people are a means to his ends and his idea of "peace."

Such a "peace" might be the absence of war, but it is often cruel toward the ruled who are often exploited. As Augustine of Hippo wrote in *The City of God*,

> Even when men are plotting to disturb the peace, it is to fashion a new peace nearer to the heart's desire; it is not because they dislike peace as such. It is not that they love peace less, but that they love their kind of peace more.[1]

In the state of nature, leaders are sovereign. Followers sacrifice their own desires to those of the leader in exchange for protection. They might find some degree of liberty and happiness under the rule of the sovereign if the sovereign is good or rewards them for loyalty. But, one's life is not one's own; one's fate is determined by the one who controls power.

The Right to Life

Most people are not content to live under the arbitrary rule of a leader. They want to live in a dependable society that treats them fairly, with dignity and respect, and with rules they can trust. The demand for justice follows by comparing one's life to that of others. Young children display this trait at an early age, often saying to parents things like, "It's not fair, you gave him more than me." We compare how much money or how many things we have, but most important is how we are physically treated. The right to live and not to be killed is primary, because without our life, no other rights mean anything.

Heads of families, tribes, and gangs, bound to protect the lives of their members, react strongly to the murder of a loved one or loyal follower. Revenge is often personal in this case. But, the murder of one member of a group is a threat to the entire group. The typical response is to eliminate the threat by killing the perpetrator as a way to protect the group from future attacks. In either case, killing the perpetrator is the common response. The perpetrator does not have equal rights before some abstract law.

Universalizing this distaste for murder is the natural consequence of reason. "Thou shalt not kill" is one of the basic commandments of all civilizations. This commandment preceded the Ten Commandments of the Abrahamic faiths in Mesopotamia, and it is taught in nearly all societies. By saying the commandment not to kill comes from God, it becomes a universal law with respect to all human beings. Inherent in this commandment is the idea that all people, regardless of the tribe to which they belong, have a basic right to life. While religions can implant commandments on the human conscience and tell people that it is wrong to take the life of another human being, they lack the mechanism of physical force.

> In the state of nature leaders are sovereign. Followers sacrifice to the leader in exchange for protection. They might find some degree of liberty and happiness under the rule of the sovereign. But, one's life is not one's own; one's fate is determined by the one who controls power.

The protection of one's life, as well as the protection of other rights accorded an individual, requires not only values that proclaim equal rights, but also a government that can enforce the protection of such rights through law backed by power, not the arbitrary will of a conqueror.

Thomas Hobbes

One of Thomas Hobbes's contributions to modern political theory was the use and development of terms like right, law, sovereignty, contract, and commonwealth.[2] He developed these terms with a realism that saw the most brutish behavior of human beings not as "sin," but as the "state of nature," based on our individual insecurity and desire for protection. Hobbes argued that the power of the sovereign was absolute and that any attempt to divide it would dissolve it because the powers would "mutually destroy one another."[3] Sovereignty, for him, did not reside in the individual, but in the commonwealth, or state.

It is no more coincidental that Hobbes's *Leviathan* was published soon after the Treaty of Westphalia than that Augustine's *City of God* was written after the sack of Rome in 410 A.D. Augustine's work was an attempt to articulate a society in which the Christian Church and the Roman State could be synthesized. He needed to defend Christianity, which was accused of weakening the empire through its emphasis on love and eternal life. Hobbes, on the other hand, wrote after the rise of modern science and the idea of the nation-state, as the Dutch were forging a society collectively after Spanish rule was overthrown.

Leviathan contains the idea that a commonwealth is born through the consent of the governed (a social contract), who give their consent in exchange for safety. But, because Hobbes wrote that once a sovereign is established, it has absolute power, his political theories posed little threat of revolution to existing rulers. It is thereby viewed by some as a practical capitulation to the existing order. However, following Machiavelli's *Prince,* Hobbes argued that it is in the interest of the sovereign to dispense liberty and justice for the sake of maintaining his own power and a stable and durable regime.

Hobbes discussed the moral duty of the sovereign to obey the ten commandments he developed for the commonwealth. Here is an excerpt from his idea of the sovereign's duty that develops the concept of protection of life, liberty, and property:

And to avoid doing injury. Again, every sovereign ought to cause justice to be taught, which, consisting in taking from no man what is his, is as much as to say, to cause men to be taught not to deprive their neighbors, by violence or fraud, of any thing which by the sovereign authority is theirs. Of things held in propriety, those that are dearest to a man are *his own life*, and limbs; and in the next degree, in most men, those that concern conjugal affection; and after them, riches and means of living.[4]

Hobbes was a bridge between ancient and modern political thought, using the political philosophy he had inherited as well as articulating these principles in terms of modern nation-states in which the rights of citizens are becoming more important. But, it was for those who followed him to develop the rights of man, the idea of a social contract, and the concept of individual sovereignty to the point where revolution against an unjust sovereign is warranted and individual human beings are thought of as ends-in-themselves.[5]

The Founding of the United States

The right to life and other modern political ideas found a new opportunity for expression in the United States Declaration of Independence when, in 1776, it was declared that "all men are endowed by their Creator with certain inalienable rights, and that among these are life, liberty, and the pursuit of happiness." The idea of natural right had been developed by John Locke, who argued in his Second Treatise of Government that men by nature have the right to Lives, Liberties, and Estates, which he collectively called "property."[6]

The founders of the United States did not accept the idea that true sovereignty existed in any human being, particularly those with political power. They had suffered firsthand the effects of King George III's power over the colonies, power which they viewed as exploitation. Jefferson wrote that "the Bill of Rights is rights that people have against every government on earth."[7] Rather than sovereignty lying in the political ruler, true sovereignty came from "Nature and Nature's God." The proper role of government was to secure these rights. When a government neglected this duty, its replacement by another government was justified.

The framers of the U.S. Constitution did not accept the medieval notion, still present in Hobbes's writing, that dividing power would destroy a commonwealth. Rather, they were influenced by Montesquieu's *Spirit of the Laws* that examined modern government as a set of institutions that work together in an organic relationship, all serving the well-being of the whole. He wrote that in every government there are legislative, executive, and judicial functions; and, when any of these functions combined in one person or group of magistrates, they would deprive people of liberty. These functions should be separated, and the legislative body should be broken into two parts, with each body having veto power over the legislation of the other:

The founders of the United States believed that sovereignty resided in individuals. This came from "Nature and Nature's God." The proper role of government was to secure this sovereignty.

> Here then is the fundamental constitution of the government we are treating of. The legislative body is composed of two parts which would check one another by the mutual privilege of veto. They are both restrained by the executive as the executive, in turn, is restrained by them. These three powers should naturally form a state of repose or inaction. But as there is a necessity for movement in the course of human affairs, they are forced to move, but still in concert.[8]

Montesquieu thus envisioned that a modern liberal political system would be rooted in a form of gridlock that would only be pushed forward by the necessities of the people. Such an idea inspired the founders seeking a way to check the powers of government. The United States Constitution was conceived as having a limited role in society, while individuals pursuing their own liberty would be the driving force.

England had a government that not only wielded political power, but also had an official state religion that imposed values and doctrines upon people. These sometimes contradicted reason and science and contributed to intellectual stagnation. In addition, the Crown owned monopolistic companies like the East India Company that was chartered by Queen Elizabeth in 1600 and was using its muscle to put U.S. tea merchants out of business (the reason for the Boston Tea Party). And, the Crown had forced the colonies to stop using their own script money that was backed by an appropriate value of goods in the economy and instead foisted the more worthless British currency, based on a credit bubble, onto the colonists.

These attempts by the political institutions to control religious and economic institutions contributed to the American Revolution. The U.S. founders believed government should keep its hands off both religion and the economy and instead limit its role to protecting life, liberty, and property by ensuring no person and no government caused any harm to citizens who were pursuing their own dreams, so long as one citizen's pursuit did not harm or interfere with that of another. In later chapters, we discuss the importance of further separating knowledge and commerce from the government.

The Right to Life in International Law

The success and prosperity of the United States has been an inspiration to people around the world. The United States Constitution has been widely studied as a model for constitutions of other countries, and the concept of a right to life is an essential right in the Universal Declaration of Human Rights adopted by the United Nations General Assembly.

Article 3 of the Declaration says that "everyone has the right to life, liberty, and security of person." The term "security of person" also occurs in many constitutions adopted after the U.N. Declaration, including Canada, South Africa, Turkey, and New Zealand. This term is used to expand on the idea of protection from being killed to protection from unlawful government detention, torture, police brutality, or other government activity that would bring physical harm to one's body.

In 1950, the Council of Europe adopted a convention on human rights in which Article 2 declared protection of the right to life. In 1966, Article 6.1 of the International Covenant on Civil and Political Rights made protection of the right to life binding on every member of the United Nations.

Pressing the Boundaries of Life

When the United States was founded, decisions on specific social issues like abortion or euthanasia were far removed from the federal government and left to families or lower levels of government. Legislation on such issues was forbidden by the Tenth Amendment to the Constitution that stated: "The powers not delegated to the United States by the Constitution, nor prohibited by it to the states, are reserved to the states respectively, or to the people." As time has passed, the machinery of the federal government has expanded and circumvented this amendment, effectively treating it as an artifact. Today, such social issues are widely discussed by federal courts and in national politics.

The question of abortion is widely debated because there is no consensus on when the life that should be protected starts. The strictest interpretation is that life begins at conception, while the most liberal declares life at first breath. Most people believe that protection should be mandated somewhere in between, for example at the first heartbeat, the first movement, the first conscious brain activity, or when it could survive birth. In the United States, a majority of the people are willing to accept abortion as legal in the first trimester.

The abortion issue is difficult because it pits the right to life of the unborn child against the rights of the mother. The situation surrounding each decision is different. Some mothers become pregnant irresponsibly by having sex even though they do not want a child or have the means to care for one. Some women conceive after a criminal rape, a situation beyond their control, when they are not prepared for children. There are also medical cases in which allowing the child to develop to birth might kill the mother, and the right to life of the mother must be weighed against that of the child. Finally, there are medical cases when it is known that the child has some abnormality that will make it dependent on other people and have a substandard life. These difficult and highly personal decisions are often not well served by impersonal federal law.

Euthanasia is another widely contested issue. This issue relates to a range of concerns about the end of life and the means by which death takes place. Some people believe that prolonging death in hospitals, using expensive medical treatments, prolonging pain and suffering, or anything leading to a humiliating and undignified death is unnecessary, perhaps even morally wrong. Some see hastening death as merciful. Others believe that families and doctors ought to do everything possible to prolong life and see failure to do so as immoral. The case is sometimes made for euthanasia immediately after the birth of a child born with severe deformity.

In most countries where law supports a "dignified death," objective conditions of severe pain for terminally ill, or "brain death," or other limited conditions must be met. In the case where one has mental faculties intact, one must voluntarily request a physician-assisted suicide. Some cultures, the Japanese for example, have a long cultural tradition of dignity in death. How well one dies is seen as the final act of one's character and how well one lived. The Federal Republic of Germany holds the principle of human dignity in higher regard than the right to life. However, there are serious issues in defining human dignity, and the chance for abuse if one person makes that decision for another who expressly wants to pursue his or her own life, liberty, and happiness.

In the next chapter, the principle of subsidiarity is developed, and this principle will help to clarify why laws at the federal level regarding such controversial and varied issues relating to abortion and euthanasia should be minimal if they are allowed at all. Subsidiarity places responsibility for such decisions at the lowest level of governance possible. Asking a federal level court to make explicit rulings on such varied and personal matters as abortion and euthanasia can be harmful to society as a whole, especially when that decision is not accepted by the overwhelming majority of citizens.

In a peaceful world, human beings and social groups are happiest when they can exercise self-determination. The role of government should be to protect that self-determination while being prohibited from forcing its will upon citizens, except to restrain people from causing obvious harm to the pursuit of life, liberty, and happiness of others.

Protection of Property

The Declaration of Independence specifically mentions "Life, Liberty, and the Pursuit of Happiness." This was a departure from the normal trinity of "life, liberty, and property" in Locke's *Second Treatise of Civil Government* (1690) and resembles the statement by Aristotle that "the end of politics...is happiness."[9] This concept was becoming widespread in the eighteenth century through the writings of Jean Jacques Burlamaqui, James Wilson, Sir William Blackstone, John Adams, and George Mason.[10] While the pursuit of happiness refers to a broader goal than the acquisition of property, the right to ownership and protection of property must be considered a fundamental right from the standpoint of motivation for a prosperous political economy. Locke's use of the term "property" had been derived from the Latin *proprius,* meaning "that which is appropriate to a person," and included life and liberty.

Following Locke was the growing new field of political economy related to the establishment of banking, large corporations, and commerce. This new discipline led to theories and legislation that, in the later writings of Sir William Blackstone, had come to mean "the sole and despotic dominion which one man claims and exercises over the external things of the world, in total exclusion of the right of any other individual in the universe."[11] This definition did not automatically sit well with many religious and collectivist sentiments of the American people at that time, and one can imagine Jefferson used the term "happiness" in the Declaration rather than the more vulgar term "property" with hopes of the widest acceptance possible.

Modern economic laws have been studied and developed since the time of the founding, giving us more knowledge about economics than was available to the founders. The increased industrialization in the nineteenth century led to many theories of political economy, from laissez-faire capitalism to communism, National Socialism, and fascism. Citizens under governments that tried to control economies through any of these theories, including laissez-faire capitalism, have eventually been deprived of their liberty and property. Where economies are centralized under the political system, the government deprives citizens of liberty and property. In laissez-faire and fascist systems, the result is oligopolies that control the fate of individuals.

> **Aristotle observed that, unless one owned property, one could not care for family, provide hospitality to friends, or perform the acts of giving that engender happiness.**

Over two millennia ago, Aristotle discussed reasons why ownership of private property was necessary for happiness. He observed that, unless one owned property, one could not care for his family, provide hospitality to friends, or perform the acts of giving that engender happiness.[12] These are basic aspects of being human that lead to happiness that neither another person nor a state can perform on one's behalf. Communism, being an abstract theory of economic justice decoupled from a thorough understanding of human nature, failed to account for this. The collapse of communism at the end of the twentieth century in the Soviet Union enabled modern society to relearn this principle.

Less well understood are problems with doctrinaire uses of laissez-faire capitalism, or appeals to organize government for greater industrial efficiency. Friedrich A. Hayek discussed in his 1944 book *Road to Serfdom*[13] how the deprivation of liberty can come from the political economy of the right, as in Hitler's Germany. He warned that many of the forces that led to Nazi Germany are unchecked in British and American society. In 2007, Robert B. Reich analyzes these trends today in his book *Supercapitalism: The Transformation of Business, Democracy, and Everyday Life.*[14] Reich argues that the large flood of money from "supercapitalist" conglomerates overwhelms and displaces the citizen in federal legislation.

The protection of individual property from both the anarchic right and the socialist left requires the separation of commerce and the state.

The protection of individual property from both the anarchic right and the socialist left requires the separation of commerce and the state, just like the protection of free thought requires the separation of church and state and the separation of the media from the state. This separation is discussed at greater length in a later chapter, but here it should be recognized that the primary role of government is protection of those rights essential for life, liberty, property, and the pursuit of happiness for citizens—not for the state, the corporations, or other special interests.

Promotion of Good

In addition to protecting us from harm, we want governments to promote good, or at least not prevent good from being done in the general society. Can governments be good? Is this their role, or is their only role protection of life, liberty, and property?

Bureaucracies are impersonal and, by nature, they cannot "care" in the way one individual can care for another. As a rule, members of a bureaucracy use their position to care for themselves first, and then perform the job function for which they were hired. Does this mean that governments cannot be good? Clearly, there seems to be a difference between free societies like the United States and totalitarian regimes like the Soviet Union. What we can conclude is that, while bureaucrats can be expected to put their own interest first, even though we see more altruistic behavior in some societies than others, governments can be structured in ways that promote different ends. States can be structured to promote better or worse ends. We can say, in general, that a good state will protect citizens from harm, and a bad state will use them as a means to its own end.

Parents want their children to be good. We want our neighbors to be good. We want good leaders, good citizens, good doctors, good soldiers, good mothers, good fathers, good teachers, and good students. We want everyone to be good. Religions, philosophers, politicians, and educators encourage us to be good.

Not everyone defines good the same way, but over the years, as civilization has developed, some formulations have lasted. For example, the "Golden Rule" in the Bible reads:

> So whatever you wish that men would do to you, do so to them; for this is the law and the prophets.[15]

The Golden Rule is a statement of virtue, a statement that tells the reader to serve others in a way that would be pleasing to one'self. It is moral encouragement to perform beneficial actions for others. These are the type of actions one would want a government to encourage as well.

Immanuel Kant formulated a rational version of the Golden Rule in his categorical imperative:

> Act only on that maxim through which you can at the same time will that it should become a universal law.[16]

Both the Golden Rule and the categorical imperative encourage individual behavior in which one acts towards others in a way that can be applied universally to others as a good action. People can be encouraged to love others, to serve others, and to do good things for others. The public presentation of medals, awards, and monetary prizes in addition to praises and thanks are forms of reward for heroic behavior. In the field of ethics, this is called supererogatory behavior, action above and beyond the call of duty.

The U.S. founders believed that religions, families, and education in the private sphere were indispensable for the creation of the type of citizens a democracy requires. Ben Franklin wrote:

> Think how great a portion of mankind consists of weak and ignorant men and women, and of inexperienced, inconsiderate youth of both sexes, who have need of the motives of religion to restrain them from vice, to support their virtue, and retain them in the practice of it until it becomes habitual, which is the great point of its security.[17]

George Washington also spoke of a relationship in which the role of government is to protect religion, but religion, in turn, supports the government:

> [W]hile just government protects all in their religious rights, true religion affords to government its surest support.[18]

Ultimately, government can only provide a platform upon which citizens can perform good and altruistic acts. Government, as an instrument of force and rational justice, does not raise children to become men and women who are responsible, civic minded, and of good character. This can only be done by individuals who care for the nourishment and education of children— parents, churches, and schools. And teaching rational knowledge is different from the instilling of character which comes from the conscience and from habit.

Theologian Reinhold Niebuhr was one of the most articulate spokesmen on the relationship among love, power, and justice. He explained that rational justice can only be an approximation of love and only fulfilled by love. Yet, love without a rational justice rooted in power will become irrelevant, and the world will not be a place where love can be practiced. The following is a sample of his writing:

> The final law in which all other law is fulfilled is the law of love. But this law does not abrogate the laws of justice, except as love rises above justice to exceed its demands. The ordinary affairs of the community, the structures of politics and economics, must be governed by the spirit of justice and by specific and detailed definitions of rights and duties....
>
> The effort to substitute the law of love for the spirit of justice instead of recognizing love as the fulfillment and highest form of the spirit of justice, is derived from the failure to measure the power and persistence of self-interest.[19]

Government, as an instrument of force and rational justice, does not raise children to become responsible, civic minded, and of good character. This can only be done by individuals who care for the nourishment and education of children.

For Niebuhr, the Marxist idea of redistribution of wealth in the economic sphere is not a satisfactory definition of "justice." Justice is based on the freedom and equality of all human beings in the eyes of the law and in the hearts of fellow citizens. The freedom to pursue self-interest and happiness is the basis of a society in which creativity and full humanity can flourish. Self-interest drives all people, and justice requires that self-interest be curbed when it would harm others. It is arrogant to think that any system of government can achieve perfect justice by merely controlling self-interest.

Not even the best system of politics can be completed without the love which is cultivated in the cultural sphere. Love creates perfect justice, as only in love can another be truly served. Take, for example, a family with members from 6 months to 90 years of age. Will giving them each the same amount of food, the same amount of money, or the same amount of medicine create ideal justice? It would be rational justice, but only the knowledge of the other based on love and continual interaction will know what each member of the family needs best. Even then, Niebuhr saw perfect love as only something we could strive for in history, but that its perfection is "beyond history." A good government should encourage culture to best perform its task of creating responsible people who love and care for one another. And, the counter-role of good government is that it must not fail to curb the excesses of religion and acts done in the name of love that cause harm to others.

Preventing excesses is not a violation of the separation of church and state; it is rather the act of preventing the church from taking excess power that would reduce the protection of citizens from harm to life, liberty, or property.

Preventing Good

A state cannot force its citizens to do good, but it can prevent them from doing good. One way is for the state to take all of the resources necessary for people to help one another. Aristotle criticized communism in Plato's *Republic* for this:

> So excessive greed to acquire property is condemned, though every man, we may be sure, likes to have his bit of property. And there is this further point: there is a very great pleasure in giving; helping friends and associates, making things easy for strangers; and this can only be done by someone with property of his own.
>
> None of these advantages is secured by those who seek through the abolition of private ownership of property the extremest unification of the state.[20]

Pew Research Center surveys of human happiness around the world give us information about which things states should not prevent people from having. At the top of the list are basic economic necessities, family, and community.[21]

Financial Income

According to this research, financial income and happiness is most strongly correlated for people living in poverty who do not have the basic necessities for physical sustenance, particularly for people earning under $10,000-$15,000 per year. People earning between $15,000 per year and up to $150,000 per year expressed some increased happiness with income, but this was not as important as some other factors. People earning more than $150,000 per year did not report much increase in happiness, even with larger amounts of money.

Marriage and Family

Surveys show that married people are, on average, considerably happier than single people. Close and enduring relationships are the most important factor in happiness once people have the basic necessities for subsistence. People enjoy sharing their life with others, both as intimate partners and lifelong friends. They enjoy raising children who will carry some legacy of theirs into the future.

Statistics show that married men live an average of 15 years longer than non-married men, and earn 10 percent to 30 percent more than their single counterparts. Marriage encourages them to settle down and take responsibility. Boys raised by single mothers are 50 percent more likely to be incarcerated in prison before age 30 than boys growing up in homes with both fathers and mothers. They are also less likely to hold productive jobs.

These surveys and statistics indicate that government policies should not discourage marriage or family. Such discouragement can come in the form of income taxes on married households that provide economic incentives to remain single. It can also come in the form of welfare payments as aid to dependent children of single mothers. Another way to discourage marriage is to provide large subsidies for college tuition to young single mothers who could not afford college if they did not have the child. If the subsidy is too high, it encourages the woman to make a rational economic decision to have children out of wedlock, even if the end result is increased government debt and likely to create problems for society.

Community

Another source of happiness on the Pew surveys was church attendance. Reflection on these survey results indicates the importance people place on community. In the extremely poor country of Senegal, over 90 percent of the people feel church is important. In such impoverished countries, where families cannot survive alone, people need to help one another to survive. Churches and other community organizations make this possible. Church attendance also provides a way to collectively cope with poverty and offer people hope for the future.

In the United States, nearly 60 percent of those interviewed felt that church attendance is important to happiness, while in Western European countries, with official state churches, the number was closer to 10 percent. This difference likely reflects the fact that in the United States, there is freedom of religion and churches have to compete with one another to provide the type of spiritual community that people find enriching. More surveys could be done around the world relating to other types of community than churches, but certainly ethnic, tribal, and religious loyalties seem strongest in countries where the state does not provide equal protection to social groups.

State policies that undercut community, or that create artificially engineered communities through state churches, appear to reduce people's ability to pursue happiness. This can be viewed as a public harm. The principle of subsidiarity discussed in the next chapter sees responsibility on the community level as more personal than the state, if it is possible. Community is most supportive of human happiness when it is organized freely "from below" rather than imposed "from above" by the state. A government that tries to engineer a community prevents the good that natural communities can produce.

Promoting Harm

A state can adopt bad policies that create harm to citizens. This usually occurs when the government tries to increase itself at the expense of its citizens. Examples are state-sponsored gambling and some types of taxes. The first is an example of the state impeding the transmission of cultural values necessary for a good society. The second is an example of state interference with economic laws that make the economy less competitive, reduce employment opportunities, and harm the pursuit of personal livelihood.

Gambling

A good state should encourage productive economic behavior and good citizenship. The state needs these things from its citizens for its own long-term survival. Gambling provides a form of entertainment for most people; however, it can be addicting, or even become a false substitute for earning a living by producing real goods and services. Those who are addicted may lose their jobs, harm their loved ones, succumb to stealing to recover losses, and need counseling and recovery that costs families and states a lot of anguish and money.

A state can put a "sin" tax on gambling, like it does on cigarettes, to discourage it. Many economists recommend giving individuals a gambling license that is revoked if the gambler suffers a problem associated with gambling, such as bankruptcy, theft, or a court judgment resulting from the addiction.[22] Such state actions provide disincentives for irresponsible behavior without eliminating the freedom for many people to gamble for entertainment, if that provides a form of happiness.

State-sponsored gambling is more socially destructive than allowing and regulating private gambling. One reason is that the state encourages citizens to engage in behavior that could be harmful to both themselves and the state. It gives people false hopes by promoting, through state advertising, the idea that people can get rich quickly. Such advertising is a form of deception, and governments should not deceive their own citizens; it is not moral behavior. In addition, gambling is a zero-sum game. It simply redistributes a pie. By promoting participation in a zero-sum game rather than productive work that expands the economy, the state impedes the economic growth that would improve the lives of all citizens.

> **State-sponsored gambling is more socially destructive than allowing and regulating private gambling. One reason is that the state encourages citizens to engage in behavior that could be harmful to themselves and the state.**

State lotteries pay the salaries of bureaucrats whose members want to have a better life each year. As we discuss in Chapter Three, there are only three things a bureaucrat can do to help increase his own financial situation: (1) raise more funds, which in this case either means putting more of the budget into advertising the lottery or expanding the number of gambling outlets, both having negative social consequences; (2) spend less on the programs the lottery was supposed to fund, or (3) eliminate the competition, for example by putting private casinos out of business. Rent-seeking incentives that help bureaucrats at the expense of the citizens and the state they are supposed to serve should be discouraged.

Another argument against state-sponsored gambling is the principle of separation of state and commerce. Just as people find greater happiness in free churches, they will find higher efficiency in free commercial enterprises. With respect to gambling, this principle applies as well. States are very inefficient as businesses.

A sin tax on private competitive gambling raises money for the state more efficiently than government-run monopolies.

Whatever program a state wants to fund with lottery income would be better obtained in almost any other way than a state-run lottery. A state lottery is a symptom of a political system on its way to collapse, with the short-term income of departments or staff a higher priority than the long-term health of the state. State-run gambling should be illegal in a state seeking to promote life, liberty, and happiness of all citizens.

Income Tax on Wages

Another way a state can promote social harm is an income tax on the wages of factory laborers. This is harmful because such a tax raises the cost of production and the price of the final product. In a global market, this reduces the economic competitiveness against other countries that do not add tax burdens to the cost of products. Such taxes contribute to unemployment and loss of jobs to other countries. To compete, our workforce has to be much more efficient to offset the tax burden. Chapter Eight explains how sales taxes would reverse this trend.

Conflicts of Interest

A conflict of interest is when anyone in a position of trust as a decision-maker for an institution has an opportunity to gain personally from that decision. For example, a government purchasing agent has a conflict of interest if he is deciding on awarding a contract for a product from which he or a member of his family stands to make profit. Preventing and eliminating conflicts of interest is one of the foremost concerns of an impartial government. Many possible conflicts of interest were not identified by the founders or existent in their time. In a government where defense is the primary purpose, rather than redistribution of wealth, fewer conflicts of interest arise.

An elected representative has a conflict of interest if he takes a financial campaign contribution or other gifts from a company that would benefit from legislation he could introduce. A university trustee has a conflict of interest if the board awards a service contract to his own company. A conflict of interest occurs when legislators set their own pay or reimburse their own expenses through legislation they pass. This is a problem in the United States in which Congress is set up to be self-regulating on issues of personal benefit from the public funds they are entrusted to watch.

Without a majority of citizens being self-regulating a democracy or republic cannot exist—it requires them. However, political and economic realism must assume that self-regulation will be inevitably abused.

Self-regulation is an ideal that should be encouraged in all areas of life and by all professions. Families, churches, and the private cultural sphere have a responsibility to produce self-controlled and generous citizens. Without a majority of citizens being self-regulating, a democracy or republic cannot exist—it requires them. However, political and economic realism must assume that self-regulation will be inevitably abused, and if a few can get away with such abuse it will spread, eventually leading to concentrations of power and tyranny. Therefore, checks against abuses of self-regulation should operate in all social institutions.

Conflicts of interest also exist when large corporations acquire companies to eliminate competition. Or, if one acquires other types of businesses to serve a captive market. For example, if an insurance company buys a hospital, it might only reimburse insured clients that receive treatments at their hospital where list prices for these services might be inflated.

The Glass-Steagall Act of 1933 was designed, among other things, to separate banking from investment so that stock market crashes would not cause bank failures. While it did not address the primary reason for the bank failures during the Great Depression, it addressed a conflict of interest that was a possible source of public harm—bank investment policy that would put deposits held in trust for depositors at risk. This Act was repealed in 1999 to make way for the Citibank and Travelers Insurance merger. Reinstituting this once-banned conflict of interest would help reduce the possibility for an unfair economic playing field. One way the government can protect citizens from harm is to forbid these financial conflicts of interest.

The Control of Information

Harm is not only inflicted on citizens through the abuse of political and economic power, but also through the control of knowledge and information. On Wall Street, knowledge of a corporate decision before it is public encourages the one who possesses that knowledge to buy or sell large amounts of stock for personal gain. But this is unfair. Public investors may lose money as a result of this insider trading.

Most people are aware of fraud, deceit, and other tactics in the use of misinformation in which one person takes advantage over another. Swindlers often hide behind freedom of contract as a shield for their scams, saying that in a free society, it is the responsibility of the consumer to understand all of the fine print. Fine print accompanies the issuance of credit cards, prescription drugs, stock purchases, and all types of financial activity in which the dangers of fraud are present. Most people don't have the time or legal experience to read fine print, so the government has an obligation to enforce minimum standards of economic behavior, regardless of whether the fine print supposedly makes it legal.

Newspapers and major television stations also have conflicts of interest in reporting news, especially if the news report would adversely affect the business of the conglomerate that owns the news company. There is also a temptation to make news sensational to generate higher sales. The commercial interests of mass media often conflict with reports of truth. These can be balanced by publicly funded media companies whose interests are different than commercial companies that rely on advertising. Consolidation in the control of information can be just as socially harmful as consolidation of political power or economic power.

Conclusion

The main role of government is to provide an environment that protects the citizens in their pursuit of life, liberty, and happiness. This requires not only the defense against invading armies, but also the elimination of all consolidations of political, economic, or information power that will allow those who hold such power to use it for personal gain at the expense of the citizens.

Questions for Review and Reflection

1. Describe what Hobbes called the "state of nature." Why is a laissez-faire economy a "state of nature"?

2. Why is peace not the same as the absence of war?

3. Why is the commandment "thou shalt not kill" an inadequate basis for protecting one's right to life?

4. How did Hobbes's concept of sovereignty differ from that of the U.S. founders?

5. Why do some people believe in abortion and euthanasia even though there is right to life? Where do you stand on these two controversial practices?

6. Explain why bureaucracies are unable to care for people according to their personal needs.

7. Explain how communism, which maintains state ownership of property, prevents people from caring for one another.

8. What is "rent-seeking" behavior? What are the ways a bureaucrat can improve his own financial income? Which of the ways you listed do not treat the citizens for whom they work as sovereigns?

9. Do you believe individuals and organizations can be self-regulating? Should government act in ways that assume self-regulation will work?

10. List three examples of a conflict of interest that are not mentioned in this chapter.

3

The Principle of Subsidiarity

Subsidiarity

1 : the quality or state of being subsidiary 2 : a principle in social organization: functions which subordinate or local organizations perform effectively belong more properly to them than to a dominant central organization.[1]

Natural Subsidiarity

Human beings depend upon air, water, earth, sunlight, and plant and animal life that they did not themselves create. They require the earth's complex environment they are a part of, and if it is altered too much or destroyed, they will die. Like other animals, human beings are *subsidiary* to nature. Nature came first. The human mind can be similarly understood as subsidiary to the human animal body. It cannot exist without our body. Awareness and thought are stimulated by impulses from sensory perception, from experience, from training, and from reason.

Attempts to defy the laws of the environment upon which we depend can be fatal. If we jump off a cliff, try to breathe under water, walk into a den of hungry lions, or in some other way act contrary to the natural laws upon which we depend, then our bodies will perish. Even though our egos, and often our sacred scriptures, say that human beings are the crowning of creation, or have dominion over it because of our superior thought and skills, when we act so as to defy the laws of our environment, we suffer serious consequences. Our bodies' higher form of complexity depends upon the lower forms of complexity. When we abuse those lower forms, we threaten ourselves. Destruction of our natural environment is a form of suicide.

Furthermore, entities in each level of natural complexity have to perform their "responsibility" for the next levels to function. For example, the earth has to stay in its present orbit to maintain temperatures necessary for the life that lives on it. The oceans need to maintain their chemical composition for current species of fish to live in them. In symbiotic relationships, each has to perform its role. For example, bees require plant nectar for food; the plants require bees for pollination. Within a cell, the various organelles (like human organs) must cooperate according to function for the cell to retain its structure, process food and waste, create energy, and reproduce. If one organelle fails, the cell will be handicapped or die. In humans, if the organs of the body fail to perform their function, the individual will be handicapped or die. This is also true of human societies, which are social organisms.

Social Subsidiarity

Human societies are more complex forms of organization than individual human beings. In a society, individual human beings are analogous to the individual cells that make up the human body. Human beings can form social institutions to perform various roles within a society, for example political, economic, and cultural institutions. In simple societies, human beings live in small family groups and forage for food or live on small subsistence farms. In more complex societies, higher institutions like states are composed of other institutions like cities, corporations, and universities with each performing roles like the organs of a body. These intermediate institutions, like human organs, are composed of individuals and families that are the basic cells of society.

When any of those resources necessary to support life are in short supply, there is competition for them, and violence often results. In what Thomas Hobbes called "the state of nature," the strongest will inevitably try to control scarce resources, and the weak will have to try to live without them or die. Even though human beings are able to interact with and shape their environment significantly, the attempt to transgress the natural laws of subsistence has dire consequences. In the "state of nature," survival is determined by the brute force of the individual. As such, a society cannot grow larger or more complex than the abilities of the strongest individual to direct others. Such is a society of force.

The creation of a harmonious and peaceful society superior to one based on force requires the cooperation of individuals and the division of social labor, with each unit assuming a responsibility in relation to the whole society. The entire social organism has to respond to a body of proper knowledge, analogous to the human brain's regulation of the human body and all its organs, or the information stored in the DNA and RNA of a cell.

In the natural world, for example, by understanding the strength of materials and how loads are carried through beams, we can design a bridge that will make our travel across a river much more pleasant than in a state of subsistence where we would wade through muddy water swinging sticks at predators. However, if we fail to build a bridge that obeys the laws of physics, it will collapse, and we might find ourselves in the muddy water below, injured and surrounded by predators, thereby creating a worse situation.

> **The creation of a harmonious and peaceful society superior to one based on force requires the cooperation of individuals and the division of social labor, with each unit assuming a responsibility in relation to the whole society.**

These principles apply in a similar way to human society. If human beings make decisions or laws that attempt to defy the laws that govern the entities upon which they depend, they will collapse. However, for reasons of selfishness, power, superstition, and ignorance, shortcuts that ignore the principle of subsidiarity are often attempted, with great human suffering as the result.

The consolidation of power, wealth, or information that deprives the individual members of society the essentials they need to be strong social building blocks can be compared to a rancher who takes all the water for his family and lets his cattle starve. This is poor governance and leads to social collapse.

The constitutions of modern democratic and republican political states attempt to thwart the consolidation of power that is experienced in Hobbes's "state of nature." However, various "Leviathans" appear no matter how carefully a constitution is crafted. In creating the U.S. Constitution, "consolidation" was the primary evil of concern for Thomas Jefferson.[2] While the founders' primary concern was the consolidation of political power, consolidation can also occur in economic power with the tendency toward monopoly, in knowledge with the tendency toward orthodoxy and fundamentalism, and in the family with wife-beating, yelling, and intimidation.

The principle of subsidiarity is the opposite of the principle of consolidation. It is associated with decentralization, pluralism, freedom, and personal responsibility.

The principle of subsidiarity is the opposite of the principle of consolidation. It is associated with decentralization, pluralism, freedom, and personal responsibility. In short, it is a principle required for life, liberty, and the pursuit of happiness. It is a principle that urges all people to do their part, both maintaining their individual strength and happiness and serving the larger purpose of the whole. The principle of consolidation is associated with selfishness, control, economic stagnation, and death.

There are some cases in which more consolidation is necessary to be the most effective. For example, we could not expect small counties to maintain or coordinate an interstate highway system. However, it would not be very pleasant if we depended on the federal government to maintain our own driveways. The history of the United States, the history of General Motors, and the history of many human endeavors is one of consolidation. It is central to the process of the rise and fall of empires, both ancient and modern. And "the bigger they are, the harder they fall" is a truism when the size is a result of consolidated power, because the rulers of such institutions consume the resources that individual members need to make the social institution operate according to its principles of organization. Governments and social institutions built on subsidiarity are inherently stronger and more durable than top-heavy institutions controlled by force.

Use of the Term Subsidiarity

The concept of subsidiarity dates to antiquity. It was present in the foundations of the Babylonian and Roman Empires and absent in their demise. The principle was advocated by the Catholic encyclical *Rerum Novarum* issued in 1891[3] that discussed economic justice as industrial development posed new social issues related to the consolidation of economic power. The term "subsidiarity" was used in *Quadragesimo Anno* in 1931.[4] The principle of subsidiarity gradually gained wider public acceptance and it became an important principle, at least in theory, in the creation of the European Union. Every nation joining the Union wanted to protect its own integrity and sovereignty. Protocol 30 (1997) specifically adopts the principle of subsidiarity in the European Union:

> THE HIGH CONTRACTING PARTIES, DETER-MINED to establish the conditions for the application of the principles of subsidiarity and proportionality enshrined in Article 5 of the Treaty establishing the European Community with a view to defining more precisely the criteria for applying them and to ensure their strict observance and consistent implementation by all institutions;...HAVE CONFIRMED that the conclusions of the Birmingham European Council on 16 October 1992 and the overall

approach to the application of the subsidiarity principle agreed by the European Council meeting in Edinburgh on 11-12 December 1992 will continue to guide the action of the Union's institutions as well as the development of the application of the principle of subsidiarity...[5]

Freedom and the Principle of Subsidiarity

While the principle of subsidiarity was developed in the context of the economic and social problems that arose with the development of large industrial manufacturing during the nineteenth century, it is a principle that can be more widely applied to any social responsibility generally, whether it falls in the realm of government, the economy, or culture. It is a principle associated with building complexity from the free and voluntary organization of smaller social units, the smallest being free individuals.

Subsidiarity is a principle that the Church has not always implemented in its own history. The Protestant Reformation was, in part, a reaction to excessive centralization of the Church. The political ideas of a "social contract" developed by Hobbes, Rousseau, and modern political philosophers, was a similar reaction to political tyranny.

The Late Middle Ages

The modern ideas of personal responsibility and individualism can be found in several developments in the Late Middles Ages that accompanied the breakdown of feudalism. One was the increase of towns in which new and sometimes experimental social arrangements were formed. Many people, freed from bondage to the land, expressed creativity in literature, art, and invention, promoting the Renaissance. The development of the printing press freed written knowledge from the captivity of the Church and paved the way for widespread public education. The Protestant Reformation reformulated religion for the new social conditions in which ideas of humanism and personal responsibility were developing.

In the feudal world, the serf was bound to the land and its prince, and the prince to the emperor. The Catholic Church had developed a hierarchy that mirrored these social arrangements. Priests were intercessors for the people and could forgive their sins. Salvation could be bought with indulgences. The priests were bound to obey their bishops, and the bishops the Pope. In this world, the Pope was the spiritual emperor and controlled the direct pipeline to God.

Protestantism, on the other hand, taught that individuals are personally accountable to God and that the Church and priests do not bestow salvation but merely assist the individual in the development of his or her faith. The impact of the Protestant faith on the human psyche and work ethic was revolutionary. Typically, a serf working someone else's land was motivated to do no more than necessary. This attitude could be found more recently in the highly centralized Soviet Union where people were working for the state rather than themselves. There the saying emerged, "We pretend to work, and they pretend to pay us." However, a Protestant believed that work was a glorification of God, and that everything one does should be pleasing to God.

For the Protestant, how the landlord or supervisor judges your work is secondary. Primary is the fact that God is watching everything you do and will judge your life for eternity. The Protestant conscience is a slave driver stricter than any earthly boss. A Protestant believer dares not violate any of the Ten Commandments for fear of eternal damnation. He believes that a confession to the priest is not sufficient. As a result, strict Protestant believers are less likely to try to bend rules for personal selfishness. They are, rather, known for the principle of "delayed gratification," which produced great economic output and savings. The consequence of these beliefs was often great productivity, high quality work, and personal wealth.[6]

The Protestant Reformation took root in growing European cities and towns. Martin Luther's father was an entrepreneur in the walled city of Mansfeld, Germany. He had developed a foundry with a partner and a capital loan.[7] John Calvin was born to a prosperous father in Noyon, France who sent him to the Sorbonne in Paris. By age 23 he was a Doctor of Law.[8] These men had been freed from the constraints of the feudal world and were able to study the arts and the sciences that sprung from the Renaissance. They were men of learning who promoted the reading of books. Before the development of the printing press, most people were illiterate. Large scale democracies require literate and self-motivated masses. Protestantism was a vehicle for producing a culture appropriate to democracy. Each person was to be a responsible citizen, not dependent on those who controlled property or knowledge.

Self-governance based on education, personal skills, and respect for the rights of others gave birth to the Enlightenment and ultimately to modern democracy. The power flow in the hierarchical top-down society of the feudal world had been reversed, and the modern world was born as subsidiarity became a tacit principle in the quest for personal freedom and happiness. It generated political structures upon which a new world could begin that could support large populations in Europe unknown since Roman antiquity.

The Pyramid as a Symbol for Subsidiarity

A social system based on the voluntary federation of smaller social groups into larger, based on the principle of subsidiarity, can be thought of as a pyramid of responsibility. The pyramids in Egypt were more than simple burial sites; they were sophisticated architectural accomplishments based on mathematics. They also symbolize an enduring human society and a microcosm of the cosmos. They were precisely made and have existed longer than most other large human artifacts. They have stood much longer than any modern skyscraper will stand.

A pyramid is extremely strong and is viewed by Masons as a symbol of order and strength. It is not the type of geometric structure that can collapse, because each layer of blocks is supported by a layer of blocks that is wider. The founders of the United

Figure 1: The reverse of the Great Seal is on the back of the U.S. dollar. A pyramid is a stable structure that cannot collapse because each layer rests on a layer larger and stronger than itself. The triangle with the eye represents the providence and self-evident truths enshrined in the Constitution that guides and watches over all the levels of human government.

States designed the reverse of the Great Seal with a pyramid. Their description from 1782 is as follows:

> The pyramid signifies Strength and Duration: The Eye over it and the Motto allude to the many signal interpositions of providence in favour of the American cause. The date underneath is that of the Declaration of Independence and the words under it signify the beginning of the new American Æra, which commences from that date.[9]

The words *annuit cœptis* mean that the eye of providence "favors our undertakings," or smiles upon the new society created in America. The Great Seal was designed in 1782, before the Articles of Confederation failed. However, the philosophy of the founders and the concepts contained in the Declaration of Independence were retained as the framers attempted to create a "more perfect union" in the Constitution drafted in 1787 and adopted in 1789.

The Family at the Base of the Pyramid

In a pyramid, there is a wide square base of blocks on the ground. Think of each block on the bottom level, sitting on the earth living in harmony with nature, as responsible citizens and families that support themselves. Each family is a like a cell that is self-sufficient, gathers its own food, disposes of its own waste, maintains its form, and regenerates. A family in society acts like cells in our body. In Thomas Jefferson's view, each of these little

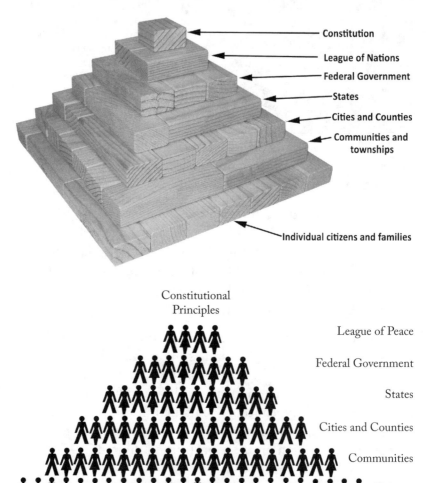

Figure 2: The layers of a stable and enduring society can be represented by a pyramid. Above is a three-dimensional representation of a social pyramid in blocks. Below is the same pyramid represented two-dimensionally. The U.S. founders viewed the entire social experiment to be guided by the Constitution which was above the entire human enterprise and consistent with self-evident truths and natural law.

social units would be subsistence farmers or run small businesses in towns that supported an agrarian society. His vision was a very lateral society in which most social units exist side by side. A traditional agrarian family was a political unit, a cultural unit, an economic unit, and a voting unit in early America. Jefferson feared the accumulation of people in cities as a precursor to the consolidation of power in government. His acquisition of large amounts of land in the Louisiana Purchase was to provide room for the westward expansion of the American experiment.

But human beings organize into more complex social units than families. Like cells, they form into more complex bodies with specialized tasks and division of labor. In the human body, an individual cell does not have to seek food; it relies on a portion of the meals eaten by the body. The various organs of the body are composed of cells that specialize in performing tasks for the whole, and they, in turn, are cared for. Many of the U.S. founders like Alexander Hamilton believed in large scale commerce, industry, and building great cities. They set the stage for the large scale financial and industrial system that eventually emerged in the United States. Such systems work well when each contributes its portion to the whole. It is a problem, however, if the part of the system that has the most power begins to consume other parts. This is what happens with unchecked power and bad governance. It is the breakdown of subsidiarity.

The Organization of Families into Tribes and Communities

Basic survival is a constant struggle for individuals and families that cannot depend upon any other level of government for protection. In a "state of nature," some people or families, in an attempt to improve their own situation, will abuse, exploit, or conquer others who are more helpless. A larger and more powerful social organization, with laws and a policing mechanism, can deter and punish those who would interfere with the well-being of its members.

Most cultures develop social values and laws like the Ten Commandments that, when obeyed, lead to a strong harmonious society. The problem is getting people to voluntarily follow such rules without trying to bend them or get around them for personal advantage. In face-to-face communities, it is easier for people to conform through peer pressure than in large impersonal societies where people feel they can get away with bending the rules without getting noticed. Where laws treat everyone equally and are policed enough to deter violation, there is little need for police force to keep social order. Most people will obey the rules. On the other hand, when many people in society prosper from illegal behavior or when laws are passed that treat some people better than others, many people will try to disobey rules.

Many great societies like ancient Babylon, Rome, or the United States prospered at their founding because they were fair and each person voluntarily performed his or her role in the larger society. Protestantism provided cultural underpinnings for such behavior. This existed to an unusual extent in the Puritans of early America who emphasized extreme self-discipline and personal autonomy. At the inception of the United States, families organized into communities or townships and developed their rules collectively. These groups, like tribal societies, are based on face-to-face relationships in which every member of the community knows every other member.

Community organizations traditionally care for individuals and families in need. They find ways to help widows, orphans, and others who cannot provide for themselves. Communities also come together for rites-of-passage to adulthood. Such rituals reaffirm a person's responsibilities as an adult or marriage partner. Funerals provide an opportunity to lift up noble traits of the departed to which all should aspire. Communities work together on large projects that families cannot easily accomplish themselves, like raising a house or a barn when a new couple begins married life or collecting a harvest together when crops are ripe. They may also create some limited physical infrastructure like wells, irrigation, roads, and bridges.

The community that best supports the pursuit of life, liberty, and happiness of each of its members is a community that promotes a system of values in which the individual becomes a responsible social unit, guided by his or her conscience to serve the wider community voluntarily, while at the same time pursuing his or her own life and happiness.

Because care for others is a burden, community members are motivated to get homeless, unemployed, or unskilled people functioning on their own as quickly as possible. Churches do not want the indigent to remain that way; the sooner they get the needy back on their feet, the easier it is for all of the members of the community. This is often not the case when a community pushes off such tasks onto higher levels of government. Social workers in many cities and states have the opposite motivation. They need indigent clients in order to get paid. If they succeed in returning them to normal, self-sufficient life, they lose their income. This is a clear example of an area where subsidiarity makes a society stronger.

> **The community that best supports the pursuit of life, liberty, and happiness of each of its members is a community that promotes a system of values in which the individual become a responsible social unit, guided by his or her conscience.**

The Conditions for Democracy in America

The first factor was the religious culture. In New England, the religious values of the early Puritan settlers had left their stamp on colonial culture. People were strongly motivated by their conscience to work hard, take care of themselves, and to help their neighbors. Such values contributed significantly to the possibility that democracy could work in America.[10] Each person was not only prepared to care for himself or herself, but also to care for others, creating the Kingdom of God on earth[11] and building a "new Israel."[12]

Another factor that enabled democracy in America to prosper was the wide availability of land. Thomas Jefferson believed that as long as land was available for people to settle and create a subsistence life, they would not feel it necessary to try to acquire part of someone else's fortune for their survival. Frederick Jackson Turner, an influential American historian in the early twentieth century, developed the "Frontier Thesis,"[13] in which the American frontier promoted freedom, self-reliance, and innovation as it allowed people to escape the shackles of civilization. Each new generation reared in America, or each new immigrant arriving from foreign lands, could freely pursue his dreams on the frontier with his own piece of land, on which he could build a house and raise a family. The frontier society was a very flat society, with primarily community level organization. It was quite different from hierarchical European civilization. It allowed the United States to develop between these two worlds.

Figure 3 contains a model of a pyramid and a two-dimensional representation of early American communities where subsidiarity was extremely high and the foundation upon which the state and federal government rested is very strong and secure.

Observations of Alexis de Tocqueville in Early America

After historian Alexis de Tocqueville's visit to the United States in 1831, he wrote his classic work *Democracy in America*. It remains one of the most insightful descriptions of life in early America, how the young democracy differed from other societies, and what its strengths and weaknesses were. His analysis is helpful for any student of democracy. One aspect particularly striking to him was decentralization of power and the assumption of responsibility and obedience to the laws by the citizens:

In no country in the world does the law hold so absolute
a language as in America; and in no country is the right
of applying it vested in so many hands. The administrative
power in the United States presents nothing either centralized or hierarchical in its constitution; this accounts for its
passing unperceived. The power exists, but its representative
is nowhere to be seen.[14]

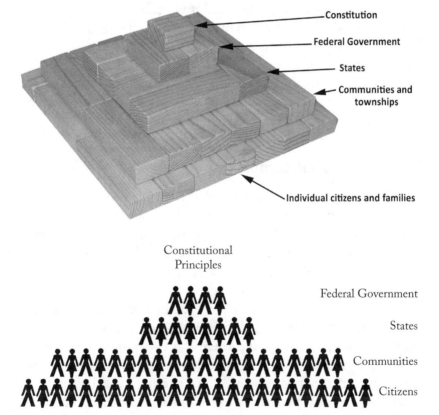

Figure 3: Early American society can be represented by a relatively flat pyramid in
which the family and community levels composed most of the society. There were very
few large cities, and the state and federal government was very small. Strong values and
a frontier where people could spread out required relatively little government.

The legal system of the United States was simple. It gave power to the people who ran their societies themselves and with the help of their representatives. De Tocqueville observed that laws were respected because each citizen regarded the law "as a contract to which he is himself a party." Thus, the situation is unlike Europe, where "a numerous and turbulent multitude" regard law "as their natural enemy" to be looked upon with fear and distrust.[15]

De Tocqueville also noticed that the United States of 1831 was composed nearly entirely of a middle class who owned their own property and organized into small units called townships. "The New Englander is attached to his township, not so much because he was born into it, but because it is a free and strong community, of which he is a member."[16] He felt that one of the chief reasons that republican institutions remained in the United States was because there was "no great capital city, whose direct or indirect influence is felt over the whole extent of the country."[17]

Cities and Social Complexity

In early American society, most people were self-sufficient, and the presence of government was minimal. Except for the post office, voting, registering deeds to land, and obtaining legal certificates, government was nearly absent from people's lives. This began to change with immigration and industrialization, which increased and concentrated population.

Cities and counties are symbolized by the third level in the block pyramid in Figure 2. Industries, cities, and states contain many levels of hierarchy, and there is a division of labor where people perform different functions required by the organization. The same is true of large organizations like an established catholic church or an army. With this degree of social organization, there are generally subunits that specialize in function like organs in the human body. These subunits handle functions like water, sewer, schools, roads, and parks more easily than individual families because of their larger size and impact on a larger population. They are usually larger than face-to-face communities and employ less personal bureaucratic processes of administration.

Individuals that move to large cities for jobs often lose their connection to family and community and experience a kind of anonymity as they leave their traditional community and become a "cell" in a business or organization that is not related to a physical neighborhood. When large bureaucracies of city management displace the more personal face-to-face relations in towns and townships that de Tocqueville studied, the social pyramid can become less stable.

Figure 4 shows a pyramid in which the third layer is larger than the second. A system based on subsidiarity would devolve more city administration to the neighborhoods and face-to-face

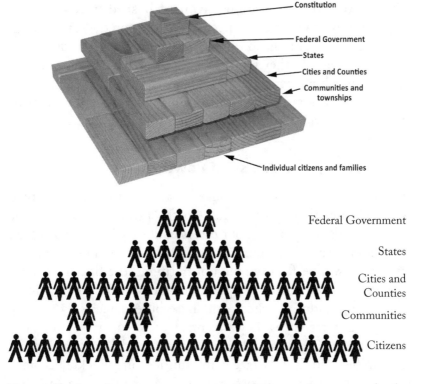

Figure 4: The above diagram represents a society in which power is concentrated at the city level and begins to overwhelm community, making the society less stable.

communities than is usually observed in modern cities. The larger third layer portrays a city administration that minimizes community, and often tries to bypass community relating directly to individuals.

Without strong communities below the city level, it becomes less stable and less caring. This happened, for example, in New York when government poor houses were established to replace programs run by religious and community charities. A city soup kitchen or homeless shelter is more likely to treat individuals bureaucratically than would a church or other community organization. If the people working for the city services are being paid to serve people they don't know, their motivation will be different than community members who want their neighbors on their feet. Also, people working in large-scale relief will generally be told to give everyone the same care, based on established procedure. They will not know the particular needs of the person they are serving. Because large centralized service programs are often driven by statistical analysis, they tend to be less humane and less just. By nature, such bureaucracies cannot "care" for people in a personal way, as families and communities do. It is harder for them to address the variety of special cases and different needs.

Bureaucracy and Abuse of Power

Bureaucracies are easier to abuse because of their large impersonal nature. They typically rely on the processing of paper or computer data, often without direct contact with an individual. Individuals can abuse bureaucracies through fraudulent claims and paperwork—for example not notifying the Social Security Administration when a recipient has died or filing false Medicare claims. Administrators can abuse bureaucracies by secretly sidetracking resources they are entrusted to supervise into bank accounts for themselves, their relatives, friends, or ethnic group. In families and face-to-face communities, one quickly becomes suspicious of such activities, because they see that someone has acquired wealth disproportionate to their job, or they quickly notice the community accounts don't balance. However, when administrators live in impersonal cities, in different neighborhoods from co-workers, such anomalies are not so easily noticed.

This problem of abuse of bureaucratic institutions becomes more severe the further they are removed from the people they serve. It is easier to defraud the U.S. government on a more massive scale, for example, than it is to defraud a state or a city. And it also takes larger and more expensive bureaucracies to police such abuse. Special agencies, like the FBI, with large budgets are required in such societies, making them less economical to operate than societies formed with greater subsidiarity.

Abuse of public trust can be deterred by harsh laws that assure abusers of strong punishment when such abuses are uncovered. In some societies like Hammurabi's Babylon or some Islamic societies in which a hand is chopped off a thief, the deterrence of crime can be more effective than in a society where the wealthier citizen can afford to hire a lawyer with skill to get punishment dismissed. In societies like Hammurabi's Babylon, in which government leaders receive greater punishment than the average citizens because of their greater level of responsibility, leaders are less likely to abuse power. Today, the justice system found in the United States is quite ambiguous. Laws have been written that allow all kinds of exceptions, rules of evidence, and procedures that convey a sense of greater immunity for the privileged. This undermines government legitimacy.

Anonymity in mass society has been exacerbated and partly shielded in some rights to privacy that have been developed by the courts. Some "rights to privacy" merely prevent the transparency that is self-evident in face-to-face community, making white-collar crime easier. In *Law in a Democratic Society*, Morton A. Kaplan argued that "the right to be left alone is the right to be no one."[18] When individuals are treated as autonomous individuals whose only necessary social relationship is the state, they lose the essence of humanity that is created in the relationships of people with one another. The right to privacy also shields others from knowledge of improprieties that might take place through bureaucratic abuse or fraud. The right to privacy, carried to an extreme, conflicts with the demands for justice, transparency, and humanity.

Corporations, States, and Federations

Large corporations, states, and federations are all bureaucratic and impersonal in nature. The large corporation is to the business as the city is to the township or the religious denomination is to the parish. The large corporation has departments that specialize in function, for example, design, production, sales, accounts payable, accounts receivable, customer service, building management, etc.

> **When individuals are treated as autonomous individuals whose only necessary social relationship is the state, they lose the essence of humanity that is created in the relationships of people with one another.**

In a small business, the owner is in charge of all these functions personally, thus you do not run into a problem where the "right hand doesn't know what the left hand is doing." Customer care in large bureaucratic organizations is often impersonal and may greet customers with a series of telephone prompts, privacy notices, and disclaimers before contact with a real person is possible. And even then service is still long-distance and impersonal.

Similarly in a religious denomination there might be departments specializing in doctrine, in music, in foreign missions, in disaster relief, etc. In a local congregation, the pastor is involved in all of these aspects and, in addition, he provides personal care through home and hospital visitation, marriage officiation and counseling, and personal testimonials at funerals. A denominational headquarters cannot perform such tasks in a personal way. If a representative would be sent from headquarters to conduct a funeral, it would be officious in nature, and any semblance of a personal touch might be provided on cue cards prepared by the local pastor.

The larger and more centralized an entity becomes, the less chance there is for personal connection to the individuals the organization is intended to serve. Perhaps worse than the impersonality of service in a large organization is the greater possibility of abuse of power. In a centralized bureaucracy, chances of escaping detection seem greater. In addition, the only way a bureaucrat can improve his situation is by being promoted within the system or by keeping more of the organization's resources originally intended for others. Consolidating power (e.g., taking over the responsibilities that could be delegated through subsidiarity) is an inevitable result of unchecked human nature in a bureaucracy.

In drafting the Constitution, the founders of the United States, were primarily concerned about the relationship between the individual states and the federal government. But Jefferson had a clear understanding of the principle of subsidiarity and its relation to liberty as it generally refers to levels of government:

> What has destroyed liberty and the rights of man in every government which has ever existed under the sun? The generalizing and concentrating all cares and powers into one body, no matter whether of the autocrats of Russia or France, or of the aristocrats of a Venetian Senate. And I do believe that if the Almighty has not decreed that man shall never be free (and it is blasphemy to believe it), that the secret will be found to be in the making himself the depository of the powers respecting himself, so far as he is competent to them, and delegating only what is beyond his competence by a synthetical process, to higher and higher orders of functionaries, so as to trust fewer and fewer powers in proportion as the trustees become more and more oligarchical.[19]

All people, bureaucrats and self-supporting citizens alike, want to expand their dominion and improve their lives. There is nothing morally wrong with this natural desire. However, it is problematic when the pursuit of your own happiness interferes with that of another or takes place involuntarily at the expense of another. The problem for bureaucrats is that they are not economic producers, so any expansion of their power not given by those citizens who support them is a form of theft from them. This principle not only applies to governments, but also to corporations and other organizations that have expanded to levels of bureaucracy beyond face-to-face relationships. Excessive CEO pay is an obvious example of such abuse, with the restructuring of pensions, the award of stock options that dilute shareholders' worth, and other rationale aimed at enriching CEOs when the individual stockholder or employee has little power to challenge the legal and financial power at the disposal of the CEO.

The Problem of Centralized Power

The temptation to centralize is always strong. It is a way for the centralizer to increase his power and wealth. Centralizing occurs in the name of efficiency or in taking responsibility over from the citizen to make his life easier. Centralization of some functions is appropriate, for example, a highway system. However, centralizers are prone to centralize functions more appropriate to lower levels. And, people at lower levels with hopes of getting more for doing less are often happy to let the centralizer do their work. However, such schemes always come with a price that is ultimately high for those in the lower levels. Higher taxes, exploitation, and bankruptcy are frequent outcomes.

Individuals and smaller social units are tempted to hand over their responsibilities to larger social units. People are happy to let the government pay for their medical care or retirement when politicians tell them they will provide it. Likewise, a city is happy to build a commuter rail line that employs citizens and provides transportation if the state and federal governments promise to pay most of the costs. However, these things cannot be accomplished without somebody paying for them. As such, they are a form of economic redistribution and some form of theft. It is one thing if those paying the bill are being served or if the recipients are viewed by those paying as needing their aid. However, it becomes a moral problem if the recipients are already living better lives than those paying the bills, or if those paying are forced to do so involuntarily.

For example, would rural farmers in Minnesota have any desire to pay for a commuter rail system used for the citizens of Minneapolis or visitors to Minneapolis who spend their money there? Would the citizens of Toledo want their federal tax dollars to pay for a rail system in Minneapolis instead of one in their own city? Is it right for the United States government to borrow the money from a Chinese investor to pay for such a system? At their core, such systems of redistribution are similar to a Ponzi scheme,[20] which has long been outlawed for individual citizens. However, the government itself frequently attempts to foist such schemes on citizens in the process of trying to centralize power. Such schemes are unsustainable and cause financial bubbles and government collapses that ruin many of the people they were intended to support. Often those who have profited from such schemes, whether legislators or their cronies, have fled with the money or moved it offshore before the collapse, leaving the citizens to pay for the mess.

People are happy to let the government pay for their medical care or retirement when their politicians tell them they will provide it. However, these things cannot be accomplished without somebody paying for them.

In a democracy, these schemes reflect the irresponsible behavior of people, both at giving and receiving ends. Everyone is hoping to get more for less, and a pyramid or Ponzi-type political culture is adopted instead of the principle of subsidiarity. Higher levels of government are seen as more responsible, when the opposite is actually the case. Higher levels of government are only necessary for administration appropriate to their level. For example, when natural and social disasters that are unforeseen wipe out entire communities, outside aid is necessary. Often political leaders at lower levels are tempted to ask for more money than necessary when disaster hits, using it as an occasion to get extra funds for their supporters. Conversely, administrators in higher levels use such occasions to increase departmental budgets by deceiving legislators and taxpayers about the true necessary costs. They will oppose the principle of subsidiarity to consolidate power, and they will oppose the principle of transparency to hide their plots.

This principle of consolidation was well understood by Thomas Jefferson and many of the U.S. founders who fought against it in the creation of the Constitution. It is how people tend to operate in a "state of nature" unless they have an unusually strong moral conscience. Social institutions need checks and balances on power and moral education in order to prevent consolidation that eventually leads to political or economic collapse.

Everyone is hoping to get more for less, and higher levels of government are seen as better providers, when the opposite is actually the case.

In the nineteenth century, mainline Christian churches in America promoted a "social gospel"[21] rooted in the idea that governments could better perform the duties of social welfare than churches and community organizations. The case was not hard to make in areas of squalor like "Hell's Kitchen" or the lower east side of Manhattan, where the human need far surpassed the capability of the churches located in those areas. Providing for the homeless, for orphans, and for widows could be very burdensome on churches, especially when and where the needs were very high. It can be argued that in these particular locations, government aid was necessary to supplement the efforts of the churches.

While there are times and places where the outside assistance of larger social units are required to address the human needs that are beyond the ability of the local level, there is a tendency to demand more than necessary. The slippery slope of avoidance of responsibility, combined with the tendency to centralize power, leads eventually to massive welfare programs and entitlements that are unsustainable by anyone. This slippery slope runs counter to the principle of subsidiarity, which is required for a durable society that promotes life, liberty, and happiness.

In a society where a centralizing process has gone on over a long period of time, the families and values that were nourished by community begin to disappear. This results in more individuals becoming directly dependent on an impersonal bureaucracy. However, the bureaucracy is itself unsustainable without the layer of society that undergirds it. The fewer self-sufficient families and communities at the bottom of the pyramid of responsibility, compared to those only dependent on higher bureaucracies, the more unstable the society. An example of this erosion of social stability might begin with a single woman on level one, who becomes pregnant and a ward of the state. Instead of her family and community helping her care for her child, the state has to raise money for its welfare program through increasing taxes on those families that are still strong. As larger numbers of people leave the realm of self-responsibility on the lowest level of society and depend on the state bureaucracy, taxes get raised to the point where taxpayers can no longer support the system, and the society becomes unstable or collapses.

Figure 5 (on the following page) represents a pyramid in which community has eroded, and many of the self-reliant individuals and families have moved into positions of dependence at the city or state level. The load carried by self-supporting people is much greater, and these people are constrained by taxation and have less freedom to pursue their own life, liberty, and happiness. In this diagram, the pyramid is becoming inverted and is quite unstable. This illustration conveys a system in which the welfare state is quite large and is under increased strain.

Realism and Centralized Power

Modern political science begins with Machiavelli and Hobbes, who emphasized the analysis of political power. Preventing the abuse of power was the single most important goal of those drafting the United States Constitution. The goal of maintaining the freedoms necessary for individuals to pursue life, liberty, and happiness required as much decentralization of power as possible. Respect for the principle of subsidiarity is evident in their work.

Curbs on the consolidation of political power were important to all of the founders. They knew that the American experiment could not succeed without free people pursuing their happiness. However, they also knew that cultural values were required to foster an individual moral conscience that restricted people from attempting to consolidate power at the expense of others. At the founding, religious values that nourished such a conscience were inherited by most Americans from their Protestant ancestors and Enlightenment contemporaries.

Maintaining these values voluntarily in larger impersonal society over time is difficult. They are very potent when they are widely accepted and taught in the face-to-face relations of families and local communities. However, the more impersonal the relationship, the easier it is to rationalize behavior that improves one's own condition at the expense of people you may never meet.

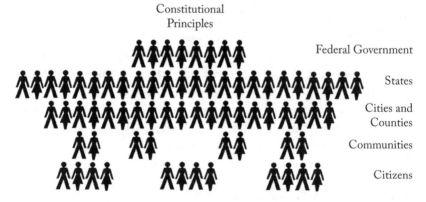

Figure 5: The above diagram represents a society in which power is concentrated at the state level and city level and begins to crush the shrinking number of self-reliant citizens that can care for both themselves and contribute something to the larger society.

In his book on this subject, *Moral Man and Immoral Society* (1932), Reinhold Niebuhr stated:

> In every human group there is less reason to guide and check impulse, less capacity for self-transcendence, less ability to comprehend the needs of others, and therefore more unrestrained egoism than the individuals, who compose the group, reveal in their personal relationships.[22]

As a theologian, Niebuhr wrestled with the problem that moral values by themselves are inadequate to check abuses of power. He had encountered this problem as a pastor in Detroit where he witnessed the Ford Motor Company putting profits above the well-being of workers. Both executives and workers at the auto plant were good members of his congregation. On a personal level, both groups seemed pious and devoted to the greater good of society. However, the corporation, guided by the logic of money, did not behave with similar altruism. His naïve view of government power was shattered during World War I when political leaders on both sides declared war for less than noble reasons.

Pacifists who had supported the League of Nations and the Kellogg-Briand Pact witnessed their total failure to deter Mussolini's invasion of Ethiopia. Niebuhr realized power could not be held in check by legal and moral institutions that were not backed by force.

Niebuhr and many in his generation had passively accepted the rhetoric of the United States' leaders to enter World War I, and later felt betrayed when they discovered the U.S. entry to the war had largely been pushed by bankers who had convinced President Wilson that the economy depended upon a British victory. Later, Niebuhr and other pacifists who had supported the creation of the League of Nations and the signing of the Kellogg-Briand Pact witnessed a total failure of these legal agreements to deter Mussolini's invasion of Ethiopia. Niebuhr realized power could not be held in check by legal and moral institutions that were not backed by force. He developed his "Christian realism" analyzing the sinful nature of human beings, making frequent reference to the writings of Augustine and the need for checks and balances on power emphasizing the writings of Thomas Jefferson.[23]

Niebuhr's Christian realism and the amoral nature of human institutions influenced Hans Morgenthau's political realism, which had the effect of separating morality from U.S. foreign policy or the policy of any state. In his *Politics Among Nations,* a classic book on political science during the Cold War period, Morgenthau wrote:

> Political realism refuses to identify the moral aspirations of a particular nation with the moral laws that govern the universe. As it distinguishes between truth and opinion, so it distinguishes between truth and idolatry. All nations are tempted—and few have been able to resist the temptation for long—to clothe their own particular aspirations and actions in the moral purposes of the universe.[24]

Political realism, like its European counterpart known as *real-politik,* had the unfortunate effect of further legitimating the idea that foreign policy is the mere projection of power in the pursuit of national self-interest. It helped shape a political culture that justified the actions of an impersonal bureaucratic institution in the pursuit of its own interests, regardless of the consequences for people in other nations. It was amoral, if not immoral. In practical terms, such political thought has led to the promotion of military doctrines such as the justification of a preemptive war on Iraq or quantifying collateral damage that justifies the killing of many innocent foreign civilians to save one U.S. soldier's life.

The United States and the Inversion of Subsidiarity

Figure 6 represents a society in which the federal government consolidates power in areas of responsibility that could be accomplished by individual states. This occurs when there are insufficient checks on the consolidation of power at the federal level, and when states would like to let someone else pay for what they could do more efficiently. The blocks show a massive load being carried by those producers on the lower level which ultimately support the entire social system. Add to this the weight of foreign empire building, which requires support of armies overseas, and any additional burden placed on the lower level might cause the entire edifice to collapse like a house of cards.

Figures 6 and 7 portray the United States system of government in the beginning of the twenty-first century. Government has grown to the limits of possible expansion and is far different from what the founding fathers sought to create. This is not a society in which the principle of subsidiarity dominates, but one in which the principle of consolidation has greatly replaced subsidiarity. It is no longer a society built from the bottom up by representative systems of government, but one that restricts the realm in which citizens are free to operate and provides them "options" to choose from that are largely determined by those in power. The movement towards further consolidation must be reversed or the entire system will break apart with the extended corners at the top of the inverted pyramid breaking off first.

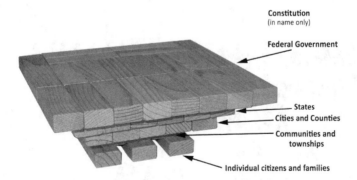

Figure 6: The above inverted pyramid of blocks represents the layers of society in which the principle of subsidiarity has been maximally violated. The power is concentrated at the federal level and it is extremely unstable, ignoring the role of community and honoring the principles of the Constitution in name only.

Subsidiarity in Culture and Economy

Subsidiarity applies to the cultural and economic spheres as well as the political sphere. Freedom in the cultural sphere includes freedom of belief, thought, speech, and assembly. Consolidation occurs in religion, the educational system, the media, and in popular culture. It also occurs in the economy through acquisitions, mergers, monopoly, and protectionism. The principle of subsidiarity applies to all spheres of human endeavor and cannot be left to politics alone.

In the realm of culture, consolidation attempts to control knowledge and impose beliefs and values. Examples of this include the Medieval Catholic Church, the doctrine of Divine Right of Kings, Marxism-Leninism, and nationally syndicated news programs aimed at mass markets. The control of knowledge is a significant form of control over others because, lacking access to alternative knowledge, official knowledge is all people know. Such knowledge stifles creative thought and the discovery of new knowledge that could make life happier. Official knowledge usually subsumes the individual pursuit of happiness under some other good like "country first." Official knowledge, even

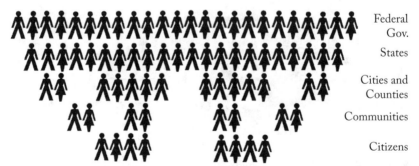

Constitutional
Principles (ignored)

Federal
Gov.

States

Cities and
Counties

Communities

Citizens

Figure 7: The above diagram represents a society in which power is concentrated at the federal and state levels, creating a huge bureaucratic edifice that places a maximum burden on its few producing citizens. It is extremely unstable and not durable.

if well-intended, often evolves into a body of "truth" that favors the interests of the ruling elite over the interests of the citizen.

The First Amendment of the United States Constitution, which guarantees freedom of religion, freedom of speech, freedom of the press, and the right to free and peaceful assembly, was intended to prevent consolidation of the control of knowledge or truth by a government or to allow a religion the power of physical force through the assistance of a government. Large commercial interests often succeed in buying government support for truth about various commercial products by influencing regulative bodies that make official statements about products or by influencing the nationwide media to promote biased reports instead of acting as watchdogs. This can happen particularly when the media are part of a financial conglomerate and not financially independent.

These problems did not exist at the time of the founding because the financial sector was decentralized in the hands of millions of independent farmers, tradesmen, and shopkeepers. There was little consolidation of economic power. However, as industries developed and capital accumulated under the political freedoms that existed in the new Republic, small enterprises became a target for takeover by larger ones. These larger economic enterprises were, in turn, able to lobby for laws that favored further consolidation.

No government has by itself been able create a society in which the economic needs of citizens have been abundantly and justly met unless they possess some large supply of a natural resource like oil, of which the revenues can be redistributed in large amounts to all citizens. However, such redistributive action does not motivate individuals

> **The First Amendment, which guarantees freedom of religion, freedom of speech, freedom of the press, and the right to free and peaceful assembly, was intended to prevent consolidation of the control of knowledge.**

to be economic producers, but makes them dependent on the government that controls the resource. It is a form of emotional slavery, even if physical well-being is supplied. In his book *The End of Poverty*, economist Jeffrey Sachs argues that redistributive economies, whether socialist or resource-rich, have very little economic growth. In fact, in the period from 1980 to 2000 the oil exporters Algeria, Venezuela, and Saudi Arabia had negative economic growth.[25]

Even though some redistribution, for example, to hurricane victims to help them get back on their feet, is warranted, the principles of redistribution structured in a general law do not produce the creative and dynamic forces required for economic growth. Such laws tend to be grounded in envy or ideology rather than an understanding of human nature. The assumption of a limited economic pie that must be divided by a central authority is somewhat analogous to a static doctrine of truth controlled centrally. The first leads to economic poverty and the second to intellectual stagnation. In both cases, freedom is required for human flourishing.

In economics as well as in other areas of human society, the principle of subsidiarity applies. Larger impersonal bureaucratic organizations are more likely to consolidate wealth at the expense of those producing it.

The principle of supply and demand is an economic law that neither the force of government law nor religious doctrine can change. Historically, the greatest engine of economic production has been a free market, decoupled from centralized control. Free people are motivated to produce a surplus of goods that others can use if they are free to sell those goods to others. When people produce an excess quantity of their products, economies grow. When static quantities are rationed, economies shrink. Even the most doctrinaire priests or legalistic bureaucrats will buy from people who offer lower prices. They will do this because they can maximize their own objectives, even if those objectives are to give away what they purchase to others in need.

Attempts to reduce free competition in the market will always lead to lower economic output. One common form of intervention that has led to the collapse of many states is printing extra money, thinking doing so can create wealth. Printing excess money to cover irresponsible economic behavior only causes inflation, which is another form of economic redistribution of wealth that stifles economic productivity. Inflation causes people to produce and maintain an inventory of fewer products, because the value of a good priced product today might be sold for less in real terms tomorrow after adjusting for inflation.

In economics as well as in other areas of human society, the principle of subsidiarity applies. Larger impersonal bureaucratic organizations are more likely to consolidate wealth at the expense of those producing it, whereas a system that rewards individuals with a more direct result of their own effort, and the protection of property they purchase from the fruits of their labors leads to greater economic freedom, economic justice, and state productivity. The large CEO pay recorded at the beginning of the twenty-first century was a symptom not of a new kind of greed, but of greed in the context of consolidated economic power. Clearly, companies that recorded such high profits from which CEOs could take such large amounts of compensation were not playing on a level playing field with a free market. In a truly free market, competitors would be willing to do the same work for a fraction of the pay and price their products for less to get part of the market share. Such accumulations of wealth do not occur without some kind of legal protection or monopoly power.

Stronger Societies Practice Subsidiarity

In conclusion, the strongest and most enduring societies and governments are those that rest upon the maximum distribution of responsibility to lower levels. They are in the shape of the pyramid.

While upper levels of government are necessary for purposes that transcend individual life, the pursuit of life, liberty, and happiness is best achieved when the principle of subsidiarity is maximally applied. If the lower levels of society are exploited by higher levels, the governments atop them will eventually collapse.

The principle of subsidiarity in government is like the law of supply and demand in the economic sphere. If violated, it will lead to government collapse. Just as consolidated political power leads to collapse or revolution that overthrows the regime, the consolidation of economic power leads to economic decline and poverty. For this reason, the Soviet Union could not compete economically with the West at the end of the twentieth century.

The principle of subsidiarity has been taught implicitly and explicitly by many great religions and philosophers. And the United States' founders enshrined this principle in the Constitution they created. It was symbolized by the pyramid on the Great Seal. But, the implementation of this principle requires maturity, will, and checks and balances on every possible concentration of power or wealth. It is much easier to preach than to practice. The United States has not been able to prevent the unhealthy consolidation of power. Its laws, and perhaps its Constitution, need reforms that prevent the spread of this virus that lay hidden in human society, awaiting the chance to consume the good cells required to keep society healthy and strong.

Questions for Review and Reflection

1. Describe the relationship of subsidiarity to complexity, explaining similarities and differences between a human organism and a social organism.
2. Why does subsidiarity often get replaced by centralization in a social organism?
3. What social institution developed the concept of subsidiarity, and what stimulated this development?
4. Explain developments in Western civilization that allowed individuals to take on the social responsibility democracy requires of them.
5. Explain why subsidiarity can create a more stable and enduring society.
6. Why is fraud and theft at higher levels of government easier to perpetrate and more damaging to members of society?
7. What circumstances caused many pacifists to become realists in the early twentieth century?
8. In what areas besides government is subsidiarity important to social stability?
9. With respect to the principle of subsidiarity, why do you think that countries with large amounts of oil tend to have negative economic growth?
10. Explain why subsidiarity in the economic sphere is important to a free market.

4

The Separation of Powers

One fine day it occurred to the Members of the Body that they were doing all the work and the Belly was having all the food. So they held a meeting, and after a long discussion, decided to strike work till the Belly consented to take its proper share of the work. So for a day or two, the Hands refused to take the food, the Mouth refused to receive it, and the Teeth had no work to do. But after a day or two the Members began to find that they themselves were not in a very active condition: the Hands could hardly move, and the Mouth was all parched and dry, while the Legs were unable to support the rest. So thus they found that even the Belly in its dull quiet way was doing necessary work for the Body, and that all must work together or the Body will go to pieces.

—"The Belly and the Members," *Aesop's Fables,*
Sixth Century B.C.

Society consists of three major components: (1) culture, (2) commerce, and (3) government. These functions are respectively related to (1) knowledge, (2) wealth, and (3) order. All people require these things to pursue happiness. They need knowledge and skills to reach any objective or produce any product. They need financial resources to obtain food, housing, and the raw materials or tools for what they produce. They need a social order that protects them in their pursuit of their goals and prevents others from withholding the access to knowledge or wealth that they need for whatever it is they are pursuing.

In drafting the United States Constitution, the founders were concerned about the separation of powers within the government:

the legislative, the judicial, and the administrative. In the First Amendment, they were also concerned about the separation of powers of culture and state: the freedom of religion, of the press, of speech, and of assembly. All four of these elements relate to the freedom of knowledge or information. They are intended to prevent the government from controlling knowledge, or a religion that promotes a closed system of knowledge or truth from imposing that truth on society. However, they did not implement any constitutional limits on monopolies on wealth, the control of which is another form of power that can restrict citizens in their pursuit of happiness. Restricted access to money, like restricted access to information, can prevent people from the pursuit of life, liberty, and happiness.

Knowledge and information transcend traditional religious doctrines. Religions traditionally emphasize values and knowledge related to the way we live: self-motivation, relationships with others, service to the larger society, and other "truths" about human life learned over centuries of human experience. However, curiosity and the desire to create and produce lead to scientific knowledge and other objective information that can help people reach their goals. Religion has frequently suppressed scientific knowledge, and science often closes off religious knowledge. Political tyrants will suppress both if they feel threatened by it, or they will attempt to create a cult of their own personality to prop up their power. Businesses will also try to suppress bad information about their products and good information about competitor's products. They will try to embellish knowledge about their products to increase sales. Knowledge and information are power. This power should not be controlled by either the political, commercial, or religious sectors if citizens are to freely access it in the pursuit of life, liberty, and happiness.

The economic sector should be separated from domination by a particular organ of society, just like access to knowledge needs to be kept free. Wealth is a form of power. People in all sectors of society will try to consolidate and control wealth in order to have advantages over others. Free access to the economy by human beings is essential for their pursuit of life, liberty, and happiness. Monopolies are the most frequently cited form of consolidated economic power that prevents free and equal access to the economy. They enable those in charge to fix prices, inflate profits, and prevent competitors from entering the market. A monopoly in industry parallels a monopoly on truth or absolute political power.

The U.S. Constitution placed limits on the consolidation of political power and control of knowledge. However, it did not provide guidelines for the control of economic power. Throughout the history of the United States, this power has grown uncontrollably, resulting in concentrations of economic power that have trumped the power of voters in politics and restricted free enterprise in the economic sphere. In a free society, the separation of powers must refer to the separation of all powers, not just political powers.

Each organ of society, like each organ in the human body, has a separate function to play in the well-being of each individual cell and of the society as a whole. The role of the Constitution and legal system is to create the structure of the social organism so that each organ can obtain the necessary elements to perform its function and has proper checks and balances so that it does not grow like a cancer and destroy the entire society. The economy is like the blood in the body, the system of exchange of elements among all cells that must take in nutrition and convert it to something useful. Every individual and each social institution needs access to the economic system in order to perform its function.

> **The Constitution placed limits on the consolidation of political power and control of knowledge. However, it did not provide guidelines for the control of economic power. Throughout the history of the United States this power has grown uncontrollably.**

THE ECONOMY IS THE THIRD SECTOR

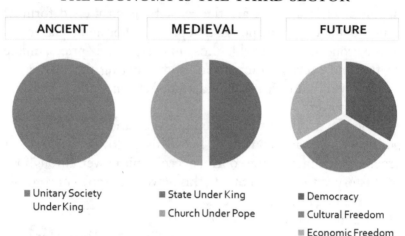

Figure 10: The above diagram represents the evolution of society from the ancient unitary society, to the medieval two-organ society, and the transition to a three-organ society.

Specialized Components in the Social Organism

In a simple family or tribe, all social components and functions are integrated into the parents or elders of the group. They relate to other members of the group in open face-to-face and transparent relations. In such societies the results of decisions and actions are quickly known to all members. In a small family farm or business, the owner has necessary knowledge, economic skill, and political impact to successfully run his enterprise. These people have to educate their own children, get products to market, and protect the family from intruders. Each adult can be considered "a jack of all trades and master of none." This is how a single celled animal like an amoeba operates.

Human societies, like multi-cellular animals, consist of organs or components in which the individual members perform specialized tasks and more complex functions than a single cell. In both an animal body and a human social organism, there are symbiotic relationships where the cells serve both themselves and the larger organism. In an animal, the lung cells specialize to provide oxygen to the blood, the stomach cells provide nutrition from food, the liver cells process waste, and the heart pumps blood throughout the body, making the nutrition available to all cells. The blood also carries waste products to the liver, where the blood is purified. The brain and the central nervous system serves as a coordinator. Sensory organs like eyes and ears appear in higher animals to provide information from the environment. In such evolved organisms, no single cell can govern the whole and no single cell can live in isolation from others.

As human societies have evolved, they have developed specialized sub-societies to perform specialized functions like the organs of an animal. Each of these social organs is constituted by principles and structures appropriate to its function. Like the organs of a human body, they each have a role to play in the maintenance of the overall society. Culture, commerce, government, education, transportation, police, science, industry, and health are all examples of areas in which people specialize. In healthy societies, each cell must have what it needs to do its job both in relation to its own happiness and to the happiness of the entire society. Cells function as semi-autonomous units in relation to a larger whole. If one of the functions performs badly, all the cells in the organism are weakened. For example, if the transportation system of the nation breaks down, it could be compared to reducing the flow of blood in the human body.

Human societies can be considered abstractions from nature, in that individual human beings have similar genetic makeup and learn specialized skills. In the animal, a liver cell produces other liver cells. However, the children of a doctor could be lawyers, engineers, or artists. Their talents are not genetically predetermined. Human beings are very adaptable because much of their mental growth occurs after birth, while receiving emotional, sensory, and educational feedback from their parents and environment. Because of this, human beings have freedom,[2] and human societies are amorphous and fluid. Individual people are able to pioneer new territories, develop new technologies, and contribute to society in various ways that change it. They are not locked into one destiny, and they can create and develop new social organs.

However, freedom in a society is constrained by both natural laws and the laws of the social organism. If one walks off a cliff, he is killed by natural law. If one kills another person or steals from them, he defies social law and must be punished by the society. This is because the larger social organism is threatened when the individuals that make it up run amok. Social breakdown can occur when the individual citizens stop performing necessary functions that their predecessors performed or if one social organ tries to grow at the expense of the others. This is what happens when government tries to control religion or the economy through force.

> The type of agrarian society Thomas Jefferson envisioned is a horizontal society of human "amoebas" living side by side. Alexander Hamilton and his followers imagined a more vertical society with cities, banks, industries, and more complex social institutions.

Government's proper role is protection of all the components of society and all the individuals that make it up. If government oversteps its proper role and attempts to control culture, run the economy, or restrict personal freedom, it becomes like a cancerous organ that ends up destroying the entire organism. Conversely, if the government fails to adequately perform its role of refereeing a free market and allows corporate greed to run rampant and unpoliced, then the economic sector will develop a cancer that can immobilize the social organism. The same holds true for other social institutions including families, churches, schools, and highway departments. Each component has to perform its task within the operating limits set forth by its role in the entire social organism. Failing to do the minimal requirements of the job will lead to weakening of the institution in which one is employed. Attempting to use one's position to become wealthy at the expense of others is like a cancer that will also weaken and possibly kill the social organism.

If one is a self-sufficient, rugged individual—a jack of all trades like an amoeba—one doesn't have to worry about limits within the social institution, because one is not part of any society. Like a wilderness frontiersman, one is a society unto oneself. To some extent, this is the type of agrarian society Thomas Jefferson envisioned, a horizontal society of human "amoebas" living side by side. Alexander Hamilton and his followers imagined a more vertical society with cities, banks, industries, and more complex social institutions. The United States Constitution can serve the Jeffersonian society well, but it is not sufficiently detailed to handle the complex social development that followed. This is why constant updates and upgrades to the legal system, comparable to virus updates for computer software, are required. Proper separation of the components of society with the operation of the whole is necessary, with the most primary being the proper separation of church, state, and commerce.

Separation of Church and State

In strongly hierarchical societies ruled by a king or a small group of people on the top, the leaders try to control all sectors of society. These are not organic societies grounded in freedom and diversification of knowledge, but societies limited by the knowledge, wealth, and legal skill of the ruler. These rulers function as a jack of all trades, like a head of household or tribal leader, trying to direct all citizens that surround them. Their rule is inadequate because they are attempting to transplant the principles of small personal societies into larger impersonal societies. The physical force possessed by the ruler is used to impose his limited knowledge of religion, economy, and the needs of each individual through the government he rules. Such governments are generally static and only marginally functional compared to a well-oiled social machine in which each individual can serve as a specialized part.

In authoritarian societies, there is generally very little liberty or pursuit of happiness for the people living under the regime; the values of the ruler become the official values for all citizens, whether they believe them or not.

The separation of church and state is a relatively new feature of human society that developed out of the collapse of Western Empires. In antiquity, there were altars and temples built by social groups for collective worship and the care of the helpless. These were less differentiated than in our modern world where there is a plurality of religions and cultures competing within the wider culture. The Roman Empire absorbed a plurality of cultures, and in its height, there was generally a freedom to express particular cultural values and practices so long as one recognized the supreme political rule of Rome and its laws. The collapse of the empire was accompanied by the development of a single official religion (the Catholic Church) that was relatively independent and paralleled the state. It was a spiritual empire, organized hierarchically like the temporal empire, and was the official repository of truth, whereas the temporal ruler was the official embodiment of temporal power.

> **The parallel system of Church and State, hierarchically organized, was unresponsive to changes in the external environment. The unwillingness of the Church to accept new ideas, and the impoverishment of most people earned this period the name "Dark Ages."**

Through the various Church Councils and the decrees of the Popes, official doctrine was developed that supported the feudal agrarian system that came after the Roman Empire. It created a body of teachings that provided meaning in this life and hope in the afterlife. It created spiritual orders and monasteries that both guarded and disseminated this official knowledge and provided refuge for impoverished or unattached single people who could be part of the Church family in exchange for devotion to God. This parallel system of Church and State, hierarchically organized from the top down, was very unresponsive to changes in the external environment. The burning of ancient "pagan" books, the unwillingness of the Church to accept scientific discoveries or humanistic ideas, and the impoverishment of most people earned this period the name "Dark Ages." An estimated 65 million inhabitants of the Roman Empire in the second century A.D.[3] declined to about 18 million by 650 A.D. and did not recover until the fourteenth century[4] after the rise of independent city-states and the Renaissance.

The Reformation did not challenge the idea of an established religion. Martin Luther, under the protection of Frederick the Wise, was able to guide the establishment of a reformed church in his political jurisdiction. The pattern in Germany, which had hundreds of small principalities, was to establish a *landeskirche* or official church in each jurisdiction. The Northern provinces were generally Reformed, while Bavaria and areas near France and Belgium remained Catholic.[5] In 1534, the Act of Supremacy declared that the King, then Henry VIII, was "the only supreme head in earth of the Church of England," and the Treasons Act of 1534 made those who did not recognize his religious authority guilty of treason, punishable by death. Sometimes new rulers changed the official religion back and forth from Protestant to Catholic, causing chaos for the members of society.

Freedom of religion first appeared in Holland after the defeat of the Spanish Empire. Most people in Holland were Protestant, and when the Netherlands became an independent republic, it became officially Dutch Reformed. However, it could not garner enough support from its citizens for its Constitution without a guarantee of religious freedom. The Dutch prospered and developed an empire very quickly. Holland became a haven for those who, like the Puritans, suffered religious persecution.

As with Holland, it was practically necessary for the United States to frame its Constitution with the separation of church and state. Several states had established religions and did not want another state's religion to become official in the new nation. The founders did not want any religion to have undue influence on government or attempt to impose an official truth on the state. Thus, the First Amendment contains the clause, "Congress shall make no law respecting an establishment of religion, or prohibiting the free exercise thereof." They left the option of separation of church and state within states to the states. However, by 1828 all states had decided to abandon the establishment of religion.

Disestablishment of religion had some unexpected positive effects. Ministers and churches found themselves competing for voluntary adherents on the open market of religion. Many established churches attempted to promulgate doctrines and traditions developed for a previous era when free thinking was discouraged or forbidden. However, in the new democracy, conditions were very different. To win church membership, ministers had to provide services and teachings useful to the people. Therefore, they thought long and hard about ways to improve church teachings and provide spiritual nourishment to members. After the founding, U.S. church attendance grew dramatically, making it one of the most religiously rich and diverse countries of the world.

> **In the new democracy, conditions were very different. Ministers had to provide services and teachings useful to the people. Therefore, they thought long and hard about ways to improve church teachings and provide spiritual nourishment to members.**

During that same period of time, church attendance in Europe, where there are state churches, dramatically declined, and churches were increasingly viewed as irrelevant by the masses. New churches have had a more difficult time forming in Europe because of state registration and tax subsidies that create a financial bias towards established churches and against new competitors. There is less incentive for established church leaders to revise what they teach or go out of their way to serve others, since they are paid by the state whether they innovate or not. As in the economy, a monopoly on religion leads to the increasing irrelevance over time of the usefulness of the monopoly. As with the communist economy in Russia, when the official market cannot serve its social function satisfactorily, a black market arises to fill its place.

The "Wall of Separation"

The "wall of separation" so often discussed in the United States was never intended by the founders to be an absolute wall. Religion was viewed as the primary means of implanting the values of self-governance and respect for others that a democratic republic requires of its citizens. The founders were not opposed to the open promotion of religion in the public sphere. The Constitution did not bar the individual states from having established religions if that is what they wanted. What they opposed was the federal government establishing or providing financial support to any particular religion or providing any impediment towards the free exercise of religion. They also opposed any institutional church using the federal government for achieving its own religious ends.

The separation of church and state was not intended to undermine religion. Most founders would have considered that to be socially destructive. Nor was it intended that religion could be used as a shield behind which people could hide from the crimes they had committed. An absolute wall can do that. Government has a valid role to protect its citizens from harming one another and has the right to prosecute the perpetrators of murder, theft and other criminal acts; a "religious" reason for committing such crimes is not an adequate defense. Such arguments had been used to burn heretics and witches in Early America and to carry out wars, crusades, and religious and ethnic cleansing in the Middle Ages. These acts are still carried out in the name of *jihad* and other religious doctrines in parts of the world where there is no separation of religion and the state.

As a protector and referee, governments must identify objective crimes like murder, theft, rape, and fraud. These crimes must be nearly universally recognized as crimes and not "crimes" that impede a particular religious or minority group from achieving their particular ends. Immanuel Kant's *Groundwork of the Metaphysic of Morals*[6] provides useful guidelines for sifting through the inherited world's cultures to determine which crimes are universally considered crimes. Generally, they are acts which make some people suffer as a means to another's end. To be viewed as legitimate, governments must treat all citizens equally before the law. When governments pass laws that redirect wealth or power from one group to another, they undermine their universal legitimacy.[7] Without government acting as an impartial referee related to protection of life, liberty, and property, it will not be respected by a majority of citizens.

The Separation of Church, Commerce, and State

The remainder of this chapter develops the idea that commerce and state should be separated in a manner similar to church and state. Church, commerce, and state are separate organs of society just as the head, the heart, and the limbs are to an individual person. The head is not a heart and cannot perform the function of the heart or the limbs very well, although it can direct and monitor the function of the heart and limbs. In modern complex societies, knowledge, money, and physical power can be a rough analogy to the head, the heart, and the limbs of an individual person. Knowledge gives direction, the economy fuels the society, and the government protects and defends.

Using the First Amendment, which protects freedom of knowledge, as a model, we could propose another amendment related to the separation of commerce and state as follows: "Congress shall make no law respecting the establishment of commerce or prohibiting the free exercise thereof." Religion and the economy provide different functions in society. Economic freedom can boost economic growth in a way that freedom of thought can advance knowledge and culture.

In a large impersonal bureaucratic society, church, commerce, and state are all institutional expressions of basic social functions undifferentiated in self-sufficient individuals and face-to-face communities. The attempt by one of these organs to take over any of the others is socially destructive. It is as wrong for a government to take over religion or the economy as it is for religion or the economy to take over the government. Republican societies are systems with interconnected organs in which each organ must function within appropriate limits for the entire system to operate.

The founders separated church and state with the U.S. Constitution, but no such action was taken with respect to the separation of government and the economy. As the American economy has evolved from its original agrarian shape to the modern industrial state, new concentrations of wealth and power have emerged. They have run roughshod over the citizens of the United States, and held government legislators hostage. Rather than creating updates and upgrades in our legal system to prevent such activities, legislators have been bought off and the legal system bent to provide benefits to special interest groups at the expense of the citizens as a whole. This has led to economic recessions and depressions, mass consumer culture, excessive CEO pay, welfare dependency, economic consolidation on Wall Street, and the real estate bubble of 2008.

> **We could propose another amendment related to the separation of commerce and state as follows: "Congress shall make no law respecting the establishment of commerce or prohibiting the free exercise thereof."**

We need to examine these harmful developments more fully, as they are more a by-product of the freedoms created by the Constitution than inherent economic trends existing in modern history before the founding.

British Imperialism and the American Colonies

When Britain ruled the American Colonies, the relationship between commerce and the crown was not absolute, but very heavily intertwined. The Charter of the East India Company, a joint stock company, by Queen Elizabeth I in 1600 gave a commercial monopoly on all trade to the East Indies for 15 years.[8] The power of the Crown was originally based on conquest of land, not commerce. But after sinking the Spanish Armada in 1588, Britain was in a position to earn wealth through global trade and commerce. Profits from trading companies enriched the investors, and the British Crown and its cronies ensured their company would enjoy monopoly status and yield them great profits. In 1609, King James I renewed the charter of the East India Company for an indefinite period of time (unless it should lose money three years in a row). By 1689, the company's branch in India had become a virtual government backed by its own private army.

The employees of the company also became wealthy and bought estates and started new businesses, sometimes trying to compete with the East India Company that gave them their start. The commercial classes that arose in the seventeenth century began to overtake the traditional landed class in terms of wealth. The landed class and other "interlopers" eventually sought laws by Parliament that would allow parallel business ventures and similarly increase their wealth. Such laws would undercut the monopoly of the East India Company. In 1694, a deregulating act was passed, and the Bank of England was created to provide credit for other ventures. In 1698, a large parallel company, the English Company Trading to the East Indies, was floated with state backing of £2 million. While this was an attempt to create prosperity for more investors, the wealthy stockholders in the old East India Company quickly bought up the majority of the shares, eliminating the chance new competitors would drive prices down. The two companies merged in 1708 and loaned the British treasury a sum of £3,200,000, in return for exclusive privileges.

The buying of political power followed the consolidation of economic power and monopoly. The East India Company had a large lobby with significant financial clout in the Parliament. The Parliament did not want to relinquish its political control over the company because holding the charter hostage each time it came up for renewal was an opportunity to exploit the company's profits. So the collusion between these two entities and the monopoly company persisted, preventing all citizens from having an equal opportunity to compete in the business.

The American colonies began as a place where strong independent people sought to create new lives and communities. The Puritans, with their rigorous work ethic, were among the first to arrive. Many others who followed adopted the self-reliant lifestyle and settled on new farms or set up new shops or businesses in towns. These immigrants wanted a new life where they could own property and retain the fruits of their work, unencumbered by the official religion, taxes, or the corruption they had experienced in Europe.

However, throughout the eighteenth century, taxes and monopolistic practices of the British were increasingly imposed upon the colonies. The Currency Act of 1764 banned the colonies from using their Colonial Scrip and caused an economic depression. The Stamp Act of 1765 was the first direct tax imposed on the colonies, promoting the outcry, "no taxation without representation." Less well known is that part of the tax was to fund ecclesiastical courts, supporting a state church that many Americans did not want. The Tea Act of 1773 was an attempt to prop up the East India Company that had 18 million pounds of excess tea to sell. This act led to price subsidies that undercut the business of other tea merchants. The Boston Tea Party was a protest by Boston tea merchants and supporters that some commentators have called the first act of protest against globalization. The Hudson's Bay Company and the East India Company were banned from the United States after the revolution.[9]

The Constitution Silent on Corporate Power

At the time the Constitution was drafted, the power of large corporations was not a pressing issue. Foreign corporations like the East India Company and the Hudson's Bay Company had been banned from the U.S., and domestic corporations, to the extent they existed, were regulated by state charters and normally expired in 20 years. Most corporations were not industries, but rather local institutions like fire departments and libraries.

In *Federalist Paper No. 10,* James Madison wrote that the destructive effects of factions needed to be controlled and that either religion or economic power could be the cause of a faction. He and other Federalists (like Alexander Hamilton) thought a larger central government would be better able to contain the influence of factions. The anti-Federalists, exemplified by Jefferson, also saw the problem with factions but advocated smaller and decentralized government rather than a central government as the way for them to be best contained.

There was a major difference between the Hamiltonians who sought to develop a commercial society and the Jeffersonians who promoted an agrarian society. In Thomas Jefferson's vision of an agrarian society, each family owned its own property for its economic livelihood and had one vote. This would widely distribute wealth and political power across the voters of the nation. In a letter to James Madison in 1787, Jefferson wrote:

> I think our governments will remain virtuous for many centuries as long as they are chiefly agricultural; and this will be as long as there shall be vacant lands in any part of America. When they [people] get piled upon one another in large cities as in Europe, they will become corrupt as in Europe.[10]

This quote echoes Aristotle who, in his *Politics,* argued that democracies worked best in agrarian societies because everyone was self-sufficient and would have no motivation to try to use political maneuvering to receive an income from someone else's production.[11] Jefferson was worried that economic monopolies would impede freedom and argued that they should be forbidden in the Bill of Rights. He also suggested that the protection of copyrights or patents be limited to writers and artists in this suggested article:

> Article 9. Monopolies may be allowed to persons for their own productions in literature, and their own inventions in the arts, for a term not exceeding __ years, but for no longer term, and no other purpose.[12]

Hamilton sought a strong central government promoting the interests of commerce and industry. He advocated a central financial system that provided credit for industrial development, trade, and the operations of government. He devised a Bank of the United States, sponsored a national mint, and argued for tariffs for the temporary protection of new firms to foster the development of competitive national industries. These measures created a solid group of businessmen who stood firmly behind the national government.

Jefferson approved of a strong central government only for foreign relations, not for the domestic economy. He feared a tyranny would develop when wealth was centralized, and he sought protection of many more rights than the Bill of Rights finally contained. Hamilton feared Jefferson's society would lead to democratic anarchy, and he wanted an efficiently planned government.

Hamilton argued that a vast body of powers was implied by general clauses in the Constitution, and one of these authorized Congress to "make all laws which shall be necessary and proper." In his opinion, the Constitution authorized the national government to levy and collect taxes, pay debts, and borrow money. A national bank would materially help in performing these functions efficiently. Jefferson objected when Hamilton introduced his bill to establish a national bank, saying that the Constitution expressly enumerates all the powers belonging to the federal government and reserves all other powers, such as establishing a bank, to the states.

In the end, Washington and the Congress accepted Hamilton's view. This was an important foundation for a later and more expansive interpretation of the federal government's authority. In 1791, Hamilton led a movement to charter a federal bank. The federal government owned $2 million of the $10 million in stock. In 1792, 24 brokers and merchants signed the "Buttonwood Agreement" to trade securities on a commission basis that laid the basis for the New York Stock Exchange.

By 1811, the power of the federal bank's directors had come to frighten many people, and the charter was not renewed. Five years later in 1816, a second federal bank was chartered on arguments similar to the establishment of the first: the needs of a growing economy. Jefferson went on record in opposition. The Supreme Court, under Justice John Marshall, created legal rulings in support of the Federalists. However, a populist backlash followed in the period of Andrew Jackson, and in 1836 the second bank's charter was allowed to expire, despite the fact that many promoters of European-type banks and corporations continued to exist.

The Triumph of the Industrial State

It was the development of the railroads, the heavy steel industry, and the occasion of the Civil War that enabled the federal government to trump states' rights once and for all. In 1850, about 9,000 miles of track existed in the United States and, by 1860, more than 30,000 miles of track was in use, much of it the result of government subsidies. As railroads grew in size, they grew in political influence. Everyone wanted a piece of railroad action. Railroad money influenced legislation and the courts. By 1890, more than 180 million acres of land had been deeded to railroads.

Abraham Lincoln, one of the organizers of the Republican Party that was born out of anti-slavery activism, was elected U.S. President in 1860. Lincoln had been a lawyer for the Illinois Central railroad and received industrial backing as a candidate. He was a combination of anti-slavery activist and industrial nationalist.

While he began the Civil War to stop the South from secession for economic reasons, he signed the Emancipation Proclamation, against the wishes of his cabinet,[13] to garner popular support from the anti-slavery movement to raise an army against the South to free the slaves. The war provided arguments for creating national banks to fund war production and transportation, leading to the National Banking Act of 1863.

The "Civil War Amendments," passed shortly after the war, made it constitutionally possible for the federal government to bypass the states and directly intervene in the affairs of individuals. The stated purpose of the Fourteenth Amendment was to guarantee full citizenship to freed slaves by giving the federal government the authority to intervene when states deprived them of due process. However, the Amendment was rarely used for such purposes. Rather, it has been used by the federal government to overturn certain state laws disliked by industrial lobbyists. Lawyers for the railroad convinced the Supreme Court (which included several former corporate lawyers) to rule, in *Santa Clara County v. Southern Pacific Railroad* (1886), that the railroad would have equal protection against confiscation of property as a "person" within the meaning of the Fourteenth Amendment. This action and others stripped the states of significant power to control corporate behavior. While states continued to issue corporate charters, many of the large corporations were darlings of a federal government that could dictate to the states how they were to be treated.

Only a short time after large U.S. corporations had freed themselves from the shackles of state charters they set their sights on international commerce. This prompted lobbying for a stronger U.S. Navy and the acquisition of ports.

The Triumph of the Global Corporation

Only a short time after large U.S. corporations had freed themselves from the shackles of state charters, they set their sights on international commerce. This prompted lobbying for a stronger U.S. Navy and the acquisition of ports. The argument was made that this was how the British and had become so prosperous.[14] In the 1890s, the U.S. built up the Navy, giving the United States the power to conduct "gunboat diplomacy" to obtain naval bases that could help protect U.S. commercial shipping.

The next change was a push by large industries to put an end to tariffs and establish free trade in order to compete overseas. It is ironic that a primary factor in starting the Civil War half a century earlier had been the fear of the South establishing free trade (see Chapter 6). The problem was, without income from tariffs, the federal government needed another form of funding. The result was the Sixteenth Amendment that allowed replacing tariffs with income taxes. While this tax was not apportioned as the Constitution originally specified, it was not seriously challenged because it was originally scheduled to be a tax only on high incomes (over $500,000 in today's dollars) and not wages. Income tax was to have no effect on wage earners working to provide basic living and education expenses for their families. It was a tax on personal profits from corporate investments. Thus, the U.S. Treasury would remain funded by the commercial sector of society.

The Sixteenth Amendment opened the floodgates and that small tax grew into the monster that exists today that places a burden on the middle-class wages.[15] Such taxes on wages get factored into the cost of U.S. products. In the end, free trade benefits those countries whose products cost less. The income tax as it exists today thus put U.S. products and U.S. workers at a disadvantage compared to those countries that do not have to factor the cost of taxes into the cost of production. In this sense, U.S. workers are correct when they say their government prevents free trade.

The financial sector also drew the U.S. into World War I.

U.S. bankers with extensive international loans argued that the U.S. economic system would collapse if the loans to England and France would default if those countries lost the war.[16] Such arguments that "corporations are too big to fail" were used in 2008 by U.S. Treasury Secretary Paulson to persuade President Bush and Congress to a $750 billion taxpayer bailout of large financial institutions that had failed because of greedy and unethical financial behavior. It is not the role of the economic sector to shape government policy, but the role of the government to provide a fair economic playing field with risks of economic profit and loss clearly known by the commercial sector.

Corporations do not make "good citizens." They only seek to maximize profit as they carry out their economic business wherever it is most efficient. They follow economic laws.

Corporate expansion continued throughout most of the twentieth century. Many U.S. corporations eventually outgrew the constraints of the United States and became global economic giants. The logic of capital respects no political boundaries, and this was its logical next step. A couple of recent events show how global the economy has become. In 2007, the New York Stock Exchange merged with the European stock consortium Euronext, whose oldest historical member was the Dutch East India Company, which had been forbidden to operate in the United States at the founding.[17] Also in 2007, Halliburton, a major U.S. corporation that has provided services to the United States military, established a headquarters for its Chairman and CEO in the United Arab Emirates "to focus [the] company's eastern hemisphere growth." Halliburton used another offshore office in the Caribbean to hire U.S. workers for operations in Iraq so they could avoid U.S. tax reporting and Social Security tax payments. Meanwhile, IT giants like Hewlett-Packard, IBM, and Electronic Data Systems have moved significant portions of their operations to India. Such corporations do not make "good citizens." They only seek to maximize profit as they carry out their economic business wherever it is most efficient. *They follow economic laws.*

Government has a responsibility to ensure corporate activities are properly refereed and that behavior that would restrict freedom or bring harm to others is illegal and punished. Governments have done a pretty poor job at this to date. Rising inequality of income and wealth in the United States is accelerated by a government controlled by special interests at both the top and bottom of society. This shifts wealth from the middle class to both corporate welfare on the right and social welfare on the left. The shrinking of the middle class in the United States is not a good omen for the future of its democracy.

In his book *Supercapitalism,* former Secretary of Labor Robert Reich tells of the rapidly expanded lobbying by large corporations in Washington. This has changed Washington from a rather impoverished city before the 1970s to an expanse of high-rise glass buildings with offices for corporate lobbyists around K Street. Many of those lobbyists are former legislators wooing their colleagues still in office. They often earn significantly more money than they did when they were in office. The uncontrolled escalation of political contributions for election campaigns is the result of lobbyists trying to ensure elected legislators will act in their interest once elected.

> In the 1970s, only about 3 percent of retiring members of Congress went on to become Washington lobbyists. By 2005, more than 30 percent of retiring members turned to Washington lobbying.... The amount lobbyists charge for new clients rose from about $20,000 a month in 1995 to $40,000 a month in 2005. By 2006, starting salaries for well-connected congressional or White House staffers eager to move to K Street had ballooned to about $500,000 a year. Former chairmen of congressional committees and subcommittees were fetching up to $2 million a year to influence legislation in their former committees.[18]

The lobbying efforts of traditional interest groups like the AFL-CIO, which had strong influence in the past, pale in comparison to the money flowing from Exxon-Mobil, Microsoft, Google, Wal-Mart, and other corporate giants that want to make sure laws are passed that enable them to make ever-greater profits for their investors. Americans as investors and consumers are steamrolling over Americans as citizens. This is not a Republican or Democrat phenomenon. Many of these developments were taking place in the Carter and Clinton administrations at a rate comparable to that of the Reagan and Bush administrations.

The result is that much of a legislator's time is spent finding ways to address piecemeal concerns of lobbyists. Much legislation is passed by tacking on "pork" to get votes. This pork earmarks money, grants exemptions, or offers protection from competitors. Earmarks are continually added to bills until the sponsors have secured enough votes to pass legislation that would not pass on its own merit. Such legislation redirects tax dollars to special interests and undermines the citizens' faith in the government. The focus on special interest legislation distracts legislators from acting on the issues of general concern to the entire country and on making sure it is governed by sound principles.

The press is not promoting the end of special interest legislation. Most of the news media are owned by large financial groups that lobby heavily in Congress.[19] It would be a conflict of interest for them to criticize the system. Some legislators run on platforms saying they will stop catering to special interests. Others recommend term limits. But none of them propose a separation between government and commerce in which each social sector would perform its proper function in society. Such proposals would not have financial support from the special interests in the society some have called "the best democracy that money can buy."[20]

The Federalist/anti-Federalist debate left issues unresolved. Without guidelines as to the use of economic power and the relationship of government to the economy, decisions have been made by lobbyists persuading politicians, or politicians trying to control corporations. However, neither of these processes led to a truly fair playing field and, in the end, national productivity has been the causality. *This is an end nobody wanted.*

Government Planning for Competition

The United States founders had a sound understanding of human behavior that American citizens need to relearn. Crises pose questions that need serious thought and answers. The Constitution of the United States is silent on economic power. In order to produce a Constitution that everyone would sign in 1787, the Federalist/anti-Federalist debate was left tabled, as was the issue of slavery. Both of these omissions have come back to haunt the United States, first in the form of the Civil War and later as a consolidated and economically unsustainable government. However, the founders on both sides of the federalist debate would have easily recognized the plots by twentieth-century political lobbies to abuse the average citizen through redistribution to both the poor and the wealthy. Both types of redistribution come at the expense of a productive middle-class economy.

Both types of common state planning, oligarchy and socialism, are incompatible with economic democracy and limit economic freedom. F.A. Hayek addressed this debate when he wrote,

> The modern movement for planning is a movement against competition as such... Planning and competition can be combined only by planning for competition, but not by planning against competition.[21]

The large corporations who lobby for corporate welfare and socialists whose lobbies create social dependency plan against competition. For the monopolist, competition is not in their economic interest, for it reduces profit and requires more effort. For the socialist, a sense of economic injustice seeks immediate relief to the poor without the understanding that most economic redistribution will, in the long run, end up hurting the class of people they are seeking to help. The monopolist frequently promotes a laissez-faire market because he knows that with his size he can push competitors off the playing field. The socialist frequently promotes government regulation of the economy that inevitably saps the motive for economic production necessary to help the poor because they treat the economy as a zero-sum game. Twentieth century political debates frequently pitted these two flawed views against one another. These straw men still fuel the debates between Republicans and Democrats. Neither have adequately understood government's role as a referee or what it means to "plan for competition."

The monopolist promotes a laissez-faire market because he knows that with his size he can push competitors off the playing field. The socialist frequently promotes regulation that inevitably saps the motive for economic production because he treats the economy as a zero-sum game.

Neither a Laissez-Faire nor a Regulated Market

Many people confuse a free market with a laissez-faire (French for "leave alone") approach to the market. This is a serious mistake. A free market only functions with a level playing field, or "planned competition" as Friedrich Hayek referred to it in *The Road to Serfdom*. Laissez-faire can be viewed as what Thomas Hobbes called "the state of nature," only in the economic sphere. This is a state in which the strongest take what they can from the weak. In the state of nature, there is no supervised order. For examples of the state of nature, we can imagine the wild West in the nineteenth century or some inner-city areas where gangs freely roam today. The rise of the Russian mafia after the collapse of communism is another example of the state of nature in a vacuum of political power.

The goal of a free market, which provides the most economic democracy, is to allow everyone to compete fairly to provide the most desirable goods and services at the lowest prices. If one seller prices his goods with too much profit, another seller will be content to sell his for less profit. The "invisible hand" can work in a free market; it cannot work in a laissez-faire economy. In a laissez-faire economy, the strongest and most powerful people or corporations use force to push out players in order to earn profits higher than would occur under conditions of competition. Lobbyists for large corporations use their influence on legislators to either create a laissez-faire market, which they deceptively call a "free market," or to secure laws that give them other advantages over competitors through subsidies, tax breaks, or other protections. You will not find a lobbyist for a large corporation advocating a genuinely free market.

Many politicians will say that the answer to large predatory corporations is to "regulate them." Socialists tend to buy this form of argument, as it is designed to appeal to a sense of fairness. Various forms of regulation include taxes and fees imposed by the government, oversight committees that dictate corporate policy, or nationalization of the industry. In this case, government is the beneficiary of the regulation, imposing itself through force upon the industry and redirecting some profits of the industry for some ostensibly public purpose.

Regulation in this way transfers some control or ownership of the industry to the government, either directly through law or indirectly through taxes or fees. Such regulation does not create a free market in which the average person can move in and compete in the marketplace, but gives the hybrid government/private corporation protected or monopoly status. "Regulation" is a term used to give the public confidence that government is providing an acceptable response to whatever is not functioning correctly. However, through most regulation, the government uses its political power to forge a partnership with an outlaw corporation. The government becomes a player and abandons the role of referee. Where such forced partnerships are legal, you are very unlikely to see a politician advocating a genuinely free market.

It is useful to provide a couple of examples of refereeing competition and creating a level playing field to illustrate how a refereed market is different from either laissez-faire or regulation.

The Example of a Football Game

The first example is a Superbowl game. The Superbowl is one of the most highly watched events in the United States. The role of referee is very important in making these games competitive and successful. The laissez-faire approach to a football game would be to let all players on the field without referees. In this case, anarchy and violence will prevail until the strongest players have manhandled their way to victory. Such anarchy would not resemble the fair competitive game that people will enjoy. Such a game would not allow all players to use their specialized talents. It would not be a level playing field.

One way to regulate this game might be an attempt to weaken the strongest players by adding weight to their backs, restricting their range of motion to assigned corridors, or by mandating other actions they must take. Such actions would be a punitive method of trying to make the overall game more equal. This type of regulation fails to provide genuine free competition. Rather, it slows down the game and makes it less interesting because those with the greatest skill or strength are forbidden from using it.

Neither the laissez-faire approach nor the regulatory approach leads to an acceptable Superbowl game that people would want to pay to see or advertisers would want to support. The only way the game becomes exciting is when the game is played by rules that stimulate competition, treat all players impartially, and allow everyone to display their highest skills. Most important to make such rules work is the role of the referees who enforce them. If someone violates the rules, they are immediately and impartially enforced by prescribed penalties. The role of the referee in a football game is similar to the role of government in a free market.

Special interest lobbying is like bribing a referee of a football game. It changes the role of legislator from a noble representative to an ignoble lackey.

But referees can also be bribed, unless they suffer severe penalties for misusing their power. The acceptance of bribes by referees who throw a football game is grounds for immediate dismissal. Not only does rigging defeat the purpose of a game, it is considered illegal and immoral. If it were discovered that a Superbowl game was rigged, spectators would not want to watch it, players would have no motivation to excel, and advertisers would have no incentive to support it. It would be the end of the Superbowl.

However, special interest lobbying that turns legislators from referees to advocates does the same thing to a government. It destroys support and interest by the general population, changes the role of legislator from noble representative to ignoble lackey, reduces the incentive to create good government, undermines respect for the law, and prevents the economic sector of society from being a level playing field. This ultimately undermines the economy and the government's own tax base. If this trend continues, the government collapses.

The Example of Traffic Rules

The second example is the rules of driving on a highway. The traffic rules, which are aided by the posting of signs, enable the flow of traffic so that users can get to their individual destinations without having an accident. Absence of rules would lead to a system of anarchy on the highway that would prevent people (especially those without heavily armored vehicles) from reaching their destination in a timely manner and without vehicle damage.

The rules of a highway are considered legitimate when they apply to all drivers equally and assist drivers in attaining their destinations. If a particular class of people got shorter stoplights or access to special roads, people in other classes would not consider the rules legitimate. If some classes of drivers were forced to go a long circuitous route while others were allowed access to a direct route, the system would not be considered legitimate by those against whom it discriminated. Even people of conscience in the classes that the rules favored would be struck by guilt and not consider such rules legitimate.

Traffic is not what we call "free-flowing" without the rules that plan for its free flow. A free market, like free-flowing traffic, requires rules that, when followed, make it a free market. These rules include penalties and fines against anyone caught using their power to drive another competitor from the market by any means except selling better products at lower prices. Rules of a free market also forbid impeding the flow of traffic through some form of regulation that slows it down or tries to live parasitically on the system.

With fair rules and knowledge that fines will be enforced when the rules are violated, very little policing of the highways is necessary. Police might need to only patrol a street once a month to ensure drivers obey the rules. However, if the rules were unfair or if they were not enforced at all, people would try to get around them, requiring constant police supervision that would be too expensive to maintain.

Traffic is not what we call "free-flowing" without the rules that plan for its free flow. A free market, like free-flowing traffic, requires rules that, when followed, make it a free market.

The Role of Government as a Referee

A free market is neither a laissez-faire market nor a regulated market, at least in the sense "regulation" is usually applied, but based on a rule of law, in which the role of government is that of a referee or policeman on a level playing field that maintains the free flow of goods and services. A free market needs vigorous competition under proper rules, like a football game. It needs to be free-flowing as a result of the rules, like a free-flowing highway system. The role of government is to adopt the best rules and enforce them impartially. When the government tries to side with one of the players or becomes a player with virtu-ally unlimited power, it effectively throws the game. In practice, this is what most "regulation" amounts to. In a free market, no economic competitor suffers any disadvantage against others because of the law.

As in football, when a business violates the rules, penalties should be imposed swiftly. Government should not listen to the arguments that penalizing the business will hurt the economy. In the long run, the opposite is true; not penalizing the business will hurt the economy because it makes the game unfair and fewer people are willing to play it. Similarly, any attempt by a lobbyist to influence a government official to pass laws that "throw the game" should be harshly punished as a crime. Also, any lawmaker who introduces a bill that would give an unfair advantage to particular businesses should be punished by fine or removed from his or her legislative position.

Today, legislators in the United States are caught in a contest for control of the economy by a Republican oligarchy on the right and Democratic state redistributionists on the left. This is a direct result of a system in which nearly all lobbying represents one of these two views: laissez-faire or regulation. There is little lobbying that represents a genuinely free market. Neither political party promotes planned competition. In order to become a political candidate for one of the two major parties, one must promise to work for the goals of the interest groups that fund the Party. In the present system, a person concerned with the well-being of the entire nation is precluded from becoming a candidate unless he lies to the party leaders about his ultimate objectives. Our society, which fails to separate commerce and government, is like a football game between two teams, each of which owns half of the referees.

The reader may think that under this flawed system Congress would experience gridlock. This would be the case if the system operated as Madison and other the founders intended. But, this is not the case. Consider Figure 8 below.

This system is structured so two political parties control the legislation. However, the political parties represent the real interests of fewer than half the voters. Most voters are forced to choose between what they consider to be the least evil of two choices. On the left, special interests controlling the party represent those people who are employees of the government, those who seek government welfare, and those whose businesses serve these groups. On the right, real control is in the hands of Republican interest groups. However, the remaining middle class tends to divide the representatives relatively equally to prevent one group or the other from controlling the country.

The crux of the problem is this: the battles for government power are over special economic interests, not the interest of good government. In theory, the goal of the competition between political parties should be to compete over which party can make the government better for the entire society. The competition should be like the competition among computer operating systems:

- Who can develop the most efficient, user-friendly, and productive operating system?

- Who can protect the operating system from infection from viruses better and write patches when viruses are discovered?

BUYING MISREPRESENTATION

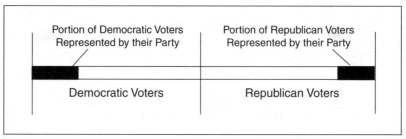

Figure 8: The above diagram represents a society in which actual power is controlled by two political parties that, taken together, represent the actual interests of less than half the people.

Legislation, particularly at the federal level, should be aimed at these kinds of issues:

- Which party can create the most efficient government that best does its job equally for all people?
- Which party can spot core problems that need to be fixed so that all citizens prosper?
- Which party can find the most qualified candidates?

When government and the economy are not separated and government does not act as a referee, then the competition between political parties is misplaced.

Today, instead of serving the citizens, the legislators representing the interest groups at both ends of the political spectrum find it easy to "reach across the aisle,"[22] and serve the interests of the financial backers of both political parties at the expense of the "forgotten man"[23] in the middle class. Figure 9 illustrates how Democratic and Republican legislators reach across the aisle and pass legislation that throws various bones to the special interests backing both parties in order to satisfy lobbyists on both sides. The result is that this collusion serves the special interests at the expense of the forgotten man in the middle.

"REACHING ACROSS THE AISLE"

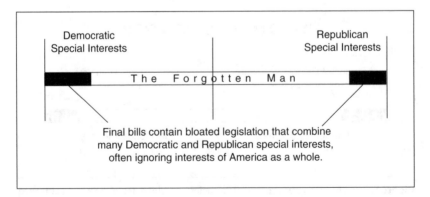

Figure 9: The above diagram represents a society in which actual power is controlled by two political parties that, taken together, represent the actual interests of less than half the people.

The TARP Bailout Example

An example of this process can be seen with the 2008 TARP legislation aimed at rescuing large financial institutions considered by U.S. Treasury Secretary Henry Paulson as "too big to fail." The $700 billion financial package requested in desperation with no strings attached was the result of fraudulent lending practices, irresponsible lending practices, and a government promising to guarantee unsound loans. These practices had made credit available to people who could not afford to pay for it, and they drove up the price of housing to nearly double its market value, creating both a credit and real estate bubble. The legislation that allowed these practices in the first place was "across the aisle" legislation such as the 1999 repeal of the Glass-Steagall Act that prevented certain financial conflicts of interest. This paved the way for the Citibank and Travelers Insurance merger and the creation of hedge funds. Banks were once again able to act simultaneously as lenders, underwriters, financial advisors, and principal investors in some transactions. Such legislation allowed the fox in the henhouse. The analysts, regulators, and watchdogs were on the payroll of those they were supposed to analyze, regulate, and watch. It wasn't two years before the Enron, Global Crossings, Arthur Andersen, World Com and other scandals broke as corporate greed fueled various schemes with layers of phony paper. Then in 2006, the credit bubble collapsed when overvalued housing began to bring down financial giants.

What did the banks do with the bailout money? They bought other banks. And, they loaned money to other large companies like Pfizer who could acquire smaller companies. What happened to loans that were refinanced? Many of them failed a second time because borrowers still could not afford the payments.

When Secretary Paulson ran to Congress in panic, there were a number of Senators on the banking and finance committee who panicked as well. Their special interest supporters had benefitted from the unsound and unsustainable credit practices. Middle-class voters around the country wrote letters to their congressmen not to vote for the bailout, but to let corrupt financial giants fall and return the economy to those practicing sound financial principles. The bailout bill failed on its own merit. The forgotten man had spoken. Therefore, "sweeteners" were added to the bill to get it passed over the will of the people. The bill that passed included a host of tax breaks, an increase in the size of bank accounts insured by the Federal Deposit Insurance Corporation, a requirement that health insurance companies provide more coverage for mental health services, a tax benefit for victims of the 1989 Exxon Valdez oil spill, and even a tax exemption for makers of children's wooden arrows.[24] Each one of these measures was added to sway the vote of one or a few legislators to whom obtaining those sweeteners were more important than voting no on the bailout.

In the end, economic principles trump political desperation. Special interests wanted the government to infuse the banks with cash, trying to force them to lend, even as property values were dropping below the values of the loans. You cannot force a bank to lend $300,000 on a $200,000 house no matter how much cash you give it. What did the banks do with the bailout money? They bought other banks. And, they loaned money to other large companies like Pfizer who could acquire smaller companies. What happened to loans that were refinanced? Many of them failed a second time because borrowers still could not afford the payments. Was cash really unavailable? Not if the borrower had 20 percent or 50 percent as a down payment to guarantee the bank that it had sufficient equity.

There was plenty of money on the sidelines for sound loans without the bailout. The TARP bailout bill is a good example of the limits of "across the aisle" economic legislation; government could not force financial institutions to make bad loans. Instead, it aided the undesirable financial consolidation of the economy. If there are 5,000 banks and one collapses, the economy is not at risk. However, if there are five enormous banks and one collapses, the economy collapses as well.

The Constitution of the United States did not directly address the proper use of economic power. It was concerned with political power and left monetary policy to the legislators. Economic power was much decentralized in 1787, and it was not considered an issue worth blocking the passage of the Constitution. In retrospect, we can see that political parties have become focused on obtaining money for special interests rather than the interest of the nation. A responsible monetary policy is not to remove government from the process nor to regulate industry in a way that impedes the economy, but to turn the government into an economic referee that enforces good rules that apply to everyone on a level playing field.

Clear Rules Will Decrease Lobbying

Creating clear and fair rules of economic competition will drastically reduce the incentives for corporate lobbying and political corruption. Today, because one company can successfully lobby for an advantage, competitors feel they must lobby as well. Robert Reich compares this to an arms race: "The more one competitor pays for access, the more its rivals must pay in order to counter its influence."[25] As long as political deals are legal and serve the interest of profit, corporations will pursue them.

It is illogical to criticize corporations for playing by the current rules of the game or for pursuing strategies that are defined as legal, even if they are immoral.[26] They are simply acting so as to maximize return. The massive legal buying of politicians in the United States and around the world is a result of the failure of government to serve as an impartial referee. As long as it is legal to pass legislation that rewards lobbying, it will persist. As long as it is legal "cross the aisle" in political horse-trading, those who are supposed to be the referees will continue the practice. However, if the clear result of lobbying is known in advance not to pay off, it will not be sought.

Do football players and coaches continually lobby to change the rules? Maybe the rules need to be reevaluated periodically, but they are never changed in the middle of a game after a coach or team owner complains about the results of a play. Rather, the persistent complaint of a coach will get him thrown out of a game. Harsh punishments are also given to football referees who accept bribes to throw a game. The same principle should apply to lobbyists and legislators.

Rules that eliminate attaching special interest legislation to other special interest legislation would greatly reduce frivolous and destructive special interest legislation. This does not mean it would disappear entirely, but that an item would genuinely have to be favored by a majority of people, including the "forgotten man," in order to pass on its own merit.

The Economy is the Third Sector

When Augustine wrote *The City of God*, Western civilization was in the process of defining the relation of church and state. The church had become a large bureaucratic institution on a scale that began to rival government. Religion and government had developed into two distinct spheres of society. They were inter-related, and both served the whole of society, but they were each specialized organs of society. The government was charged with protecting the temporal order and the church nourished the culture. Both the church and the temporal rulers owned tracts of land, and there was no separate field of economics. There were no large corporations raising social questions. Society was viewed as having two sectors. This did not allow the economic sector to develop.

Like the three legs of a stool, culture (religion or knowledge), government (protection), and the economy (sustenance) form the three main supports of a stable society. Just as people will pursue knowledge and other aspects of culture for their own development when they are free to do so, they will also pursue the acquisition of property and produce goods and services to sell to others when they are not inhibited. When the United States was founded, this is what everyone was doing. Most were doing this as individuals and families, like the single-celled amoeba. People not interested in pursuing a new life on their own in America remained back in Europe where social structures were more elaborate.

The economy of a state is only as sound as the productivity of its people. Anything more than subsistence living requires individuals to produce more goods or services than they will personally consume. The fewer restrictions on production or consumption imposed by the government, the more vibrant the economy. An individual, through free choice, is the prime mover in any society, because individuals naturally want to pursue their own happiness and well-being. This was discussed in the chapter on the principle of subsidiarity. Today, the Constitution could better serve that purpose with an amendment that says: *Congress shall make no law respecting an establishment of commerce or prohibiting the free exercise thereof.* Or, Congress should pass other laws which effectively create this separation.

> The economy of a state is only as sound as the productivity of its people. The fewer restrictions on production or consumption imposed by the government, the more vibrant the economy.

Physical Protection and Commercial Products

If the primary role of government is protection, then it can be argued that intervention is necessary when activity in the economic sphere will cause harm to one or more of the players. Can this intervention occur without the government harming fair economic competition? Can it intervene without "establishing commerce" or becoming a player itself? There is a third way for government to address such issues that is fair and still allows all players to compete aggressively, and two examples can illustrate the basic idea.

The first example of protection comes from safety practices that are proven to be beneficial and easily affordable for everyone. A requirement to wear a football helmet as safety gear does not make the game less competitive or exciting to watch. It might be viewed as a nuisance to some, but it might be an incentive for a person who might be afraid of brain injury to decide he can become a player. Similarly, the requirements for padded dashboards and seatbelts in cars can be easily accomplished by requiring all manufacturers to have them. This creates a level playing field for auto manufacturers while drastically reducing the number of deaths of auto users. Through such laws, the government performs its role as protector of citizens without harming economic competition.

However, if referees owned the company that made and sold the football helmets, or government legislators owned the companies that made government approved seatbelts, this would be a conflict of interest. In this case, they would be using the power of their position to gain economic wealth. If a government agency decides which product or provider will be used, that is a violation of the separation of the state and commerce. This is why no-bid government contracts should be outlawed. They violate the laws of the market and establish quasi-monopoly industries.

Safety rules should refer to standards of protection decided impartially and not by the lobbying of specific corporations. Further, government oversight panels generally fail when they are assigned to catch violators in advance. Like building inspectors, they can be bought. And, there are just too many daily economic transactions to assume that a government could watch them all without a huge bureaucracy that would bankrupt taxpayers. If the government is in the role of the brain and the economy the heart, we cannot expect the brain to pump blood to all the cells, but it can regulate the heartbeat and make sure it is stable. Such is the division of social labor. The most efficient procedure is for a citizen to point out the violation to an oversight committee or a court when it appears a rule has been violated; he can use the courts to resolve the problem. It is like feedback from a cell to the brain that says it isn't getting enough blood, then the brain can adjust the operation of the heart a bit—not try to become a heart. With good feedback, huge bureaucracies and intricate legislation that supervise particular businesses would not be required to maintain a healthy economy—only an objective standard by which to act as a referee. This is "planning for competition" in Hayek's words.

By nature, governments are impersonal bureaucracies and, as such, do not "care" about anything. They behave as bureaucracies. Bureaucrats suffer from sin and greed just like CEOs. In the Soviet Union, the *nomenklatura* behaved in much the same way as the CEOs of large impersonal corporations. However, a government can produce laws that protect people from such abuse in any social sector, whether it be fraud perpetrated by a church, theft by a corporate CEO, or excessive taxation by a government. If a law is fair and backed by the force of government, it will help people in their pursuit of happiness.

The Separation of Commerce and State

Modern industrial life arose as a result of freedoms available to individuals in Western Europe and the United States. However, modern states have lacked the knowledge and political will to address the effects of large concentrations of economic power on society.

No country was prepared for the impacts of the industrial revolution on modern life. In a legal vacuum, people have been selfishly trying to eliminate competition or manipulate the political system for economic gain. This is true of both monopolists and socialists. The numerous bubbles, recessions, Ponzi schemes, and financial scandals of the last century are proof that the government has not been a proper referee. It is time to sort out principles related to having an independent economic sphere on par with the culture and the government. We need a political revolution related to refereeing an economy based on planned competition. Such a revolution might be on par with that begun by Machiavelli and Hobbes regarding the analysis of political power.

Free competition has proven to be the strongest engine of productivity. In the Superbowl, the referees are few in number, yet many more players and millions of viewers find it a very exciting and productive enterprise. It is successful and exciting because of fair competition, fine tuning of human skills, and productive teamwork that brings out the pursuit of excellence. A good competitive game uplifts, challenges, and causes creative thought about ways to do things better. People become more educated and skilled when they have a fair opportunity to compete and to prosper, and the country can prosper as a result.

Governments do not need to be large to act as good referees. The swollen modern administrative states of the twentieth century were cumbersome, inefficient, and often went to war because they were acting for some special interest. Many government departments have selfishly proposed, at great expense and waste to taxpayers, to do things "for people" that most people are happier doing themselves. Governments have a definite function as a referee and a role in providing a safety net to protect people who are unable to fend for themselves. But even this role is best fulfilled at lower levels of government where real needs can be better perceived and more personal care can be delivered. This is the principle of subsidiarity.

> **Free competition has proven to be the strongest engine of productivity. In the Superbowl, the referees are few in number, yet many players and millions of viewers find it a very exciting and productive enterprise that brings out the pursuit of excellence.**

If the United States would adopt a constitutional amendment that said, "Congress shall make no law respecting an establishment of commerce or prohibiting the free exercise thereof," it would be like erecting a traffic light at an unregulated intersection jammed with traffic and gridlocked.

SEPARATION OF POWERS 121

It will take a while to clear out the congestion—to repeal legislation promoting conflicts of interest and reorienting Congress
and the courts to think in terms of being referees—not players or
power brokers—but in the end, the free flow of the economy will
bring jobs and opportunities that penalizing competition prevents.
It could help make the United States a very exciting place to live.

Questions for Review and Reflection

1. What are the three major spheres of society, and what does each provide to an individual citizen?

2. Compare the levels of social complexity between Jefferson's and Hamilton's visions of society. Which vision was the U.S. Constitution better suited to govern?

3. Explain how Western Civilization, after the Roman Empire, evolved into three social spheres leading to modern society. Where does the U.S. Constitution fit in this social evolution?

4. Explain the difference between a regulated economy and a refereed economy.

5. Why does planned competition lead to a freer flow of the economy than a laissez-faire economy?

6. Explain why special interests have more influence over legislation than individual citizens.

7. Why did the separation of church and state lead to more vibrant churches?

8. Why did the TARP bailout fail to deliver more credit to consumers? What did banks do with the money instead?

9. In what ways do the CEOs of large corporations and U.S. Senators behave like the *nomenklatura* in the Soviet Union?

10. What do you think is the best way to separate the government and commercial sectors of society?

5

Transparency

Do not ask for transparency from others unless you have provided transparency to them.

—Anderson's Golden Rule of Transparency

Knowledge is power. Information is power. Historically, people in power have sought to control information in order to reinforce or retain their power. One method of control is to limit access to knowledge. In ancient times, very few people could read, and most documents were kept by scribes who worked for royal courts. Rulers could order what knowledge to write down and declare what was true. The spread of knowledge and the existence of information that might undermine power often threaten those who hold power. Banning books, burning books, and canonizing scriptures like the Bible and the Koran are examples of attempts to limit official truth to knowledge approved by ruling powers.

However, human experience often conflicts with inherited truth. We are well aware of the conflicts between science and religion that result from attempts by the Church to promote knowledge that has been disconfirmed by science. We are also well aware of ideologies like Marxism and Darwinism that have been rigidly promoted as truth and as a refutation of inherited doctrine, even though they have failed tests of open discussion and experience. The keepers of such religious and ideological truths, theologians and ideologians, are generally required to show how their writings confirm and expound on official truth in new circumstances. A Christian theologian is required to base his writings on the Bible or church doctrine. A Muslim scholar is expected to show the truth of the Koran or the Islamic way of life. A philosopher in the Soviet Union was required to explain how his ideas conformed to the doctrines of Marxism-Leninism. Yet, human experience continues to challenge all of these closed systems of truth, creating cognitive dissonance, revisionism, repression, or revolution.[1]

The First Amendment to the United States Constitution, with the separation of church and state and guarantees of freedom of the press, speech, and assembly, was designed to counter the temptation by those in power to restrict knowledge as a way of consolidating their power or limiting the free pursuit of knowledge by citizens. In a republic, sovereign citizens need access to all knowledge possible to make the best informed decisions.

Even with constitutional guarantees for freedom of thought, control of information is an ongoing struggle. We are familiar with military and government agencies arguing that information should be given on a "need to know" basis. Control of specific knowledge is often classified for national security reasons. However, that control of information can be used to protect oneself from criminal prosecution, as was popularized in the line by Jack Nicholson,

> **In a republic, sovereign citizens need access to all knowledge possible to make the best informed decisions.**

"You can't handle the truth," in the movie *A Few Good Men*. In that movie, Nicholson plays a military leader who believes he is in a superior position to the citizens and must paternalistically make decisions on behalf of an ignorant public.

Such paternalistic restrictions on information can be well-intended or self-delusional. They might be necessary to prevent an enemy from gaining an advantage. However, they are often for the purpose of hiding unacceptable power-seeking or criminal behavior. There will always be some human beings who try to control information for their own benefit, but the basic principles of a republic require clear and transparent public information and planning. One of the most important needs for transparency is in accounting for the use of public money.

Information Asymmetry

Most people, especially managers of political and financial institutions, seek the "transparency" of other people's information but want to keep their own information private. We want to be sure someone else isn't spending our money unwisely, but we don't want other people to know how we spend their money. This behavior, while a moral double standard, often literally manifests as two sets of financial books. In 2001, Joseph Stiglitz shared the Nobel Memorial Prize in Economics for his work on "Information Asymmetry." For example, "insider trading" is a form of information asymmetry that is not allowed on the stock market because it undermines equal opportunity and investor confidence. One researcher describes Stiglitz's boldness in sounding the alarm:

> In 1997, Stiglitz began challenging the International Monetary Fund's (IMF) handling of the financial crises in East and Southeast Asia. His criticism grew to include the World Bank where he was employed as chief economist, and then the prevailing orthodoxy in Washington. He moved his criticism from economics to politics.[2]

Stiglitz raised the ire of many people in Washington and the international financial institutions when he urged greater honesty and openness than is currently practiced. The present system lacks the checks and balances that information openness could bring to democratic decision-making on issues related to economic and political justice. In his discussions of transparency, Stiglitz draws on Jeremy Bentham, John Stuart Mill, Walter Bagehot, Albert Hirschman, and James Madison. He argued that openness in public life is necessary because democracy requires informed citizens. Stiglitz argues that "the right to know" is a basic human right. A "culture of openness," or transparency, is needed in political and economic life. Laws and accounting practices are not by themselves capable of overcoming the powerful incentives for secrecy, for covering up mistakes, rent-seeking activities, and special interest policy. Stiglitz observed that even while championing freedom of the press, the press is often complicit in the "conspiracy of secrecy."[3]

Freedom of Information

"The right-to-know" is becoming increasingly demanded and accepted around the world. In 1766, Sweden and Finland were the first to enact freedom of information laws. The "International Right-to-Know Day" was established by a group of Eastern European openness advocates who met in Sofia, Bulgaria in 2002 and first celebrated in 2003. This day is now celebrated throughout much of the world, sparking Right-to-Know events and legislation.

In 1966, the United States passed the Freedom of Information Act (FOIA) after ten years of work spearheaded by Representative John Moss (D-CA). The legislation was reluctantly signed by President Lyndon Johnson. Then, after the Watergate scandal that forced President Nixon to resign, Congress passed legislation to strengthen the FOIA. This was vetoed by President Ford, but Congress overrode the veto. In 1986, legislation removed some of the records of the Central Intelligence Agency (CIA) from the FOIA, causing a setback for transparency in the name of "security."

President Bill Clinton and Vice President Al Gore were supporters of the information revolution and, unlike other administrations, they viewed the FOIA favorably. Clinton urged heads of 25 government agencies not to just formally comply with the act, but also to make more information available on their own initiative, stating,

> For more than a quarter century now, the Freedom of Information Act has played a unique role in strengthening our democratic form of government. The statute was enacted

based upon the fundamental principle that an informed citizenry is essential to the democratic process and that the more the American people know about their government, the better they will be governed. Openness in government is essential to accountability, and the Act has become an integral part of that process.[4]

Clinton wanted to develop a new model of government that learned from the impact of the information revolution on business and the growth of companies like Wal-Mart, which had put all its purchasing and inventory records online. This enabled the vendors to manage the inventory shipped to various Wal-Mart stores, increasing efficiency, reducing overhead, and thereby outperforming competitors. The information revolution in the private sector and in business forced the collapse of the centralized control of information. The Soviet Union, still trying to centrally control both information and the economy, could not keep abreast of the information revolution. This contributed to its collapse. Clinton initiated a revolution in government when he asked department heads to treat the "citizens" of the United States as "customers" to be served:

> The Freedom of Information Act, moreover, has been one of the primary means by which members of the public inform themselves about their government. As Vice President Gore made clear in the National Performance Review, the American people are the federal government's customers. Federal departments and agencies should handle requests for information in a customer-friendly manner. The use of the Act by ordinary citizens is not complicated, nor should it be. The existence of unnecessary bureaucratic hurdles has no place in its implementation.[5]

In 1996, the FOIA was amended for electronic records. In 2002 there were 2.4 million requests for information, and in 2004 there were over 4 million requests. The most frequently cited exemptions were for law enforcement and personal privacy.

As one would expect, agencies often stonewall requests. The Bush administration reversed the Clinton policy towards openness and moved to restrict some information, particularly related to federal websites, energy policy meetings, and security issues under the PATRIOT Act. On October 12, 2001, just one month after the September 11 attacks, U.S. Attorney General John Ashcroft issued a memo indicating heads of agencies should be careful in releasing information under the FOIA, promising his office would defend agencies' decisions to withhold information.[6] In 2003, the Government Accounting Office (GAO) found excessive lost requests, unanswered requests, and backlogs of requests.[7]

Over 200 million pages were declassified in 1997. However, the number of pages of newly classified information also began to increase from about 1996 as agencies began to seek to protect themselves from the effects of the expanded FOIA.

Classified documents are not subject to the FOIA but are generally released after 25 years when the principals are unlikely to be in power. Under the Clinton administration's openness policy, a huge increase in declassification occurred. From 1982 to 1994, 10-20 million pages per year were declassified. Over 200 million pages were declassified in 1997. However, the number of pages of newly classified information also began to increase from about 1996 as agencies began to seek to protect themselves from the effects of the expanded FOIA.

Under the Bush administration, the number of classified documents dramatically expanded. In March 2003, the Executive Order on Classified National Security Information was rewritten, striking the words "commitment to open government" and "if there is significant doubt about the need to classify information, it shall not be classified." Previously, if there was doubt about a document, it would not be classified. After this order, however, if there was doubt, the information would be classified. In addition to the increase in new classifications, many documents released under the Clinton administration or prior were reclassified or specific information was struck from previously declassified documents (redeclassification). In fact, some information was struck that had been available for decades, or is still available in public documents elsewhere.[8]

After 9/11, the stonewalling of FOIA requests and increased control of information and secrecy by the government were coupled with increases in the government invasion of privacy and other rights through wire-tapping, prisoner detention without trial, and no-bid government contracts in Iraq. These and other activities inconsistent with openness and transparency were major reasons that the image of the United States was transformed from world leader to world pariah under the Bush administration. While there was an initial willingness to trust the U.S. government after 9/11, the legitimacy of the administration was undermined as the personal fortunes of those close to the administration prospered under secrecy. It is a perfect example of the problem of information asymmetry and legitimacy.

This public stigma put the Bush administration on the defensive, and it eventually had to modify its position on secrecy. On December 14, 2005, President Bush issued an Executive Order titled "Improving Agency Disclosure of Information." The order had little substantial impact but opened a door to the public. In 2006, the Supreme Court ruled against illegal detainment in Guantanamo Bay. One justice warned that violations were considered war crimes. Outrage increased when Congress granted retroactive immunity to U.S. officials who may have carried out or ordered torture in the years after 9/11.[9] This was a tacit admission of guilt as government officials showed they realized the need for protection from crimes they had committed.

The elections of 2006 reflected overwhelming disappointment with the Republican administration as Democrats took control of both the House of Representatives and the Senate for the first time in a dozen years. On December 31, 2007, President Bush signed into law the OPEN Government Act, a freedom of information reform bill that would create more incentives for openness, penalties for delays, and methods to settle disputes. It would provide a tracking procedure for the handling of requests similar to Federal Express's tracking software for packages, and would penalize agencies if requests are not processed in 20 days.

The president attempted to prevent this bill from being passed by Congress with his executive order issued two years earlier. But that order was only considered window dressing that lacked real power to effect change. While the bill did not get all the transparency many had hoped for, it showed that Congress could respond to public concerns that the executive branch had become too clandestine for a democracy. It was also a response to growing international pressure for increased transparency and pressure from individual states that were implementing new transparency measures.

The Cost of Freedom of Information

The demand for freedom of information has not come without cost. In 2004, the cost of processing 4,047,474 requests cost a total of $330,175,513.[10] These costs are a reflection of government doing business as usual, in the traditional hierarchical mode of operation long abandoned in business and the private sector. Except for colleges and universities that are subsidized by government funding or large endowments, the government is the last bastion of organizational flow charts modeled on industrial production in the middle of the twentieth century. Only organizational inertia, monopoly power, and control of knowledge keep such structures in place.

Today, almost all government records are produced on a computer and could be made public without additional work. Some individual states are beginning to do this. The posting of records and access to them can be handled by software that registers users after verifying they are citizens. Levels of access are already used in most government agencies and departments for this same information. Another level of access for the public could easily be added without cost. The main resistance to this move to transparency is fear of loss of income and control of financial resources.

Records that are classified require a higher level of access. However, one professional analysis of classified documents has stated that over 50 percent are unwarranted. Rodney B. McDaniel, Executive Secretary of the National Security Council under President Reagan, said only 10 percent of classification was "for legitimate protection of secrets."[11] The problem is not one of expense, but rather of human nature, civic spirit, and creating a culture of openness inside the government. If this resistance can be overcome, the government will end up saving money, because officials would not dare make selfish and fraudulent expenses public.

Financial Transparency and Banking

Banking, like any other social institution, benefits from subsidiarity. A local banker lives in the same town as a borrower. He knows the financial reputation of a borrower firsthand and can personally watch property on which he has loaned money. Transparency is not difficult in such face-to-face community relations. A local banker will know if his borrower is suddenly living extravagantly after receiving a loan or if he appears to be using his money wisely. Local bankers also tend to have smaller levels of capitalization, and they often own a significant portion of the bank stock. Since they are spending their own money, they will be motivated to make only safe loans.

Large impersonal banks have no way to know a person's credit worthiness other than a credit score and what is written on application forms or stored in databases.

Large impersonal banks have no way to know a person's credit-worthiness other than a credit score and what is written on application forms or stored in databases. They are unlikely to ever personally meet the borrower or visually inspect the property for which they are lending money. They must rely on paperwork and data that is abstracted one or two levels from the transaction. Large banks like to buy or control smaller banks that are profitable, because profitability is a sign that the small bank is engaged in sound banking practices.

However, large banks never have the level of transparency and accountability possible with community banks. Fraudulent paperwork is easier to submit. Agents on commission are anxious to place loans and often misstate the situation to close a deal. Credit scores are manipulated both up and down by reporting that might contain incomplete information or bias. Repeal of the Glass-Steagall Act and other depression-era legislation designed to eliminate conflicts of interest makes it more difficult for large banks to trust one another.

Lower transparency due to insufficient subsidiarity is one of the primary reasons for the credit bubble at the beginning of the twenty-first century. The effect of federal banking legislation on large lenders was difficult to predict without understanding the effects that legislation would have on mortgage brokers and borrowers. In retrospect, it appeared that the legislators did not understand the effect their bills would have. Democrats thought that loosening credit would help lower-class families buy houses, but the legislation ended up hurting those people the most as they defaulted, lost any savings they may have had, and were pushed onto the street. Wealthy lenders and financial markets were more than happy to go along if their loans were guaranteed by Fannie Mae and Freddie Mac.

Those guarantees undermined the economic incentives for lenders to carefully supervise their assets, which large lenders have more difficulty doing than small lenders anyway. Giving rescue money to large banks did not give them any more confidence in lending money on under-collateralized properties. They were more motivated to act as scavengers, using the bailout money to acquire the assets of other banks in distress. The legislation did not encourage the desired financial outcome. A better solution would have been for the TARP funds to go to renegotiate loans through local banks. It would have been better yet to handle the entire situation on a state-by-state basis, because the federal legislation did not penalize those states like Florida and California where most defaults occurred but redistributed money from states with better fiscal oversight, in effect punishing the more responsible behavior that would have been another form of subsidiarity in practice. However, consolidated economic powers resist subsidiarity, and consolidated governments prefer to work with representatives of other consolidated institutions rather than devolving their own power.

Rather than encouraging consolidation, good legislation should encourage devolving large banks into smaller ones where transparency and accountability are better able to operate. If a small bank misbehaves, it is not "too large to fail." Anytime a state has institutions "too large to fail," it is in peril; it should seek to extricate itself from such encumbrances. While large businesses and financial institutions will lobby for financial incentives to consolidate, merge, and acquire smaller companies, governments should be suspicious and create legislation that encourages movement in the opposite direction— towards subsidiarity. This would mean, for example, instead of providing a tax incentive for a merger, there could be a sales tax paid to the government for any acquisition of one company by another, just like sales taxes on consumer purchases. Such incentives towards subsidiarity would reduce opportunities for large scale fraud and national level economic bubbles.

> **Anytime a state has institutions "too large to fail," it is in peril; it should seek to extricate itself from such encumbrances.**

The Agency Problem

The problems of transparency in any social institution relate to what has become known as the problem of agency. An "agent" is a person or group of people that acts on behalf of others. As with other relationships, an agent can be someone you know and see regularly, like your local insurance agent, or it could be someone you do not know personally, acting at a distance through some bureaucratic mechanism, such as the CEO of a corporation in which you own stock, or a state Senator that represents your state in Washington. One generally has more influence with an agent one knows personally and feels better represented by him or her.

In the modern corporation, the firm is owned by shareholders. A principal-to-agent relationship exists between shareholders and corporate executives. The theory behind this arrangement is that the managers of the corporation will act on behalf of the shareholders and their interests. The assumption is that investors (shareholders) invest in the firm to increase their own wealth. Thus, the role of the agents is to increase the value of the firm and the value of each share.[12]

> **In their research, Berle and Means noted that the interests of corporate managers and shareholders diverged in practice and that millions of passive shareholders translated into the "absolute power in the corporate managements."**

When shares are diversified, it is very difficult for an individual shareholder to hold the agents accountable. In 1916, in a case brought by the Dodge brothers against Henry Ford, the courts ruled that "a business corporation is organized and carried on primarily for the profit of stockholders."[13] However, in their research done in the 1930s, Berle and Means noted that the interests of corporate managers and shareholders diverged in practice and that millions of passive shareholders translated into the "absolute power in the corporate managements."[14] The "agency problem" thus assumes that (1) the desires and goals of the principal and agent diverge or conflict, and (2) it is difficult and expensive for a principal to verify what an agent is doing. Kenneth R. Gray and his colleagues concluded that the agency problem contributed to the $1.6 trillion heist that occurred with the corporate scandals at the turn of the twenty-first century. Although no conspiracy or illegality could be proven in many cases, maneuvers by agents motivated by greed led to the theft of corporate wealth from shareholders and other stakeholders.

In the 1970s, Professors Michael C. Jensen and William H. Meckling had argued that whenever the management and ownership of a firm is separate, we should expect this agency problem. However, even though agents' behavior might be wasteful and they might enjoy unwarranted perks, their retention might be economically rational. They described the difference between the maximized value of the stock for the benefit of shareholders and the actual value of stocks after such waste and perks—the "agency costs."[15] In the 1980s, agency costs soared as large public corporations began to spend more wastefully and inefficiently from the shareholders' perspectives. Leveraged buyouts, junk bond sales, and other risky managerial behavior led to corporate borrowing, and debt led to a higher cost of capital than competitor costs in Japan and Germany. CEOs often earned their reputations, high salaries, and stock options by very risky and highly leveraged (and often hostile) corporate takeovers that could lead to big gains or bankruptcy at creditor and shareholder expense.

These large bets made by CEOs with other people's money were not aimed at developing the products and sales that the corporations were founded to produce and sell. Rather the Wall Street mergers and trades had reached a level of abstraction from real production. CEOs used capital for high risk strategies with winners and losers. The results of these deals were large executive salary payouts when increases to shareholders were marginal. They persuaded investors that such agency costs were justified.

Another problem for investors is the double taxation of corporate profits. First, the profits of the corporation are taxed before dividend payouts. Then, when investors receive their dividends, they pay taxes again. This double taxation has resulted in many investors preferring not to take dividends but to reinvest the dividends in the purchase of more shares. The problem with this is an accumulation of profits in the form of increased outstanding shares and further concentrations of capital for risky CEO strategies. Further, during the 1990s, the time-honored tradition of evaluating the performance of companies by the analysis of dividend yield per share was ignored. From 1871 to 1980, the dividend yield per share had averaged around 5 percent. However, from 1980 to 2000, this yield had dropped to less than 1 percent and dividends accounted for less than 10 percent of the distribution of profits, as opposed to the historic average of 35 percent of profits being distributed to shareholders.[16]

The difference accounted for increased value of the company on paper that corporate managers had at their disposal for more acquisitions, corporate buybacks, and CEO stock options. The buyback strategies were often done for the purpose of giving CEOs stock options without reducing the short-term price of the stock. The Financial Accounting Standards Board (FASB) had ruled that such options were not technically compensation and therefore need not be expensed. These schemes avoided shareholder concern and legal penalties while they transferred corporate value to the "agents" at the expense of the principals.

Not only did the government fail to referee this behavior, but it also contributed to the problems by passing legislation, proposed by special financial interests, which rewarded mergers and acquisitions with tax breaks rather than disincentives.

As the scandals emerged and many giants collapsed at the turn of the twenty-first century, the agency cost turned into the "$1.6 trillion heist."

The problems associated with agency, lack of subsidiarity, lack of refereeing of corporate behavior by the government, and lack of separation of commerce and government all enabled corporate greed to reach extraordinary levels of concentration. Not only did the government fail to referee this behavior, but it also contributed to the problems by passing legislation proposed by special financial interests, which rewarded mergers and acquisitions with tax breaks rather than disincentives. Further, by putting income taxes on corporate profits before they were distributed, the government incentivized corporate managers to spend any profits in ways that would be of more rational economic benefit to the corporations or their managers than paying taxes. Income taxes on corporate profits are an unsound form of tax, as they encourage corrupt corporate behavior. Such taxes, created by governments that do not understand corporate behavior, created greater opportunity for corporate greed, while the shareholders and the company employees turned out to be "the forgotten man."

It would be far more just if the government required all profits to be distributed to shareholders as dividends and then taxed the shareholders only in a one-time tax. Corporate managers would be less likely to spend their time evading taxes and sidetracking profits to themselves. Investors would receive regular and dependable disbursements, and while they would be considered taxable income, they would be protected by not allowing 20 years of accumulated equity to be lost with one act of corporate greed. Further, by discouraging the leveraging of capital for acquisitions, the cost of capital could be more on par with competitors in Japan and Germany. Finally, by discouraging the accumulation of corporate war-chests that create a climate for hostile takeovers and other acquisitions, corporate executives could focus on producing and selling their products in a more competitive market place, allowing more players on the field, bolstering the size of the middle-class, and creating more wealth based on real productivity rather than consolidating wealth that exists into the hands of ever fewer players.

The agency principle applies to all other social institutions, not just corporations. Elected representatives in government, school principals, leaders of nongovernmental organizations (NGOs), church leaders, and lawyers are all examples of agents that act on behalf of citizens in the performance of some social good. However, agents, as human beings, are rational maximizers just like principals. Many agents are altruistic and self-regulating, just as are many principals. However, a society that imagines all agents will perform altruistically is naïve. Even if 80 percent behave altruistically, the other 20 percent must be checked from abusing their power as agents. Otherwise, they will bring an entire social institution to the point of collapse as they enrich themselves.

The founders of the United States did not imagine or guard against all the problems of agency in government or other social institutions. They had an understanding of human nature which curtailed the problems of agency in government when they drafted the Constitution. The society prospered greatly under that Constitution, but the principles for which it stands were not carried out satisfactorily with laws and constitutional reforms that updated and upgraded their "Version 3.0." Instead, laws have often been passed that reversed or moved away from the United States' founding principles, leading to many of the social problems that exist today such as the increased gap between rich and poor, a shrinking middle class, and huge wastes of money through misdirected agency.

Government Transparency and Corruption

Taxpayers, like banks, need financial transparency from their governments, their agents, to whom they entrust their money. They need good information on how political agents are spending their money, just like banks need good information about the property they mortgage. Corruption can be boiled down to selling the influence of an agent's office for personal gain rather than using their power in accordance with the social purposes for which their office was created. Corruption can be significantly reduced through transparency, even though it is more difficult to control corruption as power or wealth become more consolidated and farther removed from the principals, the citizens.

Financial transparency is considered a key component of good governance. Since the 1990s, especially through the work of Stiglitz, the World Bank has taken the lead in promoting financial transparency. Many of its loans given to governments for the purpose of economic development were not repaid. These loans were made without understanding the problems of agency coupled to political power. In 1949, the United Nations General Assembly had overwhelmingly voted that all technical aid from the World Bank was to go to governments.[17] The members of the General Assembly were motivated to pass this measure because they represented the heads of government who want to control the money entering their country. There were no checks and balances on this international assembly of various state regimes who were all motivated to prevent the flow of money from going around them through direct loans to citizens or businesses in their countries.

The charter of the United Nations recognizes all states as sovereign entities. It treats what goes on inside a state like a black box. There was a naïve faith that government representatives represented the interests of all citizens equally, regardless of religious, ethnic, or tribal affiliation. There was a belief that such leaders would use loans for their stated purposes. There was an assumption that states leaders would repay all loans. Of course, some states represented their people better than others and repaid loans better than others. But history has now proven that government leaders often used this aid money for personal purposes, depositing much of it in Swiss bank accounts and letting the citizens repay debts after they left office.

Corruption can be significantly reduced through transparency, even though it is more difficult to control corruption as power or wealth become more consolidated and farther removed from the principals, the citizens.

Many countries that were great supporters of the UN Universal Declaration of Human Rights in 1949 had become the largest violators of human rights by 1965. The concentration of funding for economic and social development flowing through political leaders made the possibility of using those funds for personal power and wealth too tempting. Even if the political leaders of 1949 retained their moral values, those who succeeded them were often motivated to capture the office to seize a portion of international aid. Coups were instigated for the very purpose of seizing the positions that were connected to international funds.

In a market economy, the flow of money follows the laws of supply and demand. However, in government, the flow of money follows the channels of power. Leaders who have seized power would have to be altruistic to spend their money on citizens. This seldom happens. Most people responsible for government spending are not altruistic. Like everyone else, they tend to be rational maximizers. Only leaders who are elected in competitive elections or are otherwise motivated by political structure can be expected to choose to spend money for the benefit of the larger society.

The idea of treating states as unqualified sovereign powers breaks down both with respect to political and economic power.

The idea of treating states as unqualified sovereign powers breaks down both with respect to political and economic power. Politically, the United Nations, as an alliance of world powers, helped to prevent wars among states. However, this world order has failed to prevent wars within states that have caused genocide, humanitarian disaster, and unleashed a flood of refugees on the rest of the world. Such wars are caused by the seizure of state power by one group in an attempt to control the resources of the country for itself and its cronies. This is the problem of a top-down system of government that is not built on national consensus, subsidiarity, or a pyramid of responsibility. The government does not function as an agent of the people, but at the will of the leader. In such systems, people are not treated as ends in themselves, but as means to the end of the ruling group. Such systems do not support the pursuit of life, liberty, and happiness by all.

The United Nations, like the United States or any federation of smaller states that seeks to promote the life, liberty, and happiness of all individuals under its jurisdiction, should not allow full membership to states that do not meet the test of these basic internal principles of governance related to the flow of power. Full transparency in relation to information, power, and money should be a requirement of a democratic federation of states. Conversely, such an international democratic federation would necessarily need to disclose its activity with full transparency to its members.

The United Nations, as structured, treating sovereign states as black boxes, cannot reach these goals. However, it is constantly called upon to clean up humanitarian and financial disasters after the failure of its member regimes. Secretary General Kofi Annan called for its reform at the opening of the millennium session. However, agents will not generally reform themselves. One could not expect dictatorships to suddenly allow their citizens to rule their own country, because they would likely lose their position. Immanuel Kant's *Perpetual Peace* envisioned the formation of voluntary federations of republics in the creation of greater security and efficiency, not a mixture of republics and despotisms.[18] Any non-republican form of government would qualify as corrupt from the viewpoint of life, liberty, and the pursuit of happiness. Any non-transparent government is more likely to abuse its power.

The International Trend Toward Transparency

The World Bank has contributed to the growing global trend toward transparency.[19] International development fund loans now require greater transparency, and many countries are adopting freedom of information and transparency laws. By 2009, 86 countries had some form of freedom of information laws. In China, Shanghai Municipality and other lower-level local Chinese governments have transparent government programs. Russia adopted the right to information in Article 29 of its Constitution. In July 2008, former U.S. President Jimmy Carter forwarded the "Atlanta Declaration and Plan of Action for the Advancement of the Right to Information," which considers freedom of information to be a fundamental human right, to all heads of state and leaders of the major international organizations and financial institutions.

Most countries do not have highly developed freedom of information laws, and those that do often have a difficult time enforcing them. Nevertheless, from open source software, to *Wikipedia, YouTube,* and other collaborative forms of communication on the internet, the world is entering an information revolution sometimes termed "knowledge 2," or "collaborative knowledge." This knowledge revolution that gave Wal-Mart a competitive advantage in business is impacting the private cultural sphere and government as well. Older institutional forms are resisting, as did the Luddites in nineteenth century England or traditional typesetters with the rise of computers. Openness and transparency threaten people in social institutions who thrive behind walls of secrecy to maintain or abuse the power of their public office.

Not unexpectedly, some of the loudest advocates for transparency demand transparency to get information they want from others, but they hesitate to provide it themselves.

Not unexpectedly, some of the loudest advocates for transparency demand transparency to get information they want from others, but they hesitate to provide it themselves. The World Bank, a strong advocate for the transparency of *government* borrowers, hesitates when others want to investigate its activities. Likewise, newspapers are strong advocates for government transparency and freedom of information but often do not want to divulge sources that would verify the truthfulness of their stories. The U.S. Internal Revenue Service demands much more information from citizens than it is able to provide about itself. Organization heads usually demand more information from subordinates than they are willing to provide to them.

Where there is a relationship between leaders and followers

that is more like that of parents and children than citizens and their agents, giving information on a "need-to-know" basis is justifiable. But often, such arguments are made by government agents who would like to reverse the principal and agent positions, improperly leaving their position. Sometimes there are other good reasons to protect information. For example, strategic military targets need to be kept secret from enemies. Personal privacy should generally be respected and limited to what individuals authorize in order to participate in other social institutions. However, institutions generally have an obligation of transparency to all members who create and fund them. Corporate executives have an obligation of transparency to board members and shareholders. Governments have an obligation to show citizens how they are spending their money.

States Take the Lead in the U.S.

In the United States, individual states are adding to the pressure for transparency on the federal government. In 2002, the Florida Society of Newspaper Editors created "Sunshine Sunday" in response to efforts by Florida legislators to pass over 300 new exemptions to Florida open government laws. This movement expanded to the American Society of Newspaper Editors in 2003, and by 2005 had attracted financial support from foundations. They inaugurated "National Sunshine Week" in 2005 to fall on National Freedom of Information Day, which is celebrated on James Madison's birthday, March 16.

In 2006, Texas Governor Rick Perry began posting all of his office expenses on the internet, kicking off the financial transparency trend among states. Since then, eleven other states passed financial transparency laws, placing records of government expenditures on the internet. Oklahoma Republican Senator Tom Coburn and Illinois Democrat Barack Obama introduced a federal bill that requires full disclosure of all entities or organizations receiving federal funds. Senators Stevens and Byrd tried to hold up this bill, but once their holds were identified publicly, making their behavior transparent, they relented, allowing the Coburn-Obama transparency bill to sail through the Senate.[20] Just as these senators were embarrassed when their behavior became public knowledge, posting amounts of all checks written for public expenses on the internet can help reduce expenses because non-competitive, wasteful, or frivolous expenses will be exposed and threaten the jobs of those responsible for such expenses. The internet offers new possibilities for transparency and checks and balances on government. Hopefully, more accountability of government to citizens will be a trend that continues.

Transparency NGOs Mushroom

The number of transparency and freedom of information NGOs has mushroomed in recent years. It can be compared to the growth of the number of anti-nuclear, human rights, environment, and peace NGOs in the twentieth century. In the United States, the FOI Center was begun in the Research Library at the University of Missouri School of Journalism in 1958. This center and its founders were central to the effort to enact the national Freedom of Information Act. In 2008, 75 NGOs were listed as links on the sunshineweek.org website run by the American Society of Newspaper Editors.[21] They include libraries, democratic networks, think tanks, and activist organizations.

No one really likes being audited, and NGOs are no exception. However, a pattern emerged: the best projects were run by local organizations rather than international ones.

But, as one would expect, not all NGOs are transparent. Some NGOs have been set up to support revolutionary political movements and fronts for anti-government activities. Some are "educational" lobbies for myriads of special interests and humanitarian objectives. There are over 50,000 NGOs operating worldwide. If NGOs are watching governments, who is watching the NGOs? In "Who guards the guardians?," a phrase borrowed from Roman satirist Juvenal's question of Plato's "philosopher king," a 2003 article from the *Economist* mentions a study done on NGOs and concludes:

> No one really likes being audited, and NGOs are no exception. However, a pattern emerged: the best projects were run by local organizations rather than international ones.
>
> Not that surprising, really, but worth reminding armchair conservationists in the rich world. Local enthusiasts are highly motivated, whereas, as the report itself puts it: "Competition for funds and publicity among the larger NGOs results in a divided movement that is not making the best use of its assets. It also results in the diversion of funds from conservation to institutional survival, self-interest and a lack of transparency."[22]

The answer should not be surprising to a reader who has read through this book this far. Subsidiarity works. Local organizations, when they take responsibility, are more effective, more transparent, and more responsive to actual needs of particular situations. Large bureaucracies can only administer approximate justice based on rational goals. They require greater overhead, and they are easier to abuse and more difficult to police. The power in NGOs, as in other institutions, when consolidated, suffers from problems similar to centralization in government bureaucracy. When organizations hold funds in public trust, as does the International Red Cross or the United Way, they must also become unflinchingly transparent.

Conclusion

The control of information is one of the primary means that people have used to gain and maintain power and use others for their own ends. In large impersonal social institutions, agents are entrusted to use information, financial resources, and political power for the larger society and the principals they represent. However, a potential agency problem exists in any type of social institution where agents are designated to act on behalf of owners, members, citizens, or others. The U.S. founders understood the agency problem with respect to political power but did not have a real need to consider agency in the economic sphere in their day.

Following the rise of corporations and the expansion and consolidation of other large social institutions like NGOs, the deleterious effects of the agency problem manifested in many ways, including corporate theft, economic depression, and war. Transparency is one of the main ways to deter such abuse by public officials. It holds parties publicly accountable rather than allowing them to hide behind secrecy and obfuscation. However, employing principles of subsidiarity and the separation of government from commerce will further reduce these problems. Society should remember that the primary role of government is to protect citizens from being harmed by others, not to capitulate to the desires of special interest lobbies that hurt citizens. Society should remember that the primary role of corporations is to produce wealth for investors, not to pay taxes to government or inordinate wages to CEOs.

Questions for Review and Reflection

1. What area of control do you think would give you more power, control of knowledge, control of wealth, or control of an army? Why?

2. What is information asymmetry? Give examples of its use by a political leader, a religious leader, and a corporation leader.

3. What is "information 2" (or "knowledge 2") and how did Wal-Mart use it to become more efficient than competitors? Explain ways you think information 2 can be applied to similarly streamlining government.

4. Why do you think the number of new pages of information being classified increased, even as the Clinton administration sought massive declassification of past government documents?

5. Why do you think it is more difficult for large banks to prevent loan fraud than smaller ones? Do you think the TARP bailout funds would have worked better if they had gone to small community banks?

6. What is the agency problem? In what social sector do you think this problem causes the most harm to society?

7. Why do concentrations of power enable agents to ignore the well-being individual stakeholders?

8. What doctrine in the United Nations Charter encouraged corruption and human rights violations?

9. Briefly explain how the transparency movement has been growing in the United States.

10. The "Right to Know" and the "Right to Privacy" inevitably conflict with one another. Discuss this relationship and where you feel transparency trumps the right to privacy, and why.

6

The Right to Secede

III. That the powers of government may be reassumed by the people whensoever it shall become necessary to their happiness.

—From Rhode Island's Ratification of the U.S. Constitution

The right for a sub-unit to secede is a difficult right for any society to accept. Secession can amount to a loss of something one has come to consider integral to oneself. In the human body, you might compare secession to chopping off an arm or removing a spleen. An organ has to be seriously infected or damaged and its retention life threatening before one agrees to its removal. If you could find a doctor who could repair a gangrenous limb, you would prefer its repair to chopping it off. However, if you have flesh-eating bacteria that will consume your entire body if you do not cut off that limb, it is the measure of last resort. It is a violent act, but you can function without a limb. You might not be able to replace the damaged arm but, even without an artificial limb, you can function. You may not be whole, but you are thankful to be alive.

Secession and Divorce

Social organisms are connected by social bonds; they are not as physically linked as an arm or a spleen. However, social bonds are strong, and interdependencies develop. Breaking these bonds can be very painful and is not desirable. The death of a loved one is not easy to accept. Grief will be experienced with the loss of a parent or spouse with whom one has lived happily for many years. If a father abandons the wife and children he has been supporting, they will suffer. If they feel the new situation is hopeless, they might contemplate some violent act or crime. This will cause a burden for the entire society. Divorce can also be psychologically traumatic and create emotional scars on the partners and their children.

Great trauma can also be experienced in the breakup of countries like the former Yugoslavia. In a unified Yugoslavia under Marshall Tito, Croats, Serbs, Bosnians, Macedonians, and Slovenians intermarried. They had familial relationships that extended beyond provincial borders. Many had homes and property in territories traditionally occupied by other ethnic groups. Members of various ethnic groups became neighbors and friends who went to the same schools, played sports together, and worked side by side in businesses. With the breakup of the federation, family members and neighbors suddenly became enemies. Women were violently raped as a tactic of war. People were driven from their homes by the people with whom they went to school and worked. Refugees became wards of the international community, bringing the suffering and heartache to the entire world. The breakup of Yugoslavia was not exactly the secession of one state from a voluntarily entered union. Yugoslavia, like other empires, had been held together by force. Yet, it had become one society, and its breakup had many of the social and psychological consequences as the sudden secession of a state that was an integral part of a larger federal society.

In many societies, divorce is not allowed because the family is the fundamental social unit and its integrity considered essential

> **Members of various ethnic groups became neighbors and friends who went to the same schools, played sports together, and worked side by side in businesses. With the breakup of the federation, these people suddenly became enemies. Family members and neighbors became enemies.**

for the rearing of children and the maintenance of social order. Divorce causes damage to everyone connected to the functioning of that unit, to the spouses who were drawn to one another in love, to the children who need their parents to raise them, to the society that depends on the participation and financial support members of the family give to the community. People damaged and scarred from divorce might need more care from the community than they give to it. They might turn to alcoholism or leave their jobs in despair.

In the Catholic Church, marriage is sacred. Divorce has been grounds for excommunication. However, there is a lengthy procedure of annulment than can, in the end, separate the spouses so they can be free again to marry. It is the procedure of last resort and cannot be entered into lightly. It is a lengthy process of discovery to determine if there was something wrong at the start. For example, did one of the spouses feel forced to marry and never genuinely enter into it freely?[1]

In the annulment process, contrition should be made for past mistakes that did not make the marriage genuine. Responsibility must be accepted for children born in that relationship. A plan for their future must be made. Every effort to eliminate violence and resentment is made. The consequences of decisions and relationships resulting from the union should be addressed rather than simply abandoned, causing additional harm.

The consequences of a failed marriage can be like a microcosm of the relationships that developed in Yugoslavia. The breakdown of a social union can cause economic, social, psychological, and even physical destruction. Divorce and secession are actions that cause harm to others. It is the responsibility of a state to protect one's freedom to pursue life, liberty, and happiness, so long as that pursuit does not harm others. Allowing a no-fault divorce or the instant secession of a state from a union is a failure of government to protect its citizens. However, refusing to allow divorce or secession as a process of last resort is to force violence and unhappiness on citizens. Secession should be seen as the last step in a failed union.

Secession Considered a Right at the Founding

When an individual joins a voluntary association, they have a right
to leave that association. Freedom of assembly is a fundamental
right granted by the fourth clause of the First Amendment to
the Constitution of the United States. The founders considered
this freedom important enough to extend to religion. One is free
to choose his or her religion and free to leave it if they choose.
Americans have the freedom to choose an employer, and if they
do not like the work, the freedom to quit; the freedom to buy
property, and the freedom to sell it.

The Declaration of Independence is one of the most famous
declarations of secession in history. It asserts that a people have
the right to leave and join governments. The right to secede was
considered to be the ultimate check on the power of a government,
the withdrawal of membership could lead to its dissolution.

The founding of the United States was a unique opportunity,
rare in the history of the world, where a union of states was formed
by voluntary agreement rather than conquest or treaty. Individual
states were not forced to join the union, but it was in their interest to do so because the reasons to join outweighed the reasons
to remain independent. The Union could guarantee the common
protection of a member state in exchange for a price lower than
if the state had to defend all its borders with surrounding states,
as would be the case in an anarchic "state of nature" among states.

At the founding, the right of secession was seen as a natural
right of a free people, and a last check on abuse of power by a
central government. The ratification of the Constitution by several
states specifically made their joining the Union contingent on the
right to withdraw if they deemed necessary. In its ratification of
the Constitution, New York put it this way:

> That the enjoyment of life, liberty, and the pursuit of hap-
> piness are essential rights, which every government ought
> to respect and preserve.
>
> *That the powers of government may be reassumed by the peo-
> ple whensoever it shall become necessary to their happiness.*[2]

The ratification by Virginia was prefaced similarly:

WE the Delegates of the people of Virginia, …having fully and freely investigated and discussed the proceedings of the Federal Convention, … DO in the name and in behalf of the people of Virginia, declare and make known that the powers granted under the Constitution, being derived from the people of the United States *may be resumed by them whensoever the same shall be perverted to their injury or oppression,* and that every power not granted thereby remains with them and at their will.[3]

Rhode Island's ratification was similar, but they added the right to "property" to "life, liberty, and the pursuit of happiness," and specifically included statements that a government cannot deprive posterity of these rights or deny freedom of religion.

I. That there are certain natural rights of which men, when they form a social compact, cannot deprive or divest their posterity,—among which are the enjoyment of *life and liberty, with the means of acquiring, possessing, and protecting property, and pursuing and obtaining happiness and safety.*

II. That *all power is naturally vested in, and consequently derived from, the people;* that magistrates, therefore, are their trustees and agents, and at all times amenable to them.

III. That *the powers of government may be reassumed by the people whensoever it shall become necessary to their happiness.* That the rights of the states respectively to nominate and appoint all state officers, and every other power, jurisdiction, and right, which is not by the said Constitution clearly delegated to the Congress of the United States, or to the departments of government thereof, remain to the people of the several states, or their respective state governments, to whom they may have granted the same; and that those clauses in the Constitution which declare that Congress shall not have or exercise certain powers, do not imply that

Congress is entitled to any powers not given by the said Constitution; but such clauses are to be construed as exceptions to certain specified powers, or as inserted merely for greater caution.

IV. That religion, or the duty which we owe to our Creator, and the manner of discharging it, can be directed only by reason and conviction, and not by force and violence; and therefore *all men have a natural, equal, and unalienable right to the exercise of religion according to the dictates of conscience; and that no particular religious sect or society ought to be favored or established, by law, in preference to others.*[4]

The Constitution of the United States was designed as a league of peace. It did not define the internal structures of government of the thirteen member states. It treated the states as sovereign units of government. And, as in a marriage, that is the way it had to be, or the individual states would never have joined the Union voluntarily or happily. But ultimately, the sovereignty of the states rested in the sovereignty of the people. And, the sovereignty of the people rested upon natural laws. Their philosophy was one of subsidiarity.

The Revolution of 1776 was fought for this right of free and voluntary union. Although the states did not want the Union to fail, they did not want to be forced to remain in the Union if it failed to perform its job and turned into some monstrous Leviathan. The Bill of Rights was designed to further guarantee the Union would not turn into such a monster. In Jefferson's words, "a Bill of Rights is what the people are entitled to against every government on earth, general or particular, and what no just government should refuse."[5] The state of Virginia did not support ratification of the Constitution without a Bill of Rights that outlined the rights citizens had against governments, both state and federal.

Each of the first nine articles in the Bill of Rights was designed to protect people from the federal government by limiting its power and guaranteeing individual freedom. The Tenth

Amendment stated that if any other check on power was left out, that power belonged to the individual states. The federal government was forbidden from taking any power not given to it by the member states. It is hard to imagine any more fundamental principle implied by the formation of the Union than the right of secession.

The original Articles of Confederation were voluntarily joined by the colonies, and the members voluntarily withdrew when they ratified the new Constitution. There is no mention of permanence of the Union, only that it is an attempt to create a more perfect Union than the first one.

Views of Secession Before the Civil War

From the beginning of the Union, there was dissatisfaction and there were several threats of secession. In 1790, Pennsylvania abolitionists including Benjamin Franklin petitioned the House of Representatives to eliminate slavery. Georgia and South Carolina delegations said such an action would cause their states to leave the Union. In 1804, members of the Federalist Party in New England and New York plotted secession from the country ruled by Thomas Jefferson. In the Hartford Convention of 1815, Federalists again contemplated secession over James Madison's handling of the War of 1812.[6] Slavery and Federalism were the two most contentious issues unresolved by the Constitution that were serious enough for states to contemplate secession.

In his First Inaugural Address in 1801, Jefferson declared,

> If there be any among us who would wish to dissolve this Union or to change its republican form, let them stand undisturbed as monuments of the safety with which error of opinion may be tolerated where reason is left free to combat it.[7]

Here, Jefferson was making the point that if a member secedes from the Union, the Union ought not to object and should find a way to live without that member. The strength of the Union was rooted in its ability to tolerate such a departure. Hopefully, the member that had departed would realize what they had lost, and voluntarily return.

In 1811, Jefferson again spoke on this point saying that secession would be befriended by the Union:

> Certain States from local and occasional discontents might attempt to secede from the Union. This is certainly possible; and would be befriended by this regular organization [of the Union into States]. But it is not probable that local discontents can spread to such an extent as to be able to face the sound parts of so extensive an Union; and if ever they should reach the majority, they would then become the regular government, acquire the ascendency in Congress and be able to redress their own grievances by laws peaceably and constitutionally passed.[8]

In *A View of the Constitution of the United States* (1825), William Rawle wrote "The secession of a State depends on the will of the people of such a State." Rawle had met George Washington at the Constitutional Convention and served as a Federal District Attorney for nine years at George Washington's invitation. Even though he was a Federalist and Federalists supported a stronger federal government, he considered secession a basic right. Even though the idea of secession was growing more unpopular in some circles, Rawle's book enjoyed wide appeal as a textbook, and was vetted for use by both West Point and Harvard Law School without any dispute about its accuracy.[9]

A decade later, Alexis de Tocqueville corroborated this view when he described *Democracy in America:*

> The Union was formed by the voluntary agreement of the States; in uniting together they have not forfeited their nationality, nor have they been reduced to the condition of one and the same people. If one of the states chooses to withdraw from the compact, it would be difficult to disapprove its right of doing so, and the Federal Government would

have no means of maintaining its claims directly either by force or right.[10]

In *Life of Webster,* Senator Henry Cabot Lodge wrote,

> When the Constitution was adopted, it is safe to say that there was not a man in the country, from Washington and Hamilton to Clinton and Mason, who did not regard the new system as an experiment from which each and every State had a right to peaceably withdraw.[11]

Alexis de Tocqueville was an ardent supporter of decentralization. He wrote that those who favor centralization in Europe argue erroneously that they can administer affairs better than people can locally. However great and perfect a central power is, it is not omniscient and cannot understand local details. It will create "a very imperfect result or exhaust itself." Perhaps he foresaw the possibility of Americans forgetting the voluntary Union for which they fought the Revolution, when he wrote,

> Centralization easily succeeds, indeed, in subjecting the external actions of men to a certain uniformity, which we come at last to love for its own sake, independently of the objects to which it is applied, like those devotees who worship the statue, and forget the deity it represents.[12]

Somewhere along the way in the nineteenth century, Americans forgot that the states voluntarily joined a federation that would enable them greater protection for the pursuit of life, liberty, and happiness. The importance of the right for a state to secede was overtaken by a love for the Union that accepted centralization of federal power. The many interconnected relationships that had developed throughout the Union had caused people to rely on the Union in ways that its dissolution had become unthinkable, like a child refusing to consider the divorce of her parents. The deity of liberty was replaced by the statue of Union.

As the American experiment approached twenty years of age, Jefferson lamented that some protections had been omitted from the Constitution. He was alarmed that the Supreme Court was steadily working toward the consolidation of federal power, and he urged the states to stand up and resist this trend, which they never would have originally approved. He bitterly lamented over whether the Revolution had been fought in vain:

> I regret that I am now to die in the belief that the useless sacrifice of themselves by the generation of 1776 to acquire self-government and happiness to their country, is to be thrown away by the unwise and unworthy passions of their sons, and that my only consolation is to be that I live not to weep over it.[13]

Showdown Over Slavery and Tariffs

On December 20, 1860, just a few weeks before Lincoln was to take office, South Carolina formally seceded from the Union it had officially joined in 1788. Four days later, it issued a document enumerating the reasons it had dissolved its relations, citing acts passed by Northern states which violated their obligations to other states.

> An increasing hostility on the part of the non-slaveholding States to the institution of slavery, has led to a disregard of their obligations, and the laws of the General Government have ceased to effect the objects of the Constitution. The States of Maine, New Hampshire, Vermont, Massachusetts, Connecticut, Rhode Island, New York, Pennsylvania, Illinois, Indiana, Michigan, Wisconsin, and Iowa, have enacted laws which either nullify the Acts of Congress or render useless any attempt to execute them. In many of these States, the fugitive is discharged from service or labor claimed, and in none of them has the State Government complied with the stipulation made in the Constitution.[14]

Slavery was an intractable problem that grew more intense with the abolition movement gaining strength in the North. Northern states passed laws protecting fugitive slaves from return to their Southern owners. This was South Carolina's primary stated reason for seceding after Lincoln's election. Lincoln had told Southerners,

> The only difference between you and me is that I think slavery wrong, and you think it right; that I am opposed to its extension while you advocate it.[15]

Lincoln had inherited the presidency of a country tearing itself apart. His election only confirmed Southern fears that a resolution of differences was impossible. His supporters were Free Soilers, high tariff people, anti-slavery people, and radical abolitionists. He had made it clear that he would not tolerate secession and was prepared to use troops if necessary. He selected a predominantly Northern cabinet, with only members from two Southern border states, Missouri and Maryland, and filled the administration with Republicans, ousting Democrats. His carefully crafted inauguration address did not fully satisfy either side.[16] While slavery precipitated the secession, the reason that the North invaded the South was to keep the country together, not to free the slaves. The North did not recognize the secession, and Lincoln had taken the opposite position of the founders saying that it was unconstitutional for states to secede from the Union.[17] There were a number of developments after the founding which integrated the Union to an extent that made separation difficult. Makubin Thomas Owens at the Claremont Institute presents the argument that the Union had morphed into a new entity for which secession was out of the question:

> So complete was this transformation that even the opponents of the Constitution, the so-called Anti-Federalists, embraced the new meaning. Thus, they, as much as the Federalists recognized that the Union was far more than a league. It was a nation that could not be torn asunder at the pleasure of its component parts.[18]

This argument is comparable to those who argue that once a family is created, divorce is not allowable, or that some businesses are so important to a nation they are "too big to fail."[19] However, such arguments are hotly debated, and many believe that if a corporation is considered too big to fail, then it is too large to exist.[20] The South was defending the states' right to decide whether they would remain members of the Union, while Lincoln claimed that secession had to be prevented at all costs. The Constitution did not define any guidelines for secession, but it is clear that, at the founding, the states believed they had the right to withdraw.

From the viewpoints of freedom, voluntarism, and the principle of subsidiarity, the right of the state to secede should be upheld. The United States, in joining the United Nations, for example, reserves the same right to withdraw from the larger government body. It does not accept that being a member of the United Nations for 50 years nullifies the right to withdraw. However, this same government, as a union of member states, refused to let one of its members withdraw. It is quite predictable that if the United Nations had the power to prevent the United States from leaving and to tax it as it saw fit, it would use its power to do just that. This does not make it right, but unrestrained human nature can be expected to behave this way. With sufficient power, the United Nations might attempt to impose its will on the United States the same way the Union imposed its will on the South by force. The official U.S. positions of demanding independence from the United Nations but demanding obedience from its member states creates a glaring irrational double standard based on power.

The real reasons for the Union invasion of the South were pragmatic. Lincoln was unwilling to let down his high tariff supporters in the North. In the theoretical case of the United Nations, one can imagine the panic that administrators would feel if the United States were to withdraw all financial contributions. In such cases, when it is possible, political force generally trumps legal convention. The potential economic loss to the North if the South were to withdraw from the Union was enormous, as was the South's potential economic loss if they remained.

Tariff problems started after the War of 1812 when the British decided to carry on their battle by shutting down U.S.

manufacturing with a flood of low-priced materials. The federal government retaliated by imposing a 20-30 percent tariff on imported goods to protect U. S. industries. Ironically, a nationalist from South Carolina, John C. Calhoun, supported the tariffs while Daniel Webster in the North opposed them. The tariffs ended up being good for the North and for Union coffers, but disastrous for the South. The tariff of 1816 was raised in 1824, and then in 1828 the "Tariff of Abominations," as it was called by Calhoun, enacted a 62 percent tax on 92 percent of all imported goods.

The South suffered while the North became addicted to high tariffs. It became more difficult for the South to export cotton to mills in England and France and receive cloth made overseas. Increasingly, the Northern textile mills became the only viable market for Southern cotton. The South was not industrialized, and its economy relied on trading agricultural products for goods made elsewhere. Northern industries, on the other hand, prospered from the lack of overseas competition and were able to charge more for lower quality products.

From the viewpoints of freedom, voluntarism, and the principle of subsidiarity, the right of the state to secede should be upheld. The United States, in joining the United Nations, for example, reserves the same right to withdraw.

Calhoun, then Vice President, argued that the Tariff of Abominations was unconstitutional because it brought harm to some of the members of the Union. A precedent for this idea of nullification of federal law had been established by Jefferson in the Kentucky Resolution:

> Where powers are assumed which have not been delegated, a nullification of the act is the rightful remedy.[21]

And James Madison in the Virginia Resolution:

> In cases of a deliberate, palpable, and dangerous exercise of
> other powers, not granted by the said compact, the States,
> who are parties thereto, have the right, and are duty bound
> to interpose to arrest the evil.[22]

Secession was threatened. When Andrew Jackson failed to reduce tariffs as much as expected in 1832, South Carolina adopted an Ordinance of Nullification, declaring the tariffs unconstitutional. Congress passed a "Force Bill" that authorized Jackson to use military force against South Carolina. However, before violence erupted, Henry Clay and John Calhoun worked out a compromise that averted violence. The Nullifcation and Force Bills were rescinded, and the use of Union force was postponed, while the underlying problems of tariffs and slavery continued to fester.

Lincoln's invasion of the South was thus not the first indication that the federal government would be willing to use force against a state that desired to secede. The idea had been floating around for at least three decades. Lincoln had studied the Nullification and Force Bills and came down on the side of force.

When the South seceded, most American citizens in both the North and South believed it had every right to do so. Lame duck President Buchanan despaired but thought there was nothing he could do but withdraw federal forces from the seceding states. It was a cherished right based on the Declaration of Independence. After Lincoln's election, historian Howard Perkins compiled 495 editorials from Northern newspapers to prove that Northerners believed secession was a right.[23]

Those in positions of federal power had historically argued their resistance to secession based on their immediate interest to see a strong federal government, neither on constitutional principle nor the will of the people. It had been to the advantage of the Federalist party to consider secession in 1800 and 1812, when opposition party members Jefferson and Madison were presidents. Now the tables were turned, the federalists had power, and a Southern declaration of free trade threatened the economic empires and port cities of the North. It was in their political and economic interest to use force to invade the South.

The Triumph of Force

Since the founding, Alexander Hamilton and the federalists had pushed for a more centralized national government. Clay and Lincoln, supported by bankers and industrialists, continued efforts to create a federal government based on a mercantilist economy like that in England. They rejected the free market arguments of Adam Smith. They relied on federal protections from free international trade and government subsidies for large industries like railroads. They were large special interests engaged in "rent-seeking." They were not interested in government acting as a referee, but felt government played a central role in running the economy.

In 1816, when the Bank of the United States was rechartered, Henry Clay had added $1.5 million in construction subsidies for canals and roads. Then, on his last day in office, James Madison vetoed the bill saying that such infrastructure improvements were not authorized by the Constitution.[24] The political retaliation Madison feared, causing him to wait until his last day of office, was similar to that feared by Dwight D. Eisenhower 140 years later, when he waited until his last day in office to warn of the dangers of the "military-industrial complex:"

> In the councils of government, we must guard against the acquisition of unwarranted influence, whether sought or unsought, by the *military-industrial complex*. The potential for the disastrous rise of misplaced power exists and will persist.[25]

The industrial interests of the North showed little sympathy for the plight of their brothers in the South when taxes were debated in Congress. The North exploited the situation, which had developed over a period of decades. By 1860, when Republicans passed the Morrill Tariff Act, the South was paying well over half of the federal taxes, yet they had less than half the population of the North. The North was receiving over half of federal spending and was subsidized by the South. The industrialists were opposed to free trade for economic reasons. They sought to control the federal government to that end. While the Republican Party had been formally organized by abolitionists, the industrialists became the financial backers of the party as they had a common opposition to the Democratic Party that prevailed in the South.

Because the tariffs were harmful to the South, the Confederate Constitution outlawed special tariffs and nonuniform taxes:

> [N]o bounties shall be granted from the Treasury; nor shall any duties or taxes on importations from foreign nations be laid to promote or foster any branch of industry; and all duties, imposts, and excises shall be uniform throughout the Confederate States.[26]

The official statement of secession caused the industrial interests to panic like a trapped animal. They were willing to use any force necessary to stop the free trade that secession would bring to the South. Free trade ports would possibly mean that much international trade would move from the ports of New York, Boston, and Baltimore to Southern harbors in Charleston, Savannah, and New Orleans. The South would benefit from global free trade, while the North would be less competitive and more isolated. Furthermore, once goods were shipped to the South, preventing them from entering the North through porous borders with the South would be difficult.

The North proposed to suspend the Constitution, blockade Southern ports, and finally invade the South to prevent such a scenario from unfolding. For all intents and purposes, the secession of the South from the Union caused the Union to abandon the Constitution. When Southerners left the Congress, the Republican majority that remained passed legislation that supported the goals of the Northern industrial lobbies. Tariffs were further increased, and new taxes on Northern citizens were imposed as a military-industrial complex took control. In the words of economist Thomas J. DiLorenzo,

Great sacrifices (including the ultimate sacrifice) were being made by Northerners who were being taxed to finance the war and conscripted into the army; but most of the Northern manufacturers, who were the financial lifeblood of the Republican Party, were not only exempted from sacrifices but also thrived.[27]

The North, by invading the South, brought an end to the Jeffersonian experiment and established a new system of government in which money and power, not popular ideals or votes, would shape the future of the United States. At the center of this transformation was Abraham Lincoln, a former lawyer for the Illinois Railroad and a longtime champion of a more centralized government that he called "the American system."

As the schism widened and the war began, Lincoln rubberstamped all Republican-initiated legislation. He was a hero to his Union constituents, but a traitor to the idea that "Governments are instituted among men—deriving their just powers from the consent of the governed." That idea had indelibly impressed Alexis de Tocqueville on his visit to America, and was the hope of other foreign observers like Lord Acton, famous for his statement that "absolute power corrupts absolutely," who wrote to Robert E. Lee:

> **The North, by invading the South, brought an end to the Jeffersonian experiment and established a new system of government in which money and power, not popular ideals or votes, would shape the future of the United States.**

> I saw in the States' rights the only availing check upon the absolutism of the sovereign will, and secession filled me with hope, not as the destruction but redemption of Democracy.... I deemed that you were fighting the battles of our liberty, our progress, and our civilization.[28]

At Peoria in 1854, Lincoln had said "the leading principle, the sheet anchor of American Republicanism," was the belief that "no man is good enough to govern another man, without that other's consent." He equated the idea of the Divine Right of Kings with the proslavery theology. In both cases, he noted, the "master... governs by a set of rules altogether different from those which he prescribes for himself."[29]

Why, then, did Lincoln betray the principle of consent of the governed and claim extraordinary war powers? Why did he suspend Habeas Corpus, suppress free elections, suppress the press, impose taxes without consent, deprive trial by jury, and deport Ohio Congressman Clement Vallandigham for complaining about his abandonment of the Constitution? Why did he respond to secession with an invasion? Clearly, he was stuck between the rock of democracy and the hard place of political realism. When push came to shove, whether he wanted to or not, Lincoln ultimately was committed to his financial backers. Lincoln was able to eloquently articulate reasons for every step he took, making them sound rational and patriotic.

The consolidation of federal power seized by force during the Civil War was never fully relinquished after the exigencies had passed. The Union enacted legislation to keep much of its power through a set of Civil War Amendments that greatly altered the United States Constitution. Issued in the name of guaranteeing the rights of freed slaves, the Fourteenth Amendment opened the door for the U.S. government to intervene in the affairs of individual states, interact directly with individual citizens, and to use its power to enforce national social and economic policies. The Fourteenth Amendment became a lens through which the Supreme Court began to reinterpret the entire Constitution and Bill of Rights.

The Civil War struck fear in the hearts of those who would ever again entertain thoughts of secession. The original league of states had, at its essence, been converted to an empire of force. In the words of economist Walter E. Williams,

The War between the States settled by force whether states could secede. Once it was established that states cannot secede, the federal government, abetted by a Supreme Court unwilling to hold it to its constitutional restraints, was able to run amok over states' rights, so much so that the protections of the Ninth and Tenth Amendments mean little or nothing today. Not only did the war lay the foundation for eventual nullification or weakening of basic constitutional protections against central government abuses, but it also laid to rest the great principle enunciated in the Declaration of Independence that "Governments are instituted among men, deriving their just powers from the consent of the governed.[30]

The victors of war write history in a way that will induce the citizens to be loyal to the government. There is no political, religious, or economic power that does not attempt to control knowledge and influence adherence through selective "education." The rewriting of American history after the Civil War was no different. Lincoln became as important a president of the United States as George Washington. The common view that the war was begun to free the slaves is not correct, even though the freeing of slaves was a significant byproduct of the war. Nevertheless, the cause of freeing the slaves was a popular cause that provided moral reasons for Northern soldiers to go and fight the war against the South.

The aftermath of the Civil War was accompanied by the constitutional amendments that gave the federal government centralized power, not only to protect former slaves, but also to coerce all citizens by force if necessary. The Fourteenth Amendment has been used by the courts over the ensuing 150 years to impose the will of the federal government over the states on numerous matters unrelated to slavery, from freeing corporations from state regulation to imposing official national morality on issues like abortion. The former represented collusion between government and the economy, and the latter represented collusion between the government and the cultural sphere.

The lid on the coffin of right to secede was nailed down in 1869 by the Supreme Court in a 5-3 decision in the case of *Texas v. White*. The opinion was written by Chief Justice Salmon Chase, who had served as Secretary of the Treasury under Abraham Lincoln and was a leading figure in the centralization of the Union government. Many Southerners understandably questioned Chase's impartiality with such a historical conflict of interest and believed he should have recused himself from the decision. The decision officially stood the American experiment on its head. But he was a champion for a new "American system" in which national banks and industry would lead the country to a new and prosperous way of life.

> **Through the war, citizens of the United States were able to become used as a means to government ends—ends not controlled by citizens in pursuit of their happiness, but by the strongest lobbies in Washington.**

In his book, *Emancipating Slaves, Enslaving Free Men*, Jeffrey Hummel argues that fighting the war to save the Union was morally bankrupt. The means meant to justify the end became the end itself. A federal government that only interfered a little in the affairs of individual states "had been transformed into an overbearing bureaucracy that intruded into daily life with taxes, drafts, surveillance, subsidies, and regulations."[31] Through the war, citizens of the United States were able to be used as a means to government ends—ends not controlled by citizens in pursuit of their happiness, but by the strongest lobbies in Washington.

This overbearing bureaucracy (symbolized by inverted pyramid Figures 6 and 7 in Chapter 3) did not appear overnight but gradually grew while states and individual citizens carried out normal affairs largely unaware of what had happened. So long as the government appeared to aid the cause of the individual pursuit of happiness or only burden individuals slightly, the fact that membership was no longer voluntary was of little concern to most Americans. By the twenty-first century, this has changed. The unilateral invasion of Iraq as a "preemptive war" violating 400 years of just war tradition, and the near overnight TARP allocation of $700 billion in tax dollars to irresponsible financial institutions was so blatant that both presidential candidates for 2008 ran on platforms to fix a broken Washington. Other political leaders like Ron Paul and Jesse Ventura began to speak of political revolution.

The ultimate check on federal power, the rights of states to secede, has never been used and would invite another federal attack on American citizens if it were tried today. Just as divorce is a last chance to end a marriage and the abuse associated with it, secession is the last check and balance on the power of government in a free society, or any genuine league of peace. The proclamation that "governments are instituted among men" is nullified if those who join the federation do not have a right to leave it.

The Right to Secede

The case has been made that right to secede ought to be a pillar in the institution of any government designed for Life, Liberty, and Happiness, V. 4.0. However, secession of a state from the Union, like the United States secession from England, is not something that should be taken lightly. As in all other levels of society, from a marriage to a community and to the state, once some form of union takes place, a new and more complex entity is established.

When marriage has been entered into voluntarily by both parties, a household established, and children born, the products of that marriage must be treated responsibly. The children's future must enter into the decision to divorce, and if they become dependent on state assistance, their future is generally not as bright, and the state will have more difficulty balancing its own budget. Attempts are often made to reconcile marriages. Counseling and family therapy is often tried, and pressure from the extended family and local community is often applied. Divorce has social consequences, and the cost must be borne by more than the two marriage partners.

However, if a husband beats his wife and sends her to the hospital, or a wife repeatedly cheats on her husband, the costs of the marriage can outweigh the benefits to the marriage partners as well as to the children and the surrounding society. There comes a point where all observers consider a divorce better than the existing situation. In these cases, absolute rules like "no divorce" are not appropriate. Rather, divorce has to be considered as a regrettable last choice when all other options have been exhausted. The application of absolute force, killing one party, or beating them into submission, is not considered legitimate in a world that promotes the equality of all human beings. Allowing such beatings is not government protection of citizens' rights. And, it is worse if one government beats another into submission, killing thousands or millions of innocent people in the process.

The issues that arise in a federation of states, as in the case of the United States, once it was created, are similar. There are many byproducts of that Union that make separation both difficult and harmful to citizens. For example, if states enter into a Union for common defense, secession might require the cost of patrolling more borders, and it would be an added cost both to the seceding state and to those states it borders. Common projects like federal highway systems that help make goods more widely available at a low price suffer from secession and citizens may experience a lower quality of life. Then there are social consequences for industries and families that own property and have family members in all parts of the Union. They may fear economic loss or cultural attacks if there is secession. All these interrelationships that are byproducts of a Union make secession costly.

South Carolina made a reasonable case before the Civil War that the situation had become intolerable and that if something did not change, its economy would be destroyed. Similarly, the Northern industries that had become dependent upon the South and might quickly collapse if the South adopted free trade were panicked. The South had slaves and they were not treated as full human beings, but Northern financial policies encouraged rather than discouraged this practice. Further, the taxation practices of the Union treated the South unjustly. As in the case of marriage, one can find fault on both sides.

Were problems attended to adequately? Did both sides try to work out their differences? It seems there was significant intransigence and self-interest on both sides that made reconciliation difficult. The Constitution of the United States did not create guidelines about the process of secession or anticipate it. However, in retrospect, at some point secession should be a last option preferable to a war that beats one party into submission by the other, and kills 630,000 citizens. The Civil War was like a husband beating a wife into submission. The end product was a Union of force, not a voluntary Union.

The Civil War is now 150 years in the past. Conditions have changed so much that Republicans promote free trade instead of tariffs. Democrats have changed from representing self-sufficient agrarian populists to those who receive government payments. At the time of the Civil War, the North was Republican and the South Democrat. Today, the North is predominately Democrat and the South primarily Republican. Slavery and tariffs are both gone, and other issues divide the country along different lines. The Civil War was not a civilized or desirable response to the problems that existed in the United States. The final reflection on the War cannot rest with championing one side or the other. Nor can we rest content with the Supreme Court decision of 1869 that unilaterally forbids secession from the union whose victory was won by military conquest.

> **The Constitution of the United States did not create guidelines about the process of secession or anticipate it. However, in retrospect, at some point secession should be a last option preferable to a war that beats one party into submission by the other.**

A method for secession as a last resort ought to be a pillar in the institution of any government designed for "Life, Liberty, and Happiness, V. 4.0." Such methods can include things like higher standards of membership in the first place; e.g. a state that violates the rights of its citizens by owning slaves should not be allowed to join a true republic. A good case can be made that not all states were ready to join the Union, just like not all young adults are adequately prepared to enter marriage.

A process somewhat analogous to annulment of marriage could be developed for political unions of states and other governments. Standards of fair taxation or redress of grievances should be considered by the Supreme Court, which seems to have neglected such a responsibility. A Supreme Court that promoted the five principles of protection, subsidiarity, and separation of political, economic, and cultural spheres, transparency, and the right to secede would help produce a much happier, more fair, and more prosperous society than "judicial activism" that imposes popular culture and social fads. If that fails, some type of third-party intervention could be developed as a last-ditch attempt to save a political union.

A referendum of citizens of over 85 percent of the population of an aggrieved side might also be required before final secession as a form of check on whether the political negotiators had truly represented their constituents. A move to secede by such a large percentage would be a very good indication that citizens were feeling harmed or oppressed by the Union. This is one method to gracefully end some type of Leviathan that has transmuted into a parasite that fails to really serve its original reason for existence. In the end, secession is the method of last resort and a final check on abuse of federal power to preserve freedom and voluntary union.

Secession is a far more civilized solution to oppression than the more powerful party beating the less powerful into submission. That has been the method of tyrants, dictators, and totalitarian regimes throughout history. That method ended true republicanism in the United States, and restoration of a genuine republic would require legalizing secession as a method of last resort. Only after such legislation or constitutional reform can the United States legitimately claim to be a new light unto the world that is a model for the world's future.

Questions for Review and Reflection

1. Do you think a state should have the right to secede from a Union?

2. In U.S. history there were several threats to secede. Who instigated them and why?

3. Do you think South Carolina was correct in saying that the Northern States had already seceded from the Union?

4. Do you think Abraham Lincoln had any options left by the time he took office, or were they all exhausted in earlier decades?

5. Given that the Civil War is behind us, do you think the U.S. could adopt a right to secede, or would it take a military coup to do so? Why?

6. Why do you think the U.S. Supreme Court did not intervene when the North invaded the South, even though popular opinion held that the South had the right to secede?

7. Do you think that Lord Acton was correct to say that allowing secession would have been proof the United States was a democracy?

8. Do you think that the Civil War was the occasion that turned the United States into an Empire?

9. If you were writing a new amendment to the Constitution that allowed the secession of a state, what conditions would you say had to be met (a) by the state, and (b) by the Union?

10. Do you believe that there is any other way for states to non-violently check the power of federal growth other than the right to secession?

Part II: Implementation

The chapters in Part II discuss specific reforms that can be designed with respect to the basic principles of a government that promotes life, liberty, and the pursuit of happiness. This includes improving the function of Congress, reforming tax policies, and addressing social welfare. These do not exhaust the list of reforms needed, but in addition to discussing specific improvements, the discussion of these key issues shows how the basic principles might be applied in other areas.

7

Structure of Congress

A good government implies two things: first, fidelity to the object of government, which is the happiness of the people; secondly, a knowledge of the means by which that object can be best attained. Some governments are deficient in both these qualities. Most governments are deficient in the first. I scruple not to assert that in the American governments, too little attention has been paid to the last.[1]

—James Madison

Congress is the body that makes the laws. Its role is crucial for creating a government where the basic principles of good government are implemented. It is where the updates and upgrades to the Constitution should get approved. If the founding fathers created the government we call Life, Liberty, and the Pursuit of Happiness, Version 3.0, then subsequent legislation should create update Versions 3.1, 3.2, and other versions up to the upgrade Version 4.0. Legislators are the software programmers of government.

However, it is not clear that the work of Congress has created any real updates. Sometimes it seems the laws are reverting to earlier forms that move away from the basic principles of equal protection, subsidiarity, separation of powers, transparency, and freedom. If we are going to employ "programmers" to improve our governments' protection from legal viruses, they have to become an integral part of the society. They need to use the latest information to solve problems, not use their power for self gain or special interests.

The way Congress is structured is not a proven or universally accepted form of governance. It has always been somewhat experimental, and the U.S. founders had a harder time agreeing on it than any other issue they faced at the Constitutional Convention. It nearly caused the Convention's collapse. What is the basic role of Congress? What interests does it represent? How should it be structured to represent these interests? There were basic disagreements then, as there are today. Congress has not functioned as the founders intended, and its current low popular rating indicates the citizens are not satisfied with it either.

The basic principles of good governance must be learned by society as a whole, so that they can become the will of the people. Just like with good hygiene practices, it is for their own benefit and the future of society.

This chapter examines the history of the structure of Congress and offers some suggestions for improvement. It does not offer a structure that can guarantee perfect results. It would be foolish to attempt such a project, for, regardless of structure, a government can only be as good as the people in it. However, things can be done that improve checks and balances, subsidiarity, transparency, and accountability. This can help minimize corruption, consolidation of power, and abuse of power. Ultimately, the basic principles of good governance must be learned by society as a whole so that these principles can become the will of the people. Like good hygiene practices, this is for their own benefit and the future of society.

Experience Before the Constitutional Convention

Following the Declaration of Independence, the Articles of Confederation were created in relative haste, relative simplicity, and with little experience. The legislature was not modeled on

England's bicameral model of House of Lords and House of Commons because the House of Lords derived its power from the Crown, not the people. It was argued that there was no need for a House of Lords because there was no need for hereditary nobility. Democracy was to avoid the clashes of class interest and represent one common interest. People brought up the example that Pennsylvania, as a colony, seemed to be operating well with a unicameral legislature.

The Articles of Confederation were not very satisfactory. Many political groups felt alienated, executive power was too limited to be effective, and when states met the meetings were chaos. Benjamin Rush said that a happy government had been replaced by a mob. William Hooper called it a beast without a head. Another writer compared it to the reign of the barbarians over Rome.[2] The frenzy produced by mob interests had to be checked in some way to limit the popular will through sound and proven principles of governance.

The states had experimented with various bicameral arrangements that proved useful before the Constitutional Convention. Virginia wrestled with the issue of the origination of spending bills. In England, the House of Commons controlled the people's money, and the House of Lords was not allowed to tamper with it. But in many states, the representatives in both houses were elected by the same people, and represented the same interests. In Massachusetts, the Senate was supposed to represent the property of the state; but when English rule was overthrown, the people owned the state. The Senate usurped the power to originate money bills not granted by their Constitution. The senators, being elected by the people, were unable to protect the property of the state. Experience was proving Jefferson right; no governmental body could represent more than the will of its electors. Ezra Stiles said in 1783, "the upper house is only a repetition of the lower."[3]

Benjamin Rush called for some type of "double representation" in which the people would elect two houses that could check each other and yet both be elected by the people. Throughout the 1780s, and in the view of James Madison, the Maryland Senate seemed to be doing the best. Senators were elected for five-year terms by an indirect method of an electoral college, and reasonably competent statesmen seemed to be getting in office. But Maryland's Senate was also under attack as being elitist. There was a fear that an insufficient number of well-qualified people would continue to get appointed. Then an issue arose where that Senate vetoed bills on creating paper money, and the House said a referendum of the people should decide the issue. The Senate replied that would undermine the reason for their existence as a check on the power of the people, and return the state to mob rule. This issue was never settled before the Philadelphia Convention convened.

The Philadelphia Convention

At the Constitutional Convention in Philadelphia, the first and foremost order of business was how the federal legislature should be organized. In a government of the people, the legislature most directly represents the interests of the people. Blackstone had said the power of legislation and sovereignty are "convertible terms."[4] The delegates examined historical arrangements in Western civilization and various state arrangements. Bicameralism was assumed necessary to check and balance power, but how this would be established was not clear. The founders debated the pros and cons of the Roman system.

The Roman Republic, around 450 B.C., had created a system of legislation designed to prevent discrimination based on class interest. The Senators, known as Patricians, represented the noble landed class, and the Tribunes represented commoners known as Plebeians. Before this time, the Patricians who were the major landholders ruled through the Senate. However, they often failed to share with Plebeians the fruits of war or other endeavors to which Plebeians often greatly contributed. There was no Plebian check on the legislation of the Patricians. The Plebeian class felt this was unjust and eventually went on a general strike, like a national labor strike, until an acceptably just system of government could be created. This led to a commission of ten Patricians, known as the *decemviri*, to develop a code of laws. Eventually, Twelve Tables of Law were agreed upon. Tribunes would serve as Plebeian representatives to the Roman Senate. Tribunes, who were 2-10 in number, had the right to listen to Senate deliberations and veto legislation destructive to their class interest. This would prevent the exploitation of the common people by the more wealthy decision-makers. The Tribunes would be a check on the self-interest of the Patricians, while the aristocracy with its better education and investment in the country would remain the decision-makers.

The power of the Tribunes increased over the Republican period of Ancient Rome because of the large number of people with growing wealth that they represented. This was a period of time when greater justice was recognized in the Roman Republic than anywhere else in the known world. People in neighboring states lined up to help Rome overthrow their dictators so they, too, could experience Roman Law. However, by the third century B.C., power and wealth increasingly corrupted the Republic, and it waged wars for booty and engaged in more corrupt and immoral behavior. Eventually, the Roman Republic fell to a takeover plot by Julius Caesar, Pompey, and Crassus, who turned the Republic into an Empire in which the power of the Senate, particularly the Tribunes, was reduced to little more than a title.

The American founders also studied the merits of a British system that they knew well. England had evolved two houses of government, the House of Lords representing the Nobility and the House of Commons consisting of shire and borough representatives. As in the case of the Roman Senate, the House of Lords represented the land-owning aristocracy, who had a long-term interest in the stability of the country. The House of Commons developed from the rise of the commercial class that had greatly expanded as a result of Britain's global empire. The House of Commons was responsible for the money bills. Neither the Roman nor British system easily transferred to the American situation where there was no official landed aristocracy. Ben Franklin and

Charles Pinckney floated the idea of dividing the houses by class of wealth or property, but that idea did not take root.

On May 29, 1787, it was agreed that there would be an executive branch, a judicial branch, and a bicameral legislature. James Madison explained in *Federalist No. 10* the reason for bicameralism:

> Before taking effect, legislation would have to be ratified by two independent power sources: the people's representatives in the House and the state legislatures' agents in the Senate.[5]

But how could a bicameral legislature be composed? Who should elect members to which house? Which constituencies would representatives represent: states, the general population, or some other group? How should representatives be apportioned, in fixed numbers or proportional representation? How would they be elected, by popular vote, by electoral colleges, or by state legislatures? The discussions involved the merits of various arrangements in Greece, Rome, Britain, and the writings of Montesquieu, Hume, and Blackstone.

Alexander Hamilton supported Hume's idea that corruption had been necessary to maintain the balance of the British constitution. McDonald argues that the positions were not derived altruistically or theoretically, but that the political theorists were being cited to support the pragmatic interests of those making the arguments at the Convention.[6] Without a solution to the matter by July 2, the Convention ground to a halt. There were five states for and five states against equal representation. Hamilton had gone home to New York in frustration, and a couple of other delegates were absent for various reasons.

On July 6, Franklin proposed a compromise that states should be equally divided in the Senate and proportional in the House, but all bills for spending money had to originate in the House. After ten days of wrangling, the Convention was still divided with Virginia, South Carolina, Georgia, and Pennsylvania opposed. While it is speculated that some undue pressure may have been put on the North Carolina delegation to get their assent, Washington declared the Franklin plan passed on July 16,[7] though it was by no means a widely agreed-upon solution.

With the number of representatives decided, a debate ensued on whether there should be property holding requirements for members of the legislature, as they would have more at stake in their decisions and cast more responsible votes. This proposal did not succeed. However, the idea that different groups decide representatives in each house to provide a check and balance was agreed upon. The final result was that state legislators would appoint Senators, while the people would elect Representatives.

The Hybrid Result

The final result created a hybrid government. The Senate was a body of state representatives, while the House was a body of citizen representatives. It was not clear whether the federal government was primarily a union of states or a government of the people. To the extent it was a government of the people, the state and the federal governments became redundant bodies. However, it could not really function as a Union of states when the body that initiated spending wasn't chosen by the states. A case can be made that in a system of subsidiarity, the federal government should have remained a Union of states to which the states elect representatives and pay dues. This would be more like the United Nations, where members are governments of states, not citizens of other states.

> **It was not clear whether the federal government was primarily a union of states or a government of the people. To the extent it was a government of the people, the state and the federal governments became redundant bodies.**

The hybrid system could be compared to a military unit in which soldiers can relate directly to both lieutenants and the colonels over them, going around their superior in the chain of command or, in an industrial setting, going around the foreman and taking orders directly from the president. In such situations where the chain of command is not clear, there is confusion, misdirection, and waste. While a military unit is a chain of command that basically relays information from the top to the bottom, there is no reason to suppose that social organization should not organize according to levels forming a chain, only with information flowing from the bottom up, with each representative carrying out the will of his constituents.

From its inception, the federal government was a hybrid in which the same popular electorate would send their representatives to both the state and federal governments. This means that both levels of government will be getting requests from citizens for such things as health and human services or support for local schools. This confuses the functions of state and federal government and prompts the federal government to undertake things that states should do. From the simple size of territory, it would be more logical for the federal government to address defense of the common territory, the postal service, air traffic control, the electrical power grid, and other issues that cannot be easily confined to one state.

New Jersey's original proposal at the Philadelphia Convention and the system designed in the Articles of Confederation was a truer form of a league of states than which we now have. In that arrangement, representatives would be sent directly by states to represent them in the federal government, by whatever form the state chose to elect them. Human services and education would be kept with lower governments, where people have better access to their representatives and a greater opportunity to shape their own destiny. Further, the competition among states in these issues would cause people to "vote with their feet" and move to the states that allowed them to pursue happiness in the most satisfying way. Having federal policies on human services forms a monopoly that, by virtue of the fact that it is a monopoly, will become oppressive and inefficient.

The failure of the Articles of Confederation did not lie in the plan that states send representatives to Congress, but in the structure of the Congress they were sent to—one with no checks and balances that degenerated into an uncontrolled free-for-all. The Philadelphia Convention was not just creating a Union of states; it was the battleground between federalists who wanted to eliminate the states and create one superstate, and those advocates for sovereignty of each of the former colonies. The result was a system of checks by which no legislation would be passed unless it represented the interests of both the states and the people. In other words, it was envisioned as passing very little legislation, and what was passed would need the support of both the people and the states. If diverse interests had to agree, special interests would get thwarted, and only legislation that was overwhelmingly needed for the public good and desired by the entire society would get passed. Echoing Montesquieu, Madison summed up this concept in *Federalist No. 51:*

> In republican government, the legislative authority, necessarily predominates. The remedy for this inconveniency is to divide the legislature into different branches; and to render them by different modes of election, and different principles of action, as little connected with each other, as the nature of their common functions and their common dependencies on the society, will admit.[8]

The Senate would look after states' rights and society's long-term interests, and the House would represent the will of the people. This hybrid was a way to address both concerns, but the confusion of powers generated opportunities for consolidation of federal power at the expense of the individual states, and eventually ways around the majority were found in special interest across the aisle legislation that proliferates at the expense of both individual citizens and states.

The Bill of Rights

Virginia, one of the states that had voted against the arrangement decided for Congress, was not convinced that the checks on power between two houses were adequate. Jefferson and Madison did not want Virginia to ratify the Constitution without further guarantees that placed limits on the power of the government. As Jefferson said, "The Bill of Rights should be rights people have against every government on earth," and that includes one's own elected government. They wanted clear limits that restricted government from transgressing the citizen's right to life, liberty, and happiness. It would be the role of the Supreme Court to monitor and strike down any legislation that violated the Bill of Rights.

In practice, the Supreme Court seldom reverses transgressions of federal power over the Bill of Rights by either the legislative or executive branch. Rather, it massively expanded its own power beginning with *Marbury v. Madison* and has consistently and self-servingly promoted the increased role of the federal government. After the Civil War, it became the organ of the new Union that discarded many of the states' rights and Virginia's idea of limited federal government. It helped create a larger, more powerful, more active federal government that duplicates and competes with many activities of the states, perhaps in an effort to usurp their power and render them obsolete.

The Seventeenth Amendment

The method of representation in the Senate was changed by the Seventeenth Amendment in 1912. As early as 1826, the direct election of Senators had been proposed. Sometimes positions were vacant for over a year when state legislatures were deadlocked. Some felt a more dependable method of appointing Senators should be developed.

After the Civil War, centralization of national power led to the Senate positions becoming more important targets for special interest lobbies, and there were increased charges of corruption and bribery. Progressive Era reformers at the end of the nineteenth century believed the corruption and bribery in the state nominations to Senate could be weakened by the direct popular election of Senators and curbing corruption by bringing government closer to the people. Progressives did not understand the agency problem that would develop. It is very similar to the control an individual shareholder has over a CEO decision to take a stock option.

For several decades, some Southern Senators had blocked the direct election amendment out of fear that it would increase the influence of African-American voters.[9] In 1906, David Graham Phillips, working for publisher William Randolph Hearst, wrote scathing pieces on senator corruption and deals with corporate lobbyists in a series titled "The Treason of the Senate," which appeared in several monthly issues of *Cosmopolitan* magazine. By then, many Southern states had enacted "Jim Crow" laws to undermine that influence. The Phillips series, which Theodore Roosevelt called "muckraking," nevertheless helped open the way for the amendment's ratification in 1913.

Not all sitting senators were prepared to vote for reforms that would undercut their own appointments, but many individual states changed the way they appointed senators from appointment by state legislatures to appointment by popular referenda. By 1912, there were enough of these new popularly chosen senators to support the measure in the Sixty-Second Congress. This became the Seventeenth Amendment to the Constitution in 1913, with only Utah rejecting the plan.

George Mason University law professor Todd Zywicki's analysis shows that the corruption was nominal and infrequent. He says that the issue was not the procedural deadlock problem that some argue. That could have been easily solved by legislation that would have required only a plurality to elect a senator. Rather, he contends that the true backers of the Seventeenth Amendment were the special interests,[10] of which both progressives on the left and corporate lobbyists on the right were members. They had great difficulty influencing the system when state legislatures controlled the Senate. They would have to create lobbies at all the various state capitals to work on appointments. This was a far more difficult task than a system in which they could concentrate on Washington alone. Direct elections would require appeal directly to the electorate, which they had to do to get candidates elected to the house anyway.

The result was a system that failed to address the question of checks and balances of the two houses so important to Madison and other founders. It was similar to the problem that had developed in Massachusetts under the Articles of Confederation in which Ezra Stiles had called "the upper house a repetition of the lower house." At the bottom, both houses represented the popular interest and were redundant.

> **The Seventeenth Amendment eliminated the hybrid nature of the government by essentially freeing itself from the states and becoming a genuine parallel government that would decrease state sovereignty.**

The Seventeenth Amendment eliminated the hybrid nature of the government by essentially freeing itself from the states and becoming a genuine parallel government that would decrease state sovereignty. It created more opportunities for centralized influence by special interests. The increased concentration of power in Washington had virtually eliminated the role of states in providing any buffer in wresting the interests of society from the special interests. The further removal of the citizens from their decision-makers, and the reduced possibility of the personal influence of citizens on their government made it possible for lobbyists to have more personal, and thus more effective, influence on legislators. By bypassing state legislative appointments, citizens lost the main special interest group— the state—that could lobby on their behalf at the federal level. Instead, the strongest lobbies in Washington became those special corporate and ideological interests that were organized outside the state and represented minority interests seeking taxpayer funds and special treatment.

While the Senate still formally differs from the House in length of term and size of constituency, they do not provide a check and balance on interests that would reduce the passage of laws that are not in the interest of the general welfare. Bypassing states ignores the principle of subsidiarity. It is not only a removal of checks and balances on the two houses by one another, but a removal of checks on the federal government by states. Some have argued that the real citizens after the election are not the people, but corporations and NGOs.

Another problem with the present arrangement is that voters can bypass the state government and seek direct financial benefits from the federal government that could be more efficiently handled with greater responsibility at lower levels. "If you can't get it from the state, get it from the federal government. They have more money." The habit of pushing responsibility to the next higher level leads to something like to a Ponzi scheme where each level passes it up to a higher one. Eventually, the federal government can't pay for things like Social Security and Medicare without (1) raising taxes that reduce economic growth, (2) printing money, which reduces economic growth, or (3) borrowing from other countries, which couldn't long continue. Any of these solutions act like a credit bubble that, when it collapses, severely hurts everybody. In the end, without good checks and balances, the people become their own worst enemy. If the majority of people are taking responsibility for their own lives through personal pension plans or private insurance companies, then economic policy does not become so concentrated in one place, and such bubbles will not occur.

Republicans and Democrats against the Center

By the twenty-first century, both houses of Congress had become dominated by the agendas of special interests. Citizens still vote for candidates, but the slate is increasingly chosen for them by the Republican and Democratic Party apparatus who are heavily funded by special interests. The national party often tells the state party chairs who they want on the ballot in their state. Party chairmen move up the party ranks for finding ways to make this happen, often by orchestration of conventions so that grass roots nominations are eliminated. It is common for candidates for office to establish residency just the required length of time to qualify for office before moving to Washington.

Once a candidate gets elected, he or she works more for high paying supporters who finance campaigns than for individual citizens. Those interests tend to pay lawyers to create legislation for "their" representatives to introduce. These documents are often over hundreds of pages of technical legal language that representatives do not have time to read carefully, with important details often buried and overlooked. This high level rent-seeking behavior tends to be a sophisticated form of begging and theft from taxpaying citizens.

Most special interest bills do not pass on their own merit. For example, Cargill in Minnesota might have a hard time buying a Senator from Florida, or an auto-workers' union might have influence in Michigan, but not in Arizona. Thus strategies of combining special interest legislation into combined, or omnibus bills, is used. This is an effective way for special interests to cooperate "across the aisle" at the expense of "the forgotten man" (see Figure 9, Chapter 4). It is becoming rare to have what is called an "up or down" vote on a single item, even though that is the only type of vote that is truly and transparently accountable. The end result is that the present United States Congress, as structured, rewards the special interests on both the right and the left at the expense of the taxpayer.

Historically, when the president has been in a different political party than the majority party in Congress, budget deficits have been less.[11] This is because he can veto legislation the special interests of the majority party pass. However, the combination of interests into large bills has been refined to an art that includes the special interests of the president or a state governor.

Each year, the integrity of the government is reduced as strategies by special interests and political parties further erode checks and balances and find ways to consolidate special interests in large bills at the expense of the general well-being of society. It is Congress, above all other parts of government, where reforms must begin. Congress is the body entrusted with creating the updates and upgrades to government that will stop the spread of viruses and spam in the various forms of consolidation of power and special interest legislation. A sick society needs a doctor who is able to heal, not a doctor working for a man who wants your body parts for transplantation. Congress is currently carting off citizens' body parts to give to special interests.

Possible Solutions

From the standpoint of motivation and incentives, there are many levels of reform possible for the problems associated with the structure of Congress. They range from smaller measures that would improve the function of the present Congress to larger measures that would transform the structure of Congress. The following suggestions for improvement of the structure of Congress will not force Congress to create the best legislation, but it can reduce some of the incentives that allow the creation of socially harmful legislation.

Repeal the Seventeenth Amendment

From the discussions above, one obvious reform would be to repeal the Seventeenth Amendment. Ultimately, we have to consider the problems that were faced at the Philadelphia Convention and never fully resolved; the makeup of the Congress itself and who will elect which members. But more immediately, a check and balance that was lost by the passage of the Seventeenth Amendment could be restored.

Repealing the Seventeenth Amendment would be a way to return more checks and balances between the interests of the states and the interests of the general population. And, it would return more balance between the interests of individual states and the federal government. The Seventeenth Amendment was passed under the rationale that it would stop corruption, but it did the opposite. Failing its objective is an obvious reason for its repeal.

Campaign Finance Reform

Campaign finance laws and laws related to party funding can be reformed to ensure that the candidates have a better chance of representing the interests of a majority of citizens. This would include limits on contributions so that people of all income classes could afford to contribute on equal footing, perhaps a contribution limit of $100 per person. Donations by corporations, political action committees (PACs), and high-end fundraising dinners for wealthy supporters could be forbidden, as would any campaign support coming from the government itself.

Such reforms would encourage more grassroots candidates being selected through the bottom-up process envisioned by the founders, as it would eliminate the large flow of top-down money that parties spend on nationally selected candidates. Grassroots candidates are more likely to reflect majority interests than candidates in the present system. It is increasingly common for people to say, "I'm voting for the least harmful candidate." Perhaps finance reform would enable more people to say, "I'm voting for the best candidate." Eliminating government funding would also open the door to a level playing field for more third-party candidates because rules for government funding generally favor the major parties.

Congressional Pay

There is no check and balance on congressional pay. Congress was given the power to enact laws regarding their members' compensation.[12] Congress also has the power to raise taxes to pay for their own compensation, their staff, their offices, their mail, and other perks and benefits. This amounts to a blank check and is a direct conflict of interest. Conflicts of interest of this nature are a major vulnerability for any government.

At the Philadelphia Convention, several delegates suggested that the individual states should pay the salaries of their senators; others, including Madison, argued this would not provide enough independence from the states in looking after the common good of the entire nation. In this debate, the first view supports states' rights, and the second the common national good. But Madison still did not approve the idea that any political body should set its own pay. In his autobiography, he wrote in third person about himself:

> He highly disapproved of public bodies raising the wages of themselves, and declined receiving the additions made by the Legislature of Virginia to the wages of member whilst he was one. In this he was not singular.[13]

Madison's proposed pay amendment, which was eventually passed 200 years later as the Twenty-Seventh Amendment, contained the idea that sitting congressmen would vote for the pay of those in the following Congress. In this way, their pay would not be tied to the states, but hopefully not to themselves. The teeth have been taken out of this Amendment by the fact that many incumbents are reelected and thus only delay their own pay increase a short while.

By May 1992, when the Amendment was ratified, privileges from direct government campaign funding to indirect funding through franked mail had long been in place. Further, the Seventeenth Amendment had distanced the federal government further from the states than the founders intended. Perhaps more dangerous than their own pay raises is the ability of Congress to hire staff, build buildings, and equip offices for themselves with money they appropriate but use for their own political purposes. Even though a fear of excess state control existed at the time of the founding, the opposite has become true today. The federal government is no longer controlled by either the citizens or the states, but is becoming a semi-autonomous parasitic society.

Today, a reform measure that would restore balance to the system and encourage more responsibility to the people would be an amendment replacing the Twenty-Seventh Amendment with one that states the salaries, staff, and offices of representatives to the House would be paid by the states. After all, if the representative's role is to protect the interests of the states and people they represent, there is no more clear-cut way to implement that function than to be paid by the people for whom they work. The Senate, on the other hand, could have the type of independence from the states Madison had suggested was necessary for the good of the federal government, if they were paid by the federal government. However, it would not be prudent to have them set their own salaries and allocate their own expenses. Such salaries could be determined by the House of Representatives.

This is a perfect example of one way the two houses could be checks and balances on one another. If the Senate protected the national interest and the Representatives the state interests, this would be a way to remove some redundancy between the two houses, even if the Seventeenth Amendment was not repealed.

> To encourage more responsibility, the Twenty-Seventh Amendment could be replaced with one that states the salaries, staff, and offices of representatives to the House would be paid by the states. There is no clearer way to implement that function than to be paid by the people for whom they work.

Fines on Special Interest Legislation

Legislation on behalf of any special interest lobby can be outlawed and fined. Special interest lobbyists caught attempting to directly influence legislation could be fined for first offenses and imprisoned for repeated violations. Legislators who introduce legislation that gives any financial interest an unfair advantage over others on the economic playing field could be fined for a first offense and removed from office for repeated violations.

Legislation should be impartial and represent the will of the people and the states. The primary role of the federal government is for protection of the citizens, not their welfare, individual or corporate. The government has a role to play in the creation of a sound economy, but that role is best played by rules that protect the economic rights of citizens by creating a fair field of play. It does not help to micromanage the activities of individual players or become a player instead of a referee. It can set standards, limits, and referee economic activity, but it should recognize that commerce and government are separate organs of society that need to each perform their own role.

Eliminate Bills Combining Legislation

Perhaps a more potent way to discourage special interest legislation through horse-trading and combined across the aisle legislation would be to have up and down votes on single issues. Given the volume of legislation and the huge bureaucracy it supports, many might think this an unreal dream. However, the United States, the Ancient Roman Republic, and the demise of many countries has been initiated by the long-term accumulation of piecemeal legislation that undermined the original Constitution. In *Federalist No. 62*, Madison warned:

> It will be of little avail to the people that the laws are made by men of their own choice, if the laws be so voluminous that they cannot be read, or so incoherent that they cannot be understood; if they be repealed or revised before they are promulgated, or undergo such incessant changes that no man who knows what the law is today can guess what it will be tomorrow.[14]

In *The Other Path,* Hernando de Soto explains how 500 years of legislation in Lima, Peru, continuing since the time of the original Spanish conquest, created layers of law so thick that even the most powerful political leaders were hamstrung by laws. In that case, the informal or "black market" economy proved to be the only vibrant element in the society. Legislators were not willing to kill the black market because the entire society depended upon it.[15] The point made by him and increasingly made in the United States today, is that a lot of the legislation passed for specific purposes rather than sound basic principles could be undone without serious social harm, and likely with positive results.

It might be a good idea to have an up and down vote on each issue. In addition, the main purpose of the bill, like a well-written book or journal article, should be able to contain a one-page summary or abstract that anyone with a high school education could read and understand. The content of the bill should reflect the summary with no hidden clauses buried in the details. This is the type of legislation that would be transparent, and accountability could be assigned to those passing it.

One way to handle repeating budgets would be to set reasonable sunset clauses on items and to have up and down votes on all new items for which there is no precedent. Such strategies could allow bundled expenditures, but not bundles with surprises or pork thrown in.

The budgets of some departments, like the military, are complex and have developed over time. Some latitude would need to be given to the details of such budgets. The principle of subsidiarity is important in large institutions so that smaller budgets are contained within larger budgets rather than having large amounts of cash available in some centralized location. All public expenditures should have a method of clearly assigning responsibility and accountability and some form of check and balance, whether it is two signers on a check or public copies available for anyone to examine on request or on the internet.

Term Limits (Not the Best Option)

Many people argue that relationships with lobbyists develop over time and if Representatives and Senators have term limits, the relationships will not become so entrenched. While there may be some truth to this, term limits do not address the issue of incentives in the system itself, nor the possibility of special interests being so entrenched in the party nomination process that special interest replacements will be guaranteed before the election. However, term limits would guarantee a limit on the length of time of service of skilled and honest Representatives, whose talents are of benefit to the society. Term limits would thus "throw out the baby with the bathwater."

Former Legislators Lobbying

Term limits might remove a legislator from office, but not from the lobbying process. Many former legislators earn more money as lobbyists than they did as legislators.[16] This activity is comparable to "insider trading" on Wall Street, only it is legal on "K" street. These former legislators are not likely experts on the item being sold to seated legislators, nor its value to society. Rather, they are experts on the political process, on vote-buying, bill-packing, deal-making, and other strategies that should be eliminated by transparent legislation.

The Role of the Supreme Court

The problem of redundancy between federal and state legislation is largely a result of the federal government taking on economic and social tasks inappropriate for its level of governance. The primary role of the federal government is to protect the Union, not to perform the subsidiary social welfare and human services function of individual states and cities. However, to a large extent that has happened both through the desire of those in the federal government to consolidate power at the expense of the states, and the desire of states to push financial responsibilities onto the federal government.

This book repeatedly states why both of these tendencies make government worse and why the founders sought to limit the powers of the federal government and keep responsibility at the lowest possible level. That is a source of liberty. The enforcement of this arrangement was supposed to be accomplished by the Supreme Court. However, the Court largely failed to perform that mission and has allowed the expansion of federal power into areas not allowed by the Constitution. It has not struck down legislation unrelated to the primary purpose of physical protection of the Union and the rights of the states and the people.

On the contrary, the Supreme Court has historically made decisions to settle disputes, rather than limiting its role to a review of the proper operation of the machinery of government and the implementation of sound principles. It has frequently imposed its own values on the people like a tyranny instead of letting the people determine their own values and letting the most universal principles work their way to the top. It has created *de facto* legislation usurping the role of the legislature. And, it has reinterpreted the entire Constitution according to the "equal protection" clause of the Fourteenth Amendment. This "equal protection" has come to mean more than life, liberty, and property, but pretty much anything the Court decides it means.[17] Even though the Civil War did more than any other single event to consolidate federal power by force, Abraham Lincoln observed in his first inaugural address before the war:

> **The Supreme Court has historically made decisions to settle disputes, rather than limiting its role to a review of the proper operation of the machinery of government and the implementation of sound principles.**

> If the policy of the government upon vital questions affecting the whole people is to be irrevocably fixed by decisions of the Supreme Court...the people will have ceased to be their own rulers, having to that extent practically resigned their government into the hands of that eminent tribunal.[18]

Legal scholar Alexander Bickel, in *The Least Dangerous Branch*, argued that the judicial review process established by the Supreme Court in *Marbury v. Madison* had given the role of long-term guardian of values to the Supreme Court because the legislators are focused on immediate practical measures.[19] In theory, because the justices are appointed for life, they should counteract cultural fads and majoritarian views. A court which views its job as guardian of constitutional principles and the machinery of government should be able to do this; an activist court, on the other hand, can not. Activist courts have proven to have succumbed to majoritarian principles, being more part of the social mob than aloof from it.[20]

The founders had designed a government where the Senate was to assume the more activist role of guarding the long-term interest of the people while the House of Representatives was to reflect the immediate and practical will of the masses. Even before the Senate's role in protecting the interests of government by the passage of the Seventeenth Amendment, the Court had assumed an activist role, rather than fulfilling its own role as a guardian of the constitutional principles. Rather, it developed its own body of doctrine, creating a "living Constitution," and reinterpreted the sound founding principles of "Life, Liberty, and the Pursuit of Happiness, Version 3.0" into lesser rather than greater consistency and updating. Our present system fails to check such behavior. Congress has the right to remove justices from office but makes little effort to do so, often because they are subject to the same fads and fashions that motivate the Court's activist decisions.

It will probably take a constitutional amendment restricting the role of the Supreme Court to issues of political structure, separated from the cultural and economic spheres, to place a check on its abuse and expansion of power. It is only historical reflection

that shows the value of such a restriction and will not be immediately seen by those wrestling with an immediate controversy.

Not Perfect, Just More Perfect

The problem of the two houses has not been resolved in this
chapter, nor by any government. We have only suggestions for
ways the government can become more perfect than it now is.
This is the role of updating and upgrading an operating system.
The question of whether the federal government should be a
government of the people, a union of states, or a hybrid, has not
been solved. What was created by the founders was a hybrid that
democratically represented the citizens of the country better
than it currently does. However, any system can be improved by
insisting that it promote the basic principles outlined in Part I:
protection of life, liberty, and property, the principle of subsidiarity, separation of powers, including the three major spheres of
society, transparency, and the promotion of a free society based
on voluntary association bolstered by the right to secede after all
avenues of reconciliation are exhausted.

Questions for Review and Reflection

1. Why are there two houses of Congress? How do they differ from the House of Lords and House of Commons in England?

2. Why did James Madison, in *Federalist No. 51,* say that the two houses of government should be created by different modes of election and different principles of action, as little connected to each other as possible?

3. Explain why the government the founders created was a hybrid government.

4. What was the impact of the Seventeenth Amendment on the two houses of Congress?

5. Explain why lobbyists for special interests have more impact on legislation than the citizens who vote for representatives.

6. How does legislation get passed that serves a few people at the expense of many?

7. Why was James Madison concerned about too much legislation getting passed?

8. What do you think is the best way to reform Congress so that it functions as representatives of the citizens?

9. Do you think that the Supreme Court has performed its function as constitutional check on Congress? Explain.

10. If you had the opportunity to design a legislative system for the U.S. federal government, how would you construct it, and why?

8

Funding Government

In this world nothing is certain but death and taxes.[1]
—Benjamin Franklin

Governments need funds to operate. People need governments for protection. Therefore, it seems difficult to escape taxes. But government funds do not all come from taxes, and taxes come in a variety of forms. Before 1913, in the United States federal funds were obtained from tariffs and user fees; there were no income taxes. While there were plenty of state and local taxes that Benjamin Franklin had to pay, he did not have to pay anything to the federal government unless he imported products or used a service like the post office that was funded by postage fees.

There are a lot of things that citizens will demand from government if they do not have to pay for them. People's wants are unlimited. If citizens can get a government to fund something, they will try to do so. But citizen demands for public utilities, public jobs, free healthcare, retirement funds, unemployment compensation, free housing, and a myriad of other goods and services know no limit and cannot be funded by any institution. There is a natural law that output cannot exceed input.

People will offer to provide any service that others ask for if they can get a government budget to pay for it. They will even invent things they say the citizens will want, even if they do not ask for them. This is a way to find a secure job, because a government project is typically a monopoly and does not have to compete with other people trying to provide the same service commercially.

Many lobbyists are vying for government jobs and contracts in areas of their expertise. Governments can't afford to fund the entire range of services potential providers want. Some services are more useful than others. Some are a higher priority than others. Most importantly, the providers should not be the ones to make that choice, for in a democracy the majority of citizens should decide what services they want and what they are willing to pay for them. This is basically the definition of a social contract. The citizens should not ask for anything they are unwilling to fund, and the government should not tax for anything the citizens do not choose.

Good governance requires accountability in fulfilling the government's end of the social contract in ways that citizens can easily understand, happily approve, and easily change. In a democracy the members of government serve at the citizen's pleasure and never attempt to use citizens for their own ends. These principles are much easier to state than to realize in practice. There will always be some people who seek to prosper at the expense of others. Religion and culture should teach that is wrong, but realistically if there is an opportunity for abuse, someone will try to take advantage of another through the instruments of government.

Subsidiarity and Government Funding

Governments should design funding in ways that enable their citizens the best pursuit of life, liberty, and happiness with the least possible burden. Governments should seek to obtain funds for particular services they perform from the users of those services as much as possible, making the payments of taxes of fees more voluntary. If people want a service, they should be willing to pay for it. This is a general assumption of freedom. A citizen should be able to pursue his life as freely as possible, realizing that some things he freely chooses to have cost money to provide.

City water and sewage cost money, a national military defense costs money, roads cost money, and social services cost money. These are all things that people want governments to provide.

For some of them it is easy to assess fees, while for others it is more difficult.

Towns

Town and city costs are generally easier to understand and control than state and federal costs. The benefits of the principle of subsidiarity become readily apparent when you examine how funding operates at various levels of government. To some extent, cities have to compete with one another for inhabitants, just like churches compete for adherents or businesses compete for sales. If a city can provide equal quality schools, utilities, police protection, roads, and other services for half the price of a neighboring city, many people will leave the more expensive city and move to the less expensive city. One reason people often leave a larger and older city and move into a suburb is that expenses in the large city are higher, often due to accumulated creation of departments and services and less efficient bureaucracies. The computer software *SimCity*™ helps players to understand the forces that city managers need to understand.

Residents of towns get a property tax bill, water and sewage bills, assessments for developments like roads, sidewalks, curbs, gas lines, trash removal, and sewers. The property tax has to fund schools, police, and a fire department. The expenses are not much more difficult to understand than paying for product at a store. On the bill, you pay for what you get. If you think property taxes are too high, you can compare them to what neighboring municipalities charge for the services they provide and make an intelligent choice, voluntarily choosing to live in one place rather than another.

Cities

Some cities try to create a certain quality of life or ambience. For example, the city of Santa Fe, New Mexico requires adobe-style housing. This might add to the cost of living there, but a certain number of people will find that environment provides them happiness and is worth the extra cost. Large cities can provide many services that towns cannot provide. They might be able to have an airport, a rail depot, a shipping port, theaters, art and nature museums, and magnificent parks. They might be able to attract larger industries and provide greater opportunity for employment. Large cities can offer these things because their cost can be spread over many more people, giving advantages for efficiency through economies of scale.

However, larger cities with those economies of scale have more levels of bureaucracy and more concentrations of wealth and power. They are less personal and have bureaucracies that are easier to abuse and more difficult to hold accountable than smaller towns. Large cities are more likely to have corruption, a political machine that buys and sells offices, mafias, gangs, and welfare dependency. Getting a political job in large cities can often be based more on who you know than what you know. Corruption and incompetence cost money, and these costs get passed on to taxpayers. However, many people choose to live in larger cities despite the increased existence of corruption in exchange for the benefits and employment that they can find there.

Large cities are less personal, and have bureaucracies that are easier to abuse and more difficult to hold accountable than smaller towns.

Most cities do not have an income tax on wages, a tax that is forcefully imposed on the fruits of one's labor. Such a tax is less voluntary and easier to politicize and obfuscate in a general fund than clear-cut user fees or property taxes. The largest cities (like New York) have been able to impose income taxes in exchange for the higher wages and other benefits available to citizens who work there. Larger cities also frequently have a sales tax. These additional taxes above property tax and user fees are required to cover the inefficiencies and higher levels of bureaucracy that make them super-cities the size of states. However, such large cities are difficult to manage without implementing the principles of good governance outlined in Part I. The more the budget can be devolved to local districts and communities, the more competition can develop among them to compete for the best residents and the less overhead is required.

States

States are larger units of population, usually in the millions of people spread over a territory that might take one day to cross by automobile. It is more difficult for citizens to hold states accountable for use of funds than it is to hold towns or cities accountable, except for the super-cities, where the population might exceed that of many states. States are divided territorially into counties with the intention that counties would be able to handle personal welfare, like birth and death certificates, social welfare, roads, and jails. People can walk into a county office, learn to know the person behind the desk, and have face-to-face relationships on an ongoing basis. In county offices employees can be held personally accountable by the citizens who see them and with whom they carry out transactions.

States transcend the personal aspects of the county and function as an impersonal bureaucracy. One can develop a semi-personal relationship with the representative elected from one's local district to the state, but not the state itself.

States are more vulnerable to redistribution legislation than smaller governments, especially when special-interest legislation is legal. A large city with greater lobbying power than small towns, due to its higher concentrations of wealth, can use the apparatus of the state to redistribute funds raised from taxes on all citizens to itself. For example, in Minneapolis, state and federal funds were obtained to help build a light rail commuter line. After operation began and the system could not fund itself with fares, half of the operating costs were passed on to the rest of the state. Many citizens in other towns will never ride these rails and would rather see their earnings put to work building infrastructure in their own towns, in pursuit of their own happiness. State sales taxes and state income taxes make it possible to earmark larger portions of revenue to the stronger lobbies. When cities can honor the principle of subsidiarity and pay the costs of their own projects, and then provide something for support to the states that rest on top of them, the financial pyramid is strong. Lower social units should be the building blocks of higher social units. The inverse is socially unstable. Attempting to prop up an unstable edifice with lateral supports from the sides (see Chapter 3, Figure 7) is not a prescription for a happy, free, or durable society.

State funds should perform the mission related to the state territory, e.g., building roads, bridges and state-level infrastructure that transcend the territories of cities and counties. Rivers and watersheds, mineral resources, and other things related to state territory are appropriate to a state government built on the principle of subsidiarity. Welfare, public education, and other subsidiary functions are more appropriate to city and county levels. When states get involved in human resources issues, they not only assume inappropriate responsibilities, but also encourage unnatural migrations. I am aware of some states that promote the relocation of welfare recipients to other states to reduce their own budgets. Such cost shifting has nothing to do with personal responsibility upon which free societies are built. States also need to fund some emergency service support for large scale disasters, but such support should be available to all members of the state equally, without some residents having more of a state service available than others.

The Federal Government

In the United States, the federal system suffers similar problems as states, only magnified. It is further removed from citizens and thus it is harder for citizens to hold it accountable. The main players at the federal level will be those who can afford permanent representatives and offices in Washington where personal associations with legislators can be developed. In a free society built from the bottom up, the federal government should fund projects that occur at a level beyond the reach of individual states like defense of the entire country, an interstate highway system, coordination of waterways that transcend states like the Mississippi and Colorado Rivers, issuing passports, and providing or coordinating representation at international governmental organizations. Providing funding for social welfare, health benefits, and Social Security to individual citizens is even more inappropriate than it is for individual states. Healthy citizens should be able to find ways, as families, to accomplish these things. If they cannot, lower levels of government are more effective, and only for those who cannot care for themselves, not the entire population.

Being a hybrid system and not directly supported by contributions from the states below it, the funding the federal government receives from taxes on individual citizens undermines the proper flow of government in the pyramid-of-responsibility from individual to city to state to federation of states. In a stable pyramid structure of government, the greatest funding should be at the lowest possible level, with communities providing a portion of their income to the state, not from direct taxation of citizens by the state. The temptation to move from the hybrid system to a system which makes the funding of state redundant represents an attempt to consolidate control at the federal level, rather than having the federal government serve the states in areas they cannot handle themselves. The founding fathers were more true to the principle of subsidiarity when they advocated federal funding from contributions by states, apportioned by population, and the implementation of fees for services like passports, postal service, and other services provided at the national level. Over time, a very inefficient, overtaxed, and improper flow of power has developed into a system that cannot sustain itself for because it has undercut its own funding foundation.

Taxes and Human Incentive

Unless a government can be financed through user fees, voluntary donations, or volunteer service, some form of tax is required. When analyzing tax strategy, human nature and incentives are important. Taxes should be applied so as not to discourage economic productivity or encourage rent-seeking behavior. Like laws that require football helmets on players, taxes should not be applied in ways that reduce the competitiveness and fairness of the economy.

The present tax system arose in a relatively *ad hoc* fashion as various sources of funds were identified by governments as targets for revenue generation. Such targets are often viewed as individual pots to be raided without consideration given to the role they play in the overall society. Inept or self-serving administrators often seek to concentrate wealth to increase the amount available for their institutions and departments. However, if society is a social organism with each institution performing a necessary function, then the appropriate amount of money, like blood, is required to nourish each organ. In the human body, if one organ takes all the blood from others or a vein is cut and the blood is drained, the organism is weakened and might die. Selfish and corrupt use of public money is the social equivalent of cancer or bleeding out in a human body. Consolidation of the economy in ways that impede the free flow of the economy to all organs of society must be curtailed. As with the free flow of traffic, rules need to be created to assist a system in which all organs of society have access to the flow of funds they require, without amassing a hoard that prevents other organs from receiving free unimpeded access to the economy. Many forms of taxes do just that; they impede the free access to the economy that all parts of the social organism need to keep the society healthy.

Regardless of how funds are raised, they have to come from the economic sector of society in one way or another. However, there are some taxes that do not impede incentives and others that do. In passing legislation related to taxes, it is important to consider the positive and negative incentives those taxes will produce rather than the amount of cash concentrated somewhere that a government can use its force to seize.

For example, sales taxes encourage savings. They increase the cost of a product. People will save for, and buy fewer, but more durable and higher quality items if they are taxed. A high savings rate is the sign of a strong economy. Income taxes on wage labor are more negative because they punish production by raising the prices of products compared to products made where such taxes do not exist. In a closed domestic economy, income taxes on labor create a level playing field, but in a global economy, such taxes punish the U.S. economy by making the cost of goods higher than if produced in other countries where taxes are not figured into the cost of labor.

As with the free flow of traffic, rules need to be created to assist a system in which all organs of society have access to the flow of funds they require, without amassing a hoard that prevents other organs from receiving free, unimpeded access to the economy. Many taxes do just that.

In another example, property taxes based on land alone are superior for creating incentives to improve property than property taxes that include improvements. Taxes on land apply to the use of a natural resource that all people must share. Payments to use that land would be consistent with stewardship of the earth. Taxes on improvements, on the other hand, discourage making improvements and encourage dilapidation. Communities that want income but not dilapidated property will be better served by taxing the land only.

Early United States Tax Policy

The federal government began quite small and consistent with the principle of subsidiarity. Before the Civil War, most income derived primarily from import duties and sale of federal land.

To pay the Revolutionary War debt, Congress levied excise taxes on distilled spirits, tobacco, refined sugar, carriages, property sold at auctions, and various legal documents.[2] These taxes were on items considered luxuries, related to unhealthy behavior, or on the estates of those who were deceased; they were not on any item considered essential for the pursuit of general well-being, and they reinforced social morality. Such taxes did not try to equalize income or redistribute wealth; they were to maintain the national government and its military defense.

Many Americans resisted some of these taxes as unfair. In 1794, President Washington was forced to send federal troops to suppress the Whiskey Rebellion by a group of farmers in south-western Pennsylvania who opposed the tax on whiskey. When Thomas Jefferson took office, he sought to abolish all direct taxes, believing that government did not have a claim on the fruits of one's own industry and labor:

> To take from one, because it is thought his own industry and that of his father has acquired too much, in order to spare to others who (or whose fathers) have not exercised equal industry and skill, is to violate arbitrarily the first principle of association, "to guarantee to everyone a free exercise of his industry and the fruits acquired by it."[3]

Direct taxes were abolished in 1802 and, until the War of 1812, there were no internal revenue taxes other than excises. Additional excise taxes were imposed and Treasury notes issued to raise money for the War, but they were repealed in 1817. Until 1861, the government was funded solely by tariffs and the sale of public land.[4]

The Postal Service

In 1830, about three-fourths of all federal civilian employees worked for the post office.[5] This was the largest enterprise in the United States and was paid for with high postage fees that also paid for a system of post roads that might be seen as a precursor to the modern interstate highway system. It would not be an exaggeration to say that before the Civil War the average American's only contact with the federal government was the postal system.

The postal system was a legitimate federal enterprise because it transcended the physical territory of states and supported interstate commerce. The Post Road from New York to Boston is still visible today as U.S. Highway 1, showing the impact it had on demographic settlement in the United States. Tolls and vehicle taxes are another common method of paying for roads based on user fees. Since the invention of the automobile, fuel taxes are another way to fund roads based on use. None of these types of fees tax people who do not use the roads, and everyone who finds the road convenient to use will be willing to pay a fee that other users pay equally. Funding the construction of roads from a general fund paid into by citizens who ride a train or walk will be considered unfair by them. They might consider using their tax dollars for something they do not need as a form of theft.

The Postal Service made a contribution to creating a more unified national culture. However, it has enjoyed monopoly protections that made it inefficient and encouraged corruption. Post office jobs were often political rewards by government officials, and they did not always go to the most qualified applicants. Today, its employees earn about 40 percent more than UPS or Fed Ex employees when retirement and other benefits are included. It is now the second largest employer, having been surpassed by Wal-Mart. The Postal Service subsidizes "junk mail" from first-class postage fees. This is considered unfair to people who only send first-class mail and see junk mail as a waste of money and paper. Many economists recommend that large savings in costs and lower prices for postage would be gained by privatizing the postal system as Sweden, New Zealand, and a number of other countries have done. This would serve to separate commerce and state and encourage subsidiarity and competition. It would provide positive incentives and discourage rent-seeking behavior.[6]

The Civil War

To pay for the Civil War, Congress passed the Revenue Act of 1861, which restored earlier excise taxes and imposed a new income tax of 3 percent on all incomes over $800 a year. In 1862, Congress passed excise taxes on such items as playing cards, gunpowder, feathers, telegrams, iron, leather, pianos, yachts, billiard tables, drugs, patent medicines, and whiskey. Reforms were made to the income tax that made it progressive, taxing incomes over $10,000 at 5 percent. A standard deduction of $600 was allowed, and a variety of deductions were permitted for such things as rental housing, repairs, losses, and other taxes paid. In addition, to assure timely collection, taxes were withheld by employers. These taxes were very similar to the income taxes of today.

The imposition of these taxes was accompanied by a wartime suspension of the Constitution. Most of them were repealed by 1872, with almost 90 percent of all revenue collected until 1913 coming from the remaining excises and tariffs.

Industrial Lobbies

The railroads, like highways, were another industry that brought the nation together. They cross state boundaries, creating a network of hubs in cities that were followed by employment and immigration across the country. Railroads were often given favored status and subsidized by the federal government both in terms of land grants and guaranteed loans. In hindsight, a strong case can be made that this industry also abused its power, caused corruption and economic depressions, and contributed to the Civil War. The presence of the new railroad system was an opportunity for various forms of social and economic viruses to develop and root in the political and economic system, and made possible collusion between the two. The government did not have an immune system strong enough to ward of the corruption that ensued. The railroads influenced many of the Supreme Court decisions in the late nineteenth century that shifted political influence away from the citizens and toward corporate lobbies.

By the last decade of the nineteenth century, industrial lobbyists had succeeded in convincing the government to expand its power, build up the Navy, and make the world safe for global commerce by obtaining ports around the world.[7] However, globalization required free trade, not tariffs. Ironically, many of the same industries that had pushed for tariffs and fought a war against Southern secession to keep them, came to advocate a system of free trade when they looked toward global trade a few decades later. However, if tariffs were eliminated, a new way to support the growing federal government and its military had to be found.

> **Ironically, many of the same industries that had pushed for tariffs, and fought a war against Southern secession to keep them, came to advocate a system of free trade when they looked toward global trade a few decades later.**

The Federal Income Tax

The solution was found in the federal income tax, a tax that required an amendment to the Constitution that allowed taxes to be directly placed on citizens without apportionment:

> The Congress shall have power to lay and collect taxes on incomes, from whatever source derived, without apportionment among the several States, and without regard to any census or enumeration.[8]

The federal income tax was originally a tax on the profits derived from the sales of commodities. It was not intended as a tax on the wages one earned to live. There is a major difference between wage income used for production of goods and income derived from profits on sales. Wages are paid to workers and managers who produce a product. They are part of the cost of production. Income derived from ownership of an industry, whether personally owned or collectively owned by shareholders, is income derived from investment, not income derived from work. This is a very important distinction that has become lost on modern society.

Money used for production can be compared to the seeds a farmer sows in the field. Those seeds are nourished and transformed into crops for a harvest. A kernel of corn as a seed can multiply into thousands of kernels at the harvest. If someone takes the farmer's seeds and the fields lie fallow, the thief has a few seeds, the farmer starves, and there is no harvest to feed others. This principle also applies to industrial production. Taxes placed on the funds that could be used to produce products are destructive taxes. They prevent economic growth from taking place and producing wealth that would provide more income for taxation.

The federal income tax was originally intended to be income on profits from sales. It was not intended as a tax on the wages one earned to live.

When the federal income tax was established, it was proposed as a tax on the harvest. There was no intention to make this a tax on basic wage labor or on amounts needed for basic living expenses, but only on profits above these expenses. In 1913, when the income tax was begun, there was an across-the-board tax of 1 percent of income with a $3,000 standard deduction. There was an additional tax of 1 percent that was assessed on incomes over $20,000, and this increased progressively to 6 percent on incomes over $500,000 (over $11 million in 2009 dollars):

A. Subdivision 1. That there shall be levied, assessed, collected and paid annually upon the entire net income arising or aerating from all sources at the preceding calendar year to every citizen of the United States, whether residing at home or abroad, and to every person residing in the United States. though not a citizen thereof, a tax of 1 per centum per annum upon such income, except as hereinafter provided: and a like tax shall be assessed, levied, collected, and paid annually upon the entire net income from all property owned and of every business, trade, or profession carried on in the United States by persons residing elsewhere.

Subdivision 2. In addition to the income tax provided under this section (herein referred to as the normal income tax) there shall be levied, assessed, and collected upon the net income of every individual an additional income tax (herein referred to as the additional tax) of 1 per centum per annum upon the amount by which the total net income exceeds $20,000 and does not exceed $50,000, and 2 per centum per annum upon the amount by which the total net income exceeds $50,000 and does not exceed $75,000... and 6 per centum per annum upon the amount by which the total net income exceeds $500,000.[9]

Since the average wage in 1913 was $733 (or $16,000 in 2009 dollars)[10] and the standard deduction was four times that amount, income taxes would be paid only by about the top 5 percent of the population. This bill, also known as the Underwood-Simmons Tariff, was an expansion of the 1909 Corporate Excise Tax to include individuals who earned significant incomes. Congressman Murray presented an explanation while discussing the exemption in the 1913 Session:

There are those who would say that we should begin at $1,000 in lieu of $4,000. They forget the principle upon which this tax is founded, and that is that every man who is making no more than a living should not be taxed upon living earnings, but should be taxed upon the surplus that he makes over and above that amount necessary for a good living.[11]

And Congressman Borah later stated:

After a man pays the tax which he must pay on consumption, then give him a chance to clothe and educate his family and meet the obligations of citizenship and preparation of those dependent upon him for citizenship before you add any additional tax. That is the basis of this exemption, and it is fair and just to all and toward all.[12]

This was the original rationale behind the income tax. It was a tax on the harvest rather than the seed. Government cannot make the seeds grow. It is not structured as an income producing social organ; its function is to use taxes derived from the general economy for the defense and protection of the society. It is common sense that a tax system should tax the harvest rather than the seeds. Good government should encourage planting and productivity, creating incentives that encourage a bountiful harvest and discourage squandering.

The door was opened for income tax to expand without limits. While the tariffs had supplied a more limited amount of funds that forced government fiscal responsibility, the income tax became an easy way to add

> **The Sixteenth Amendment had the effect of further removing the states from the financial operation of the federal government. It extended the hybrid nature of representation in government to a hybrid form of taxation, with the taxes paid by individual citizens bypassing state coffers and going directly to the federal.**

incremental tax increases to compensate for government sloth, waste, pork barrel projects, and empire-building. Each year, laws were passed that added tax increases, deductions, adjustments, and loopholes. The United States became a special interest paradise. Rather than increasing the standard deduction to keep up with inflation, it was lowered until the tax applied to laborers and turned into a tax on the seeds.

By making the taxation of personal income legal, the Sixteenth Amendment had the effect of further removing the states from the financial operation of the federal government. It extended the hybrid nature of representation in government to a hybrid form of taxation, with the taxes paid by individual citizens bypassing state coffers and going directly to the federal. Rather than collecting an apportioned tax from the states to support the federal government, those who lobbied for the tax sought to tap funds held by individuals instead of tarriffs or other user taxes.

The Income Tax Leviathan

Within three decades, the federal income tax had grown into a Leviathan that looked nothing like what legislators Murray and Borah described in 1913. It was a tax that opened up the financial equivalent of the Oklahoma Land Rush of 1893. It has become the standard method of raising taxes and has shifted from a tax on the wealthy to a tax on the wage earner, from a tax on the harvest to a tax on the seeds. As Treasury official Worthington Ford warned in 1894:

> Wherever an income tax has been in practice for any time the small incomes as well as the large are taxed; and it is the small incomes which yield the largest revenue to the state.[13]

In addition to undermining the principle of subsidiarity, income taxes on wages reduce competition and economic incentive. It did not take long for the income tax to become a Leviathan consuming individual wealth and feeding corruption. It encouraged non-compliance and eventually contributed to loss of U.S. competitivity in industry, and this, in turn, led to job loss and a slowed economy.

The 1916 Revenue Act raised the lowest rate from 1 percent to 2 percent and the highest rate from 6 percent to 15 percent, and these rates still applied to a tax on the "harvest." However, it also imposed taxes on estates and businesses.[14] These were double taxes, because whoever owns an estate pays a tax on income to purchase the estate, and whoever received profits from a business paid income taxes. These double taxes were socially perverse from the standpoint of incentive.

Within three years after the 1913 income tax was passed, its mutations began to develop. In 1916, the United States entered World War I, and in 1917, the federal budget was nearly the same as the entire 125-year federal budget between 1791 and 1916.

With respect to estates, it works against the motive of creating long-term family wealth and the motivation to pass something on to one's children, something many feel is essential to the pursuit of happiness. It works against the principle of the family as a building block of society because it does not create an incentive for care of the sick, retired, or handicapped within the family unit, but treats each taxpayer as the main subunit of government. It creates greater possibilities that such people will become wards of the state, and makes it more necessary for the state to provide social security.

Taxing businesses created an incentive not to create a profit. This hurt the stockholders and reduced dividend income available for the federal income tax. Rather than generating a profit, businesses faced with these taxes are motivated to spend earnings on non-productive purposes. Such things as lavish corporate parties, sales retreats, high priced advertising that produces minimal results, and excessive pay to CEOs are the result of this law. The double taxation of business profit is one of the most destructive laws for the U.S. economy. It would be far better to provide incentives for corporations to earn profits, and mandate payment of minimum percentage of profits as dividends to shareholders and owners, who would pay an income tax on their investment income than to tax corporations directly.

Within three years after the 1913 income tax was passed, its mutations began to develop. In 1916, the United States entered World War I, and in 1917 alone the federal budget was nearly the same as the entire 125-year federal budget between 1791 and 1916, including the costs of the Civil War.[15] The War Revenue Acts of 1917 and 1918 increased the bottom rate from 2 percent to 6 percent and the top rate from 15 percent to 77 percent. However, these taxes were still taxes on the harvest and only paid for by 5 percent of the population. In 1916, the federal revenue was $761 million; by 1920 it had become $6.6 billion.

Taxing businesses created an incentive not to create a profit. Rather than generating a profit, businesses faced with these taxes are motivated to spend earnings on non-productive purposes.

After the War, there was an effort to "take government out of business" and return all social budgets back to state and local government.[16] Andrew Mellon, who was Treasury Secretary for much of the time in the 1920s, also tried to define a difference between earned and unearned income:

> The fairness of taxing more lightly income from wages, salaries or from investments is beyond question. In the first case, the income is uncertain and limited in duration; sickness or death destroys it, and old age diminishes it; in the other, the source of income continues; the income may be disposed of during a man's life and it descends to his heirs.[17]

Federal taxes were reduced five times in the 1920s to a bottom rate of 1 percent and a top rate of 25 percent. These cuts fuelled economic growth and strengthened the economy, but the size of the government was never reduced to pre-war levels. There were pay increases for federal employees, and a new system of federal aid to the states for building highways set a precedent for the reverse flow of federal funds to the states. Under the new hybrid tax structure, the public demanded more services from the federal government when states could not pay for them.[18] Coolidge, who believed "the business of America is business," approved the use of federal funds for subsidies for businesses, creating a form of neomercantilism.[19] Surplus revenues were not used to retire the debt as quickly as earlier wars, although fiscal conservatives pushed for it.

> **By the end of the roaring twenties, the states, the citizens, government employees, and the business lobbies had all come to believe that the federal budget could be tapped for their welfare.**

By the end of the roaring twenties, the states, the citizens, government employees, and the business lobbies had all come to believe that the federal budget could be tapped for their welfare. The surplus income after the war became a pot for everyone to raid. This was the decade where the role of the United States as a limited government to protect the people was transforming into a welfare state where subsidiarity was being reversed.

Herbert Hoover had the misfortune of being president when the depression hit. The Federal Reserve attempted to expand credit, but as with the 2008 TARP bailout, they could not attract borrowers. Hoover tried to fend off the idea of a federal welfare state increasingly pushed by the popular Social Gospel in the churches, socialists watching the Soviet experiment, and Democrats. In one public message in June 1931, he spoke of two views:

The first is whether we shall go with the American system, which holds that the purpose of the state is to protect the people.... The other is that we shall, directly or indirectly, regiment the population into a bureaucracy to serve the state.[20]

In December 1931, he warned:

The federal government must not encroach upon nor permit local communities to abandon that precious possession of local initiative and responsibility in local communities.[21]

But his warnings fell on deaf ears as the Democratic Congress passed a bill to bail out states with loans, setting up the Reconstruction Finance Corporation where everyone could dump their financial problems on the federal government. This act of Congress, under the opposition of the Hoover administration, put an end to the first chapter in American history where welfare payments to individuals were outside the scope of the federal government. The Supreme Court remained silent about the constitutionality of the Relief and Construction Act, even though it was 180 degrees opposed to the founders' vision for the United States.

For most of the 1920s and 1930s, people who earned less than $5,000 per year did not have to file 1040 tax forms. This was the majority of the working population. The 1930s saw increased federal deficits and sought to fill those deficits with increases in taxes and more kinds of taxes. The loans to the states under the Reconstruction Finance Corporation were forgiven in 1934 before the first payment ever came due, and most states began implementing income tax systems of their own.

In 1940, the minimum income requirement to file was lowered to $3,000, and the number of returns filed jumped from 7.7 million in 1939 to 50 million by 1945, more than a six-fold increase. It was no longer a tax paid above the normal expenses of food, housing, medical, and educational expenses, but applied to wage earners and the middle class who were unable to send their children to college. The basic form of the welfare state has continued since the 1930s, with some adjustments to taxes, depending on which party controlled Congress.

Over the years, special interests lobbied for many types of exemptions and special tax categories. Here are some interesting facts that help one to understand the behemoth the Internal Revenue Service has become:

- In 2008, the U.S. "tax army" was bigger than the U.S. Army in Iraq.

- There are over 500 forms, making the use of an accountant necessary for many people to file a return.

- The tax code expanded from 400 pages in 1913 to over 54,000 pages in 2003.[22]

In 2008, "Tax Freedom Day," the day when the average American has worked enough to pay income taxes, fell on April 23, about 31 percent of the way through the year. The income tax Leviathan is the type of structure that easily grows like a cancer, but is difficult to shrink. Those who control legislation are spending taxpayer money, not their own. There is less incentive to control spending when you use someone else's money. It is the type of tax that encourages rent-seeking by government bureaucrats, citizens wanting handouts, and corporations seeking corporate welfare. None of these things has to do with the primary role of the federal government in defending and protecting its citizens.

The United States income tax is a clear example of the failure of a democratic government to regulate itself and why checks and balances on financial power must be added to checks and balances on political power. The income tax became a drug to which the government, the citizens, and the corporations all became addicted, eventually leading to uncontrolled government growth and the collapse of the economy.

In the 1980s, the Reagan administration promoted "supply-side economics," arguing that income tax relief on the wealthy would revive the economy. Those reforms led both to increased economic growth, and increased conspicuous consumption associated with the squandering of income by many of the newly rich. Those reforms enabled income to be retained for investment but did not check the abuses of this income. If there are no penalties for squandering or incentives for investing, realistically the self-regulation of the wealthy cannot be assumed. Solutions will not come by giving morality lectures to the rich or teaching the poor the virtue of patience. Concrete economic incentives can alter the behavior of selfish people. It cannot make them altruistic, but it can redirect squandering into something that has some positive social side effect.

The Reagan reforms were one-sided and failed to create planned competition and economic subsidiarity. Instead they encouraged mergers and acquisitions that led to wealth centralization and created more opportunities for corruption that led to a short term economic stimulus followed by the creation of many companies "to big to fail." Then when corporations are mismanaged, the taxpayer is asked to bail them out. This problem would not exist in a decentralized—but not unrefereed—economy.

Increasing taxes on the income necessary for basic expenses and expanding the power of the IRS to clamp down further on the collection of the seed money citizens need to pursue life, liberty, and happiness will only further the resentment of citizens against the government, pave the way for widespread evasion (if not open rebellion) and promote the establishment of an informal "black market" economy. Today, the tax code is so large and complicated that most people who work for the Internal Revenue Service do not understand it well enough

> **If there are no penalties for squandering or incentives for investing, realistically the self-regulation of the wealthy cannot be assumed. Solutions will not come by giving morality lectures to the rich or teaching the poor the virtue of patience.**

to properly answer many questions raised by citizens filling out their forms. In addition to becoming financially oppressive, it is also emotionally exhausting for many to complete their returns.

Today, if some form of income tax is employed as a means of partially funding government, it would be most effective, from the standpoint of life, liberty, and the pursuit of happiness, to eliminate income taxes on corporations, mandate payment of corporate dividends to shareholders, and exempt the first $50,000 a person earns from the income tax. This would return the income tax to the common sense purposes that enable collection of taxes without harming the citizens' pursuit of life, liberty, and happiness, or the economy as a whole.

Sales Taxes: Tax the Harvest not the Seeds

Sales taxes, by definition, are taxes on products and not on the process that is used to produce them. They are taxes on spending rather than production. Sales taxes encourage saving and penalize squandering. Taxes on luxuries are a tax on the rich because the poor cannot afford luxuries. They reduce the gap between the rich and the poor, while the present system increases that gap. Taxes on socially harmful behavior reduce that behavior. Excise taxes on whiskey, tobacco, and luxuries paid off the Revolutionary War debt. There will be lobbies that complain about these taxes, especially from those people who earn their living by selling these products. However, these taxes are common-sense taxes that most citizens would agree to in a straight up and down vote. They are taxes more reflective of a representative democracy. Unlike the income taxes that special interests have placed on citizens, they are the type of tax that citizens could place on special and questionable interests.

A tax on non-essential goods and services is not a forced tax because the citizen voluntarily purchases the item and can voluntarily choose not to purchase it if he deems the government is misusing the proceeds. In this way, it is also a check and balance on government spending.

Sales Taxes Discourage Consumption

Sales taxes discourage consumption because they make products more costly. People enjoy buying products, and large manufacturers rely on consumption. This is one reason large manufacturers encourage the media to call people "consumers" (objects) rather than "citizens" (subjects). In a closed labor-intensive economy, increased consumption creates domestic jobs. However, in a globalized and machine-based system of mass production, goods are delivered at lower prices to consumers but do not create middle-class domestic jobs. Most of the domestic jobs created are lower-paid stock and sales clerks, rather than the higher-paid jobs associated with production. While consumption helps to fuel an economy, consumption cannot take place if all the workers are low paid or unemployed. Producers who make money become consumers. It is they who trade their earnings from excess production for the products of other people. An economy cannot be based solely on consumption.

> **Producers who make money become consumers. It is they who trade their earnings from excess production for the products of other people. An economy cannot be based solely on consumption.**

Sales Taxes Level the International Playing Field

An income tax on production labor increases the price of the products produced. A product that includes the cost of an income tax on production labor will be more expensive than one that does not. Producers have an incentive to manufacture products where taxes are lower so that they can better compete on the market. Income taxes on wages and profits encourage producers to move to other countries or retailers to purchase goods made in other countries. However, sales taxes apply equally to an imported product and a domestic product. This puts domestic production on a level playing field with goods produced in other countries, as long as all other factors are equal. While all other factors are not equal, a level economic playing field should be a primary goal of government; replacing production taxes with sales taxes is one way to make the playing field more level for American workers.

A sales tax is a tax on the harvest, wherever it was produced. If a domestic producer and a foreign producer produce goods equally efficiently, the cost of shipping will make the domestic good preferable and encourage job creation in manufacturing at home. If domestic workers are a bit more efficient and the cost of transportation getting the product to market is lower, there is some room to raise wages of domestic laborers or to realize higher profits that can be distributed to shareholders.

> **While all other factors are not equal, a level economic playing field should be a primary goal of government; replacing production taxes with sales taxes is one way to make the playing field more level for American workers.**

The current United States tax structure puts its own citizens at a competitive disadvantage with other countries, undermining the concept of "free trade," and reducing the possibility of a long-term sustainable economy and reduction of trade deficits. Eliminating taxes on production and placing them on sales would be far fairer to U.S. citizens, and thus reflect a more responsible government promoting Life, Liberty, and the Pursuit of Happiness, Version 4.0.

Effects on the Poor

The lower-middle class and lower classes in the United States spend most of their income on basics like food, shelter, transportation, and medical care. By exempting a sales tax on these basic items rather than charging taxes on the wages they earn before they ever purchase these basic goods and services, lower wage earners will have more money to spend on basic consumption. Such exemptions would also be fair to higher-income earners because they would get basic necessities at the same price as the poor and only be taxed on non-essentials.

The present system tries to compensate for flaws in the tax system by creating a complicated alternative minimum tax, providing welfare, food stamps, and subsidized housing that, when administered through an inefficient bureaucracy, yield less than fifty cents on a tax dollar. But this is an inefficient patch on a flawed system that increases the complicated tax code and places extra burdens on the people it is supposed to help. Such a system kicks the people who are already down in the name of helping them. It is a morally questionable use of the government. Sales taxes would encourage employment in manufacturing, where less labor is required. These jobs employ people in the lower and middle classes, allowing them to become productive citizens who take pride in their lives.

Sales taxes would solve the one-sided problem not addressed by the supply-side economic legislation of the 1980s.

The poor, thrust into neighborhoods with substandard facilities, have little self-respect and little hope for their children. People in lower-paid jobs like cashiers and stock clerks find themselves in the predicament of having to pay rent and never being able to afford their own home and gain equity in their future. They need to be able to move up to higher paying jobs while raising a family. Eliminating income taxes and increasing sales taxes on luxury items might enable them to more easily become middle-class citizens.

If non-basic products and services are subjected to a sales tax, wealthier people are taxed in proportion to their consumption. Since the wealthy have more ability to consume and can decide whether to acquire luxury items or reinvest their income in economic production, the economy would benefit whether they reinvested in the economy or bought yachts and fur coats. Sales taxes would solve the one-sided problem not addressed by the supply-side economic legislation of the 1980s.

Encourages Higher Quality Products

A sales tax on products encourages the purchase of high quality and long-lasting products, rather the cheapest disposable items. Sales taxes encourage people to save, plan, and shop for the best products, rather than buy on impulse. Higher quality products and more custom-made products would likely be made and lead to more highly skilled and better paying domestic jobs. This would also help to lower negative trade balances. Production of higher quality goods would also mean the availability of more second-hand items.

In addition, incentives will be created for the purchase of hand-made crafts and products with higher artistic appeal. Because sales taxes encourage people to buy higher quality products that they may need to live with a long time, people will also desire products that have artistic appeal in addition to their function. This will create more work for engineers and designers on lower-quantity factory runs of domestic products rather than inexpensive, but short-lived consumer products aimed at a global market and made elsewhere.

Reduce Tax Forms for the Citizens

Sales taxes can be collected by retailers at the cash register with computer software and require very little labor in processing. Forms are filled out and receipts sent to the government as a simple aspect of doing business. They are not filled out by the taxpayer. Imagine the reduction in staff at the IRS if most citizens filled out a 1040 EZ income tax form, in which the first $50,000 for basic living expenses was exempt, and the remainder was taxed a flat percentage with no deductions or adjustments. Supplementing an income tax on the harvest only with a sales tax would probably eliminate 75 percent of the $10.7 billion dollar per year tax army[23] and inefficient government.

More U.S. Products to Other Countries

More U.S.-made products will be purchased by other countries if the cost of the products is lower. If income taxes are not factored into the cost of the products, they will be more competitive. This will also improve the U.S. balance of trade.

Government Held to the Same Standard as Citizens

In a sales-tax based system, there is a built-in formula for fairness because government growth is only possible in proportion to the growth of the economy as a whole. The government can only spend in proportion to the people's ability to spend. If the economy is strong, people will spend more, and the government will have more to spend. If the people have no money to spend, neither will the government. Such a government will be representative of the citizens and not as likely to be as aloof as the current federal government has become. When the government suffers in proportion to the citizens, the citizens view it as more legitimate.

Avoid Unconstitutional Church-State Conflicts

In the attempt to squeeze more income taxes out of a depleted pool of taxpayers, the IRS has repeatedly tried to tax churches and non-profit organizations whose aim is to cultivate the human spirit and serve the poor. Not only are these taxes an unconstitutional violation of the principle of separation of church and state, they also reflect a last-ditch effort to extract money from an overtaxed society, or, more correctly, an improperly-taxed society.

The attempt to tax churches should be seen as a symptom of social and economic decline. Religion, a source of character building and the cultivation of human desires and aspirations, has a very positive function to play in the long-term health of the society. The founding fathers knew religion plays an indispensable role in the operation of a republic, because it teaches people to be self-regulating and act with a moral conscience. The work ethic promoted by religion and cultural institutions greatly contributes to productivity in the economy. In a sales-tax based society, pastors would pay tax for products they buy just like anyone else, but money targeted for social welfare held in a priest's account would not be taxed. In short, one of the most crucial church-state issues of our day would become a non-issue by changing from an income tax to a sales tax.

One of the most crucial church-state issues of our day would become a non-issue by changing from an income tax to a sales tax.

But, income tax should not just be eliminated on "not-for-profit" organizations. It should be eliminated on all organizations in the cultural and economic spheres, and that includes businesses and economic corporations. The only institutions that should pay taxes are lower governments to higher governments. This would follow from the principle of subsidiarity.

Returning Tax Collection to the States

Considering the importance of subsidiarity and the proper flow of taxes, it would be a positive step to entirely eliminate the federal income tax, and leave all taxes on income to the states. The federal government could collect an apportioned amount from the states for the defense of the country, and the states could pay this with either income or sales taxes collected from citizens and consumers. In addition, the federal government could receive income on user fees for the part it plays as a referee in services it performs, for example, fuel taxes to help pay for interstate highways, communications taxes on bandwidth, or airport taxes for control tower information and international customs related to the administration of services that transcend state boundaries.

Because the federal government is a monopoly, it is economically inefficient. The states, on the other hand are plural within the system, and they have a possibility to compete with one another for inhabitants. The performance of individual states will attract citizens, who have the ability to "vote with their feet" and move from one state to another. They do not so easily have that opportunity to move to other countries with a higher quality of life, at least in the current world.

The most successful states will be those that perform their role in creating a quality of life that is desirable for their inhabitants. Higher taxes create deterrent and lower taxes an incentive, but they are not the only factors. Cleaner environment, the opportunities for employment, the affordability of housing, and other factors all contribute to a person's choice of residence. States that provide the best overall quality for value will be the most successful. If taxes are removed from the federal level and left with the states, they will be more efficiently collected and administered. Imagine the reduction in the size of the IRS if the 50 states were the only "citizens" from which it collected taxes.

If taxes are removed from the federal level and left with the states, they will be more efficiently collected and administered. Imagine the reduction in the size of the IRS if the 50 states were the only "citizens" from which it collected taxes.

Of course, state revenue services would have a greater responsibility than they do now, because they would be responsible to raise the apportioned funds that would support the federal government. However, because they would be doing this on a competitive basis rather than as a federal monopoly, they would be far more efficient in performing their task.

Eliminating Corporate Income Taxes

The elimination of corporate income taxes has been mentioned several places in this book. It is useful to elaborate further on the social benefits of this at this point. Without corporate income taxes, industries in the United States would either reinvest profits in production of goods and services, which would increase employment, or they would distribute profits to shareholders. Shareholders, whose income would thereby be increased, would either pay taxes on that income if their earnings were above the minimum deduction, or they would spend it on items that were either necessary for living, or goods that are taxed.

Any tax revenues ultimately collected would be on the harvest, and any profits on which taxes were not paid would either go towards reinvestment in the economy or toward basic living expenses of the laborers or shareholders. The flow of tax revenues would thus be principled. There would not be a tax on productivity or a reason for the corporation to avoid distributing profits to shareholders.

Eliminating income taxes on businesses would also eliminate the need to worry about taxes on large inventories or depreciation of equipment. When these items are factored into corporate decision-making, they often force decisions that are not economically sound, for example, producing lower quantities at a greater expense to avoid tax on inventory, or dumping inventory at the end of the year at a loss to avoid taxes. Income tax on large corporations requires an expensive sidetracking of corporate energy and expense just to administer the most effective overall financial strategy. Lawyers are often retained for the purpose of reducing taxes. Eliminating income taxes reduces this whole parasitic apparatus that is not essential to the basic function of the corporation to turn raw materials into useful products that benefit consumers and the entire economy. Income taxes are like applying a brake to a locomotive, preventing it from delivering the greatest payload to the market.

The enormous amount of money, energy, and thought that go into corporate strategies to evade payment of taxes on profits is a loss for the corporation because it is motivated to spend capital on non-productive activity, and it is a loss to the government because taxes are avoided. Legislators complain about this tax evasion as if they should expect corporations to behave in contradiction to financial laws.

Democratic Senators Carl Levin of Michigan and Byron Dorgan of North Dakota requested a Government Accounting Office (GAO) study of how many taxes were paid by the corporations that sold $2.5 trillion in goods between 1998 and 2005. The GAO reported that 72 percent of all foreign corporations and about 57 percent of U.S. companies doing business in the United States paid no federal income taxes for at least one year in that period. Dorgan called the report "a shocking indictment of the current tax system," and Levin said it made clear that "too many corporations are using tax trickery to send their profits overseas and avoid paying their fair share in the United States."[24] These statements reveal either the ignorance of economic principles or the jealousy and arrogance of legislators who think businesses will willingly make non-rational economic decisions.

Corporate income tax causes an enormous amount of money, energy, and thought to be spent on avoiding avoiding profit, and thus taxes. Yet legislators complain about this tax evasion as if they should expect corporations to behave otherwise.

What this report failed to say is that many of those corporations that did pay taxes and had large profits were non-competitive. They had large profits as a result of some form of government protection, like government-set utility rates, patent protection, a legal conflict of interest, or some type of monopoly. Reducing these problems would help the overall economy but would further reduce, not increase, the number of corporations that pay income taxes.

When the attempt to tax corporate profits is ruinous to the economy, and thereby to overall government revenue, the solution is not to try to apply failed principles harder. The solution is to put a better system in its place. Taxing corporate profits reveals a plunder mentality and ignorance rather than an understanding of the economic laws and incentives that can make for a healthy society.

Eliminating income taxes on businesses would fulfill the goals of supply-side economics, but would work against many of the perversions and the corruption that came with an unrefereed corporate activity that led to many of the scandals at the beginning of the twenty-first century. Many of the government incentives for people to hide profit, cook the books, pay excessive amounts to CEOs, or pay for frivolous parties, luxury hotels, first-class air travel, and other marginally beneficial expenses that could be deducted as a cost of doing business before showing a taxable profit, would be eliminated.

> **Corporate spending habits will become more efficient and be motivated by market competition if taxes on profits are removed from the equation. Instead of business plans in which the end result is no profit, profit can once again become a realistic goal.**

Corporate spending habits will become more efficient and be motivated by market competition if taxes on profits are removed from the equation. Instead of business plans in which the end result is no profit, profit can once again become a realistic goal.

Sales Taxes on Mergers and Acquisitions

Another desirable form of sales tax would be a tax on the acquisition of another company, or on some types of corporate mergers. Such a tax would encourage a corporation to buy another corporation for the purpose of a long-term plan for the acquired company and discourage hostile takeovers and corporate raiding for the purpose of destroying and liquidating other companies in the quest for centralizing financial wealth and creating monopolies, or quasi-monopolies, that eventually become "too big to fail." Such centralization should be an indication that the company poses an extreme financial risk to the society in which it exists. Decentralization of wealth is a socially beneficial strategy, and sales taxes on the acquisition of companies would encourage subsidiarity in the economic sphere.

Corporate Income Tax Evasion Hurts Shareholders

Shareholders are the major losers when corporations are motivated to avoid profit. Corporate income tax is a double tax because profits not reinvested in corporate productivity should be distributed to shareholders in the form of dividends. Corporate tax avoidance strategies that avoid profits also leave nothing for the payment of dividends. This reduces payments investors deserve and discourages investing.

Less Industrial Waste

The sales tax incentives that lead to saving and the desire for higher quality products applies to corporate expenditures as well as individuals. Industries will be motivated to purchase higher quality machines, to invest more in their inventories, to produce higher quality products, and to invest in their infrastructure. There will be incentives not to waste resources built into corporate decision-making aimed at the bottom line. In a profit-based tax system, more regulatory legislation and force is required to prevent use of disposable materials and wasteful practices that a sales tax system would accomplish naturally without government interference.

Property Taxes

Property taxes, while not a federal tax, provide revenue for schools and other city and county services. Property taxes can also work with or against socially beneficial purposes. Land is a resource that must be shared in some way by all people. It is the basic natural resource shared by a community, town, city, or county. It is quite reasonable to tax land to obtain funds for local governments. Traditionally, schools, police, and fire departments that serve a local area are funded by property taxes in the area. Therefore, it is like a use tax and essentially fair when instituted at the local level.

Land is frequently zoned for different uses based on a general plan by the local government. This can be commercial, single-dwelling residential, multiple-dwelling residential, or mixed use. The value of land also depends on whether it borders a busy street, sits on a quiet lake, or is surrounded by other homes. Taxes are applied based on use and value.

Current property taxes are based both on the value of the land and the value of the improvements (e.g., buildings, etc.). Such taxes seem to be based on some form of envy or jealousy rather than an understanding of economic incentives. Taxes on improvements discourage people from making improvements. Hence, they can lead to the decline of a neighborhood.

The owner of a property, whether it be a house, an apartment building, or a commercial business will not be motivated to improve the buildings, or add new buildings if it will cause the assessed value and the tax to rise. However, a community benefits from such improvements because it attracts people with greater incomes to spend in the community. People want to live in beautiful neighborhoods, not run-down ones. Discouraging improvements is not in the interest of the resident, but tax assessments on improvements do just that. They also encourage owners to make any improvements "off the books" by not applying for building permits, thereby risking the chance those improvements will not be up to code, which is not in the interest of a future buyer or the community.

Communities could easily revise their system of taxation by placing the assessments on the land only, based on its zoning, and strategic location. Such a tax, which would be larger on the land but nothing on the improvements, would encourage people to build the maximum facility and keep it most attractive for resale. They would not be taxed on their investment, so they would be more likely to invest. For example, if a lot were zoned and taxed for a six-story apartment building, the owner would not want to only put a two-story building on that lot. He would want to build a six-story building with the maximum number of units to get the lowest tax value per unit. In this way, the city would get a well-maintained, six-story apartment building rather than a two-story building. A municipality would be able not only to build in a design for the community, but also use the capital of the builders to ensure it is built as they had planned.

> Communities could place the assessments on the land only, based on zoning. Such a tax would encourage people to build the maximum facility and keep it most attractive for resale. They would not be taxed on their investment, so they would more likely invest.

Improvements could be subjected to a one-time sales tax on the materials purchased for the improvement, and therefore, some tax revenue can be generated from improvements, even if they might be captured by the state instead of the local community. This is another reason to coordinate tax rates at different levels of government to create a harmonious system of government.

Protection of property, like the protection of life and liberty, is a fundamental principle of republicanism. When buildings are taxed every year by a government, this is not protecting property rights but taking them away. Taxes are needed to pay for water, sewers, roads, and schools that serve a community. A land tax is appropriate to pay for these expenses. But, the tax should be the same on an empty lake shore lot as the developed lot next door. This will encourage whoever buys the empty lot to put a valuable building on it and keep it in excellent shape, to offset the extra tax that being on the lake shore provides.

Conclusions

The downside of sales taxes is the same as the downside of any tax. If they are too high, people will attempt to get around them. If income taxes are high, people will have incentives to work for cash off the books. If sales taxes are high, a black market in goods and smuggling could be encouraged. If property taxes are too high, people will cram into small spaces and put a strain on community resources. The degree that these undesired consequences happen depends of the overall efficiency of the tax structure.

The Solution

The proven method of creating government efficiency is competition. And with governmental units, this means competition for residents. The federal government, as the highest level of government, has little incentive for efficiency compared to counties, cities and towns that are allowed to compete with one another in providing good schools, police, roads, and fire departments in exchange for reasonable property taxes. They also compete with one another in providing good sewers, water, and electricity for low-cost utility bills.

Great government efficiency, and thus citizen happiness and prosperity, could be derived from eliminating federal income and sales taxes entirely and allowing the states and local governments to compete with one another in providing welfare, social services, and other non-defense-related spending. By allowing residents to freely choose in which state they want to live, states will be forced to compete for the best taxpayers. This will not only make them more efficient than the federal government, but it will encourage people to become better taxpayers in order to live in the states that encourage the greatest personal productivity and responsibility and provide the greatest economic freedom.

In England, a major advance in government was created in its history when the *Magna Carta* was signed in 1215. The English barons, tired of the unilateral whims of the king, decided to take London by storm and force the king into an agreement that they would take an oath of loyalty to the king and pay their taxes in exchange for the establishment of a committee of barons that could meet and overrule the king. In exchange, the king had to take an oath of loyalty to them.[25]

When governments are forced to compete, the people win. States in a federation can be forced to compete, but the federation itself cannot, for it is a monopoly.

In the United States today, we have a similar power problem between the federal government and the states. Ideally, the United States Senate should be a place where the states can meet and overrule the administration. However, because the federal Congress has obtained taxing authority and eliminated the appointments of Senators by states, this process is broken. The equivalent of the *Magna Carta* in the United States today would be if the states banded together and forced the federal government to remove its hands from social coffers and demanded that it perform its role of protecting the entire federation in exchange for an oath of loyalty to raise taxes within the states to support that function.

Planning for competition works not only in the economic sector but, as the United States learned from the separation of church and state, in the religious sphere. This same principle applies to governments, because when governments are forced to compete, the people win. States in a federation can be forced to compete, but the federation itself cannot, for it is the top level of government in the country. As such, it should not have taxing authority, but should rely on apportioned taxes paid by the member states.

This same principle would extend to the United Nations or some other world federation. It would be a disaster to give an international government unchecked taxing authority, and wise to assess apportioned member dues in exchange for the services it provides. And, of course, whether it be the United Nations or the United States, secession should be the last option to check the consolidated power of the higher unit of government.

There will be resistance to good tax reforms by the vested interests who have, over the years, wrested the government from the citizens and used taxpayer dollars for their own ends. Such resistance does not necessarily require the overthrow of government and the military imposition of a new system. It can be implemented in the same way it was lost, one piece of legislation at a time. It is my hope that greater knowledge about government will lead people to reform their governments from the bottom up, not to have a junta impose it from the top down. After all, representative democracy is built from the bottom up by a knowledgable people who are capable of it.

Questions for Review and Reflection

1. Why is accountability in the budget of a small town easier to achieve than in a large city or the federal government?

2. How was the U.S. government funded before the Civil War?

3. Why did influential corporate lobbies support tariffs in 1850 but oppose them in 1900?

4. Why was the Sixteenth Amendment passed, and what aspect of the U.S. Constitution did it change? Do you think it was a good amendment, or should it be repealed?

5. When the federal income tax was introduced, who were expected to be the people paying the taxes?

6. How did the income tax serve to increase the power of the federal government over the states?

7. Why do income taxes, Social Security taxes, and Medicare taxes on factory workers cause U.S. products to be less competitive on world markets? Do these taxes violate the principles of free trade?

8. Discuss how changing from income taxes to sales taxes would affect production in the United States. How would this change affect consumption? How would it affect the size of the IRS?

9. Why is a property tax on improvements an incentive to let property run down? How could this problem be corrected?

10. Do you believe that the federal government should collect taxes from individual citizens, or should this be the job of the states?

9

Welfare

When states compete, the citizens win.
—Adapted from the Lending Tree slogan[1]

The Uncontrolled Escalation of Federal Welfare

Social welfare is one of the most expensive and most contentious areas of government. Traditionally, all social welfare was handled by families, churches, and community organizations. During the nineteenth century, there arose many benevolent societies in the United States, organized for purposes of fighting various social problems such as slavery, poverty, prisons, alcohol, education, women's rights, and peace. The industrialization of the United States created other problems like slums, child labor, unsafe workplaces, and low wages that people felt required government laws to protect workers. The Social Gospel movement arose as mainline churches and social progressives began to promote labor laws and welfare programs.

In the 1870s, charity organizations began to develop professional caseworkers at local government almshouses and asylums. By the 1920s, many universities began offering Social Work degrees, and a professional class of social workers that were not tied to religious and charitable organization emerged. This group of professionals constituted a special interest and resource related to improving government welfare services. They were often employed in government services at the local and state levels. Before 1920, there were no federal payments to states or individuals.[2]

Federal welfare and entitlement payments began during the New Deal. They have escalated dramatically since then. First of all, the Sixteenth Amendment allowed the collection of income tax. This provided a new source of federal revenue that citizens thought could be spent on social welfare. Secondly, the Seventeenth Amendment had allowed citizens to directly elect senators. This made the Senate accountable to citizens, rather than to states. The combined result of these two actions was to create a federal government more in direct relation to citizens than either the federation under the Articles of Confederation or the hybrid system of government produced by the Constitution. This new form of government led to direct taxation of citizens and payments to them without a state in the middle as a buffer. Rather, the states got pushed aside. The structure that was created did not have appropriate fiscal controls and easily grew out of control.

By 2008, 57.7 percent of the U.S. budget went to some type of social welfare: Social Security, Medicare, Medicaid, Welfare, Health and Human Services, and Education. Most of these expenses are classified as mandatory. Congress is contractually obligated to pay these expenses. The only other mandatory federal expense is interest on the debt. Of the $2.9 trillion 2008 budget, $1.79 trillion was mandatory, and $1.14 trillion was discretionary.[3] These mandatory social welfare expenditures are frequently referred to as entitlements. These are increasing at an unsustainable rate.

None of these mandatory expenses existed before 1935. If the percentage of mandatory expenses in the budget would continue to increase at the rate they have increased since 1962, by 2070, about 95 percent of all expenditures would be mandatory payments, leaving almost no discretionary funds for defense spending and basic government operations.[4] Social Security and Medicare expenses are expected to increase at a higher rate than this due to the increasing percentage of the retired population. In 1960 there were over five persons paying into Social Security funds for each person receiving them. In 2000, there were about 3.3 workers per recipient. By 2030, this amount is projected to drop to about two workers per recipient. At current rates, payments will exceed income in 2017. To keep the current system solvent, the percentage of Social Security tax on personal income would have to increase to about 41 percent by 2041.[5] Medicare and Medicaid are growing at faster rates than Social Security. Medicare taxes will need to increase to 8 percent by 2040 to retain solvency.[6] Medicaid would need to increase about three-fold to 4.3 percent. If you add to these increases a 28 percent federal tax and a 9 percent average state tax, the average wage earners would pay 90.3 percent of their income on taxes. This is before sales taxes, user fees, and other types of taxes.

Obviously this system is unsustainable. By 2040, the government would entirely control everyone's income, essentially making everyone a slave or forcing them into a black market. Since people need about 33 percent of their income available to secure a mortgage on a house, and one needs other money for groceries and other living expenses, if citizens are taxed over 90 percent, they will be homeless and hungry.

There is a physical law that output cannot exceed input. In the logic of the present system, that would mean more taxes for more subsidized housing and food. Where would that money come from? By 2070, the mandatory payments would consume virtually all of government income, leaving no discretionary spending, and thus little purpose for the Congress or any other federal departments, including the Department of Defense.

> **If you add to these increases a 28 percent federal tax and a 9 percent average state tax, the average wage earner would pay 90.3 percent of their income on taxes. This is before sales taxes, user fees, and other types of taxes.**

Can this dysfunctional system be fixed? Can the present system be reformed? The solution in Hitler's Germany turned to the elimination of "surplus populations."[7] This is a totalitarian government solution, a form of rationing, the rationing of human life, the ultimate progression of unchecked government. Can we return to greater subsidiarity where people, as much as possible, are responsible for their own welfare? Or, are we faced with social breakdown and genocide?

Personal Responsibility

A philosophy of life, liberty, and the pursuit of happiness is one in which people are free to determine their own future. This means they should be able to plan and work for where they live, how they will earn money, what kind of house they live in, what kind of groups they join, what kind of healthcare they desire, and what kind of retirement they will have. Freedom requires responsibility. If one cannot care for oneself or plan for future retirement, one will either become dependent on someone else or die. No society is made up of working people only. There are children, elderly, disabled, and other members of society who have to depend upon others. In traditional societies, the extended family is the basic unit of social welfare.

A system of government that takes a citizen's resources in the form of a tax and redistributes it according to a government plan is socialism. The opposite extreme is the kind of libertarian individualism portrayed by Ayn Rand in *Atlas Shrugged*.[8] In that book, there are no children, disabled, or retired people. The goal is for everyone to live for themselves, competing with everyone else through hard work and ingenuity, building their own empire. Her libertarianism presumes that this individualism will create the best goods and services and the greatest amount of national wealth and personal happiness. In reality, human beings are both individuals and social beings.

Do individuals have social responsibility, or is all social responsibility the role of the government? In a society based on subsidiarity, the answer is that individuals have the primary responsibility for both themselves and others in their community. If they cannot or do not take that responsibility, the next highest government has to step in.

Freedom and Taxes

The percentage of income that one keeps compared to the percentage one pays in taxes to government is a good indicator of where a society falls on the scale between libertarianism and socialism. With respect to the history of U.S. taxation of individuals, we could say that it has moved from the liberty of letting states determine their own taxes toward socialism. In 2008, with federal general income taxes at 28 percent, state taxes at 9 percent, and Social Security and Medicare totaling 15.3 percent, the average middle income wage earner is 52.3 percent socialized and 47.7 percent free. While he pays sales taxes, gasoline taxes, and other user fees, he is free to do as he wishes with 47.7 percent of his income; the rest are compulsory payments.

The present system represents the will of special interests at the expense of the people. One of the easiest ways to avoid this problem is up and down votes on single issues.

Some will argue that these are not compulsory payments, but payments freely agreed to in the social contract. Representatives of the people voted for these taxes and payments. Therefore, they are a result of a free democracy. By now, the reader should understand that the present system of government does not usually pass legislation on the spending of money that represents the will of the people. Rather, the present system represents the will of special interests at the expense of the people. One of the easiest ways to avoid this problem is up and down votes on single issues. Moreover, the up and down vote should not just be a simple majority, but perhaps an overwhelming majority of 75 percent or more. In such a case, the action could more believably represent the will of the people.

In the system the U.S. founders designed, individuals were 100 percent free with respect to the federal government. One's social freedom was determined by state and local governments.

The only taxes an individual paid to the federal government were elective, because there were no fees or taxes on essential goods or services. Individual states were to be freely organized social systems by residents. If people did not like the laws of one state, they could move to another. Uniform systems of welfare across the nation were not part of the plan. State and local governments could compete with one another in providing the best place for people to live. This meant the right balance of taxes and services. The people would "vote with their feet." Such a system of competition among governments enables people to choose among governments and not be forced to accept the system they live under. The United States has promoted such competition among the nations of the world; it is time to put this philosophy more fully into practice at home.

Impersonal or Personal Welfare?

If responsibility for social welfare is given back onto the states, does the federal government have a role to play? Can we be sure that the bureaucratic states will live up to their responsibilities and not overlook people's needs? After all, the reason for the Fourteenth Amendment was for the federal protection of former slaves that states were not willing to protect. If people are seriously suffering or their right to pursue happiness is violated, when should a government step in? How should it step in? What kind of system reflects the best integrity?

The simplest strategy when there is a pot of money to redistribute is to take some of the money and hand it out to the person in need. This is a form of alms-giving that many religions have taught: "Give to the poor." The difference is that religions ask the rich to voluntarily give to the poor, while government uses force to redistribute taxes to the poor. This strategy contains several assumptions that are generally false. First, it assumes there is a pie to divide rather than an economy to grow. Second, it assumes the recipient will do the best thing with the handout. Third, it assumes welfare will alleviate the underlying problems that cause the recipient's poverty. Fourth, it assumes the recipient is hopeless and cannot become productive, or that the handout will make him productive.

This strategy of welfare redistribution is simple, because no person has to take any personal responsibility to help another who is down and out. It is also a strategy people wish could be true because they would like a bureaucracy to handle it for them. However, the only way a bureaucracy, by definition, can handle anything is impersonally. If the solution is not personal, can a bureaucracy solve the problems of poverty? The answer is no. Although bureaucracies prefer to handle such problems with impersonal redistribution like food stamps, subsidized housing, or welfare payments, such payments have frequently generated cultures of dependency in which the third or fourth generation of recipients are on welfare.

When cases get too bad, the bureaucracy often assigns social workers with the idea that such workers can give some personal analysis of how to help and build some personal relationship with the recipient. Social workers are almost always employed by cities, counties, or states. The federal government is too removed from the people to have some central office that could analyze and act intelligently on social worker reports and recommendations. But professional social workers, hired by a government, form very different types of relationships and have different motives than families and churches. Professional social workers generally work in departments that receive budgets from taxpayer dollars. These budgets have traditionally been based on the number of people that are served. Hence, the more people assigned to a unit, the more income it has. The less the people in the department have to spend on the recipients, the more they can keep for themselves. This arrangement is a structural incentive to keep clients on the roster rather than to get them on their feet. It is also a natural temptation for persons controlling the budget, who have a small monopoly, to behave as monopolists rather than competing to provide the best social service.

Families and churches have an opposite motivation. They have an incentive to get the person off their welfare and out of their house or mission and on their own feet. The more responsible they can make dependents, the easier it is on the family budget or that of the church. These voluntary institutions are more structurally motivated to get unemployed to work, to find good homes for orphans, and to get widows self-dependent. This is because they are driven by a conscience that says they should not spend money on themselves when their family members or neighbors are unable to care for themselves. However, they would prefer to have everyone in the community on their own feet so they would not feel guilty about spending a bit more on themselves.

Bureaucratic welfare does not remove incentives for dependency, but supports them. The goal of government welfare should be the recipients' self-sufficiency or their support by family and community organizations.

Historically, families and churches are not motivated to help if there is a government program in place to handle the problem. They want to see the helpless cared for and would rather if someone else did it. This is why the Social Gospel encouraged government welfare at the turn of the twentieth century. This sets up a social dynamic that works against subsidiarity in the welfare system, a dynamic that leads to greater social dependency instead of greater individual and community responsibility. This dynamic is financially unsustainable and leads to social collapse.

This dynamic is due to the fact that government and culture are two different organs in the social organism. Asking government to perform the job of culture is analogous to asking your brain to perform the function of your liver. As in the relationship of government to the economy, the ideal role is for government to serve as a referee, not run a business itself. So too, in the realm of social relations, government can act as a referee. Government can seek to create incentives for all people, or at least all extended families, to become self-sufficient. It can create incentives for individuals, families, and churches to help one another and not let loved ones become wards of the state.

The best welfare is personal welfare. Personal welfare is motivated by love within a family and care for one's neighbor. Neighborhood and community welfare has not always been adequate without state help. Some people fall through the cracks when communities and churches are expected to care for them because some communities lack resources and not all people even join communities. This was especially true of poor immigrant ghettos and the unsettled frontier in nineteenth century America. However, neighborhood welfare provides a higher ceiling than impersonal or bureaucratic welfare. This follows from the dictum that love completes justice.

Bureaucratic Support for Personal Welfare

We can conclude that personal welfare should be encouraged, and impersonal bureaucratic welfare only be used as a safety net. We can also conclude that incentives should be improved so that the implementation of bureaucratic welfare does not remove incentives for dependency, but supports them. The goal of government welfare should be the recipients' self-sufficiency or their support by family and community organizations. There is much need for innovation in this area, but some efforts are promising.

Government Support of Faith-Based Welfare

One approach to solving this problem, supported by both Presidents George W. Bush and Barack Obama, is government support of faith-based and community organizations. The intention of this support is to encourage the welfare work of community organizations that is more personal, while providing them some incentive to perform this work.[9] There are three major obstacles to implementing this program as it has developed.

The first obstacle relates to the separation of church and state, since many community service organizations are driven by religious faith. This needs to be overcome by some assurance that funds do not support the establishment of religion. While there may be some tendency for recipients to join a church that has helped them get back on their feet, such joining should not be viewed as government establishment of religion, so long as funds are available to any religion that engages in this type of welfare. Such support would be religiously neutral, but contribute support to whoever is most willing to help. The faith-based recipient would need to show that the government funds were, indeed, used for the intended welfare purposes.

> **The idea of creating government jobs to save an economy is an oxymoron. It is like a government buying cars for people who do not have them.**

The second obstacle relates to various strings attached to government funding that turns faith-based welfare into another government welfare agency with fully paid social work positions based on the number of clients served. These strings might include meeting federal hiring requirements for jobs. Such jobs create bureaucratic positions and limit volunteer service strategies that might include mentoring programs, or pairing needy families with a group of families that could share responsibility within a particular community, more the way state department sponsored exchange student programs work. The attempt to use the faith-based welfare system as a government jobs creation program is self-defeating, even though some additional positions within the faith-based communities may be created. The more personal welfare comes from providers who view their role more as a moral endeavor than as a job. The idea of creating government jobs to save an economy is an oxymoron. It is like a government buying cars for people who do not have them. Without an expanded economy that generates revenue, governments will be forced to reduce jobs or print money, causing inflation and further harm to the economy.

The third obstacle relates to subsidiarity. This problem stems primarily from the fact that the faith-based initiatives program has been federal, rather than a local or a state program. The first problem is that the federal government is too removed from the source to make informed decisions based on first-hand experience. Rather grants are issued based on the quality of the proposal or national lobbying efforts. A second problem that follows from this is that there is a tendency for consolidation of grant awards to national faith-based organizations rather than individual community organizations. Federal grants stimulate the formation of a non-governmental welfare bureaucracy, which, while officially non-governmental, becomes a quasi-governmental bureaucracy that is not different in incentive from the government welfare programs that provide the rationale to change to faith-based organizations.

After the first three years of implementation of faith-based federal grants (2002, 2003, and 2004), federal grants were already markedly shifting toward larger faith-based organizations.[10] This is a predictable result. It reflects the general problem of the difficulty of the federal government in preventing consolidation because it is a monopoly. It also reflects the tendency to provide funding to active lobbyists that have a presence in Washington and can develop a personal relationship with legislators there. Community-based organizations, those that have the most personal relationships with the needy recipients, are too small to have lobbyists in Washington. They need to become part of a larger group of providers represented by a lobbyist to be cost-effective.

Overcoming this third obstacle requires decentralizing the funding and decision-making process, removing it entirely from the federal government, and leaving it to the states and local communities. To the extent the federal government is required to be involved because it, rather than states, currently collects taxes for this purpose, it would be more efficient to distribute faith-based welfare funds to the states, apportioned by population. This would give each state a level playing field on which to compete with others in providing effective social welfare support.

Technology and Welfare

Today, computers can perform much of the traditional role of bureaucracy in analyzing forms and making decisions based on information collected. They can do it more impartially than human beings. Computers do not seek to expand their personal wealth or power. They follow the program they are given. It is much easier to program a computer to maximize efficiency than to program a human being to be unselfish. Computers cannot replace government, but they can help governments become far more efficient and remove traditional bureaucratic inertia in their position.

> **It is much easier to program a computer to maximize efficiency than to program a human being to be unselfish.**

Computers created a second wave of outsourcing in business. The first wave was blue-collar work based on industrialization. The second wave was white-collar work based on information processing. Like other machines that replace human labor, computers are beneficial to the employer but can cause the loss of traditional jobs, particularly in a bureaucracy. It is uncomfortable to replace employees with machines, however it is easier for a business to do this than a government. Businesses are determined by the financial bottom line, while government is determined by law. Businesses are far more likely to respond quickly to market pressures and reassign, retrain, or fire employees than governments. Eventually, governments will be forced to make similar adjustments, but only after much money has been wasted. Technology can increase government efficiency, and it is generally easier to reduce the labor force through attrition and retirement than firing. Computers should help governments balance their budgets better in the future.

Computerized decision-making is only as effective as the input the computer receives. Therefore, it is best if the input comes directly from the social worker or community organization in a direct personal relationship with welfare recipients. However, recipients will still have an incentive to submit inflated or fraudulent reports. This problem is usually better corrected if the process is local and the size of the funding pool is smaller. Abuse in such cases is easier to spot. This is a reason for computerized allocation of resources to also be decentralized according to the principle of subsidiarity as much as possible.

The Instability of the Social Security System

The Social Security Administration was founded in 1935 with the intention of creating a government program that would insure that retired and disabled people would not be indigent. As with other government welfare programs, it has kept many people from unconscionable destitution, but it has also become an inflated and inefficient program that has caused a number of unwanted side effects. It was designed for a society with different life spans, different forms of work, and different demographic factors. Rather than being a program that encouraged people to save for the type of retirement they desired, it encouraged people to put off saving, knowing that the government program would be there for them. It also encouraged more retired people to live on their own and eventually move to nursing homes, rather than moving in with other members of their families. As a result, increased needs for state funding of nursing homes and the less personal care they provide for the elderly is, in part, a consequence of cultural changes made possible by social security.

The major problem of the present Social Security system is that it is driven by the concept of funding present retirees with present workers. In 1935, when the program was begun, there were about eight workers paying for one retiree. The burden was unusually small compared to today where this ratio is heading towards two workers per retiree. A stable system has to encourage present workers to cover their own retirement. If this is done as a free society, it should be a system that enables citizens to choose their own form of retirement at whatever age they wish. However, it also should be a system that does not allow or promote unconscionable harm to befall irresponsible citizens who do not plan for their future.

Private Retirement Insurance

Social Security is a form of social insurance. With social insurance, society as a whole insures its members against various risks they all face, and members pay for that insurance through contributions to the system. Social Security is a social insurance program through which the government assumes some of the responsibility for a variety of risks that workers face regarding their retirement income security.

It is frequently argued that people who save for their own retirement should be able to opt out of the present Social Security system, placing more responsibility on the individual and creating a much smaller government program. Critics of this argue that individuals saving for retirement bear too great an investment risk.[11] They argue that personal savings can be wiped out by a bad investment or a downswing in the economy, as in the Great Depression when the program was instituted. Both those who argue for personal investments and their critics fail to understand that investments and insurance are not the same thing. Debates about investments are straw men. It is insurance, not investments, that is important.

> In 1935 eight workers paid for one retiree. Today this ratio is heading towards two workers per retiree. A stable system has to encourage present workers to cover their own retirement.

It would not be irresponsible for individuals to buy personal retirement insurance that provides the minimum guarantee that the government now provides. This would be a true privatization of Social Security. Many insurance companies already sell annuities that do this. While a number of annuities have a maximum number of years they pay out, true retirement insurance would have to pay a minimum amount regardless of how long the retiree lived. Different insurance providers could compete to provide this insurance, making it more efficient than the present system.

If private social insurance was owned by 95 percent of the population, this would mean that the $657 billion Social Security Administration Budget in 2008 could be reduced to about $32 billion. However, this $32 billion need not be entirely funded by the general budget. Government could still tax all workers who do not take care of their own futures. When citizens file their taxes, they could be required to provide evidence they have a sufficient personal retirement account in place, and this could be cross-checked by computer software. If the citizen did not have a minimum personal plan in place, then the government could impose a tax and pay into an annuity on his behalf. Such an imposition would not only reduce the remaining 5 percent burden on the general fund, but it would also be a further incentive to have one's own retirement plan, especially if the government plans yielded a lower result per dollar invested—as they usually do.

Both those who argue for personal investments and their critics fail to understand that insurance is what is sought. Debates about investments are straw men.

Most states require auto insurance in order to purchase license plates. It should not be much different to require proof of retirement insurance when one files annual taxes. This privatization process would take some effort to implement, as benefits due from the present system would need to phase out while a privatized system is phased in. However, such a system would eliminate over 20 percent of the federal budget at current rates, and those rates are destined to rise to unsupportable levels in the near future. Therefore, the sooner such a system could be implemented, the better it would be for the fiscal health of the nation. In addition, citizens would have more control over their own futures than they do now—and people are happier when they can shape their own future.

For a system of private retirement insurance to work well, the inflation in the overall economy would need to remain at low levels. It is always difficult for retirees to pay rising costs when they are on a fixed income. Another thing the government could do is provide some federal guarantee on these retirement accounts in a way similar to the $250,000 FDIC guarantee on bank accounts.

Out-of-Control Health Care Costs

The next critical area of welfare reform in the United States is the government expenses on health care. It accounts for over one-fifth of the federal budget and is increasing. These expenses approximately equaled Social Security outlays in the 1990s but, between Medicare and Medicaid, they are rising at a faster rate than Social Security.[12] There are more advancements in medical technology being developed and more demand that government cover uninsured citizens. The current system is forcing more people to become uninsured. Many young people are only able to afford to have a baby if they are on welfare, because insurance is too high. Therefore, the people having children are often those with the least financial ability to raise them.

The failure of the present system is causing more political pressure on the federal government to pay for everything in a form of socialized medicine. However, as one would expect from studies of human incentive, those countries that have socialized medicine, while creating a safety net, inevitably ration medical services and cause citizens to seek advanced medical treatment privately.

Controlling Government Expenses without Socialized Medicine

Advocates for socialized medicine argue that England, Canada, Sweden, and Germany are countries that provide decent health care. They may not provide as much care as patients request, or immediate care. They may not allow citizens to freely pursue their own health, but they provide some care to everyone. People in those countries live at least as long, on average, as in the United States. Critics argue that these countries build very few new facilities, are slow to adopt new procedures and drugs, and cause some needless deaths by rationing care. They point to patients in Canada who have to wait for months for a CT scan when they have aggressive cancer, or to patients coming across the border to the United States for hospital beds that the market automatically creates from Canadian demand, while Canada hesitates to build hospitals in order to control budgets. They point to people who try to get x-rays and medicine from veterinarians where there is no wait because animals are treated on a market system in Canada.

The U.S. government pays for more procedures and higher-priced medicine in its Medicare program than countries with socialized medicine. The major reason for that relates to the special interest nature of federal legislation.

There are many inefficiencies and excesses in the U.S. health care system that cause prices to be much higher than in other countries. One of the reasons is that the U.S. government pays for more procedures and higher-priced medicine in its Medicare program than countries with socialized medicine. The major reason for that relates to the special interest nature of federal legislation. In addition, the U.S. and state governments mandate that insurance companies cover more procedures and higher-priced medicine than countries with socialized medicine allow. Again, this is due to special interest lobbies, whether they are drug companies, the American Cancer Society, medical rights organizations, surgical groups, or hospital groups. These groups all lobby in ways that create standards for medical care that is inconsistent with the rational and time-tested standards accepted by doctors and adopted in countries with socialized medicine.[13]

Public advertising for wonder drugs and miracle procedures that can make one happier and healthier stimulate demand for medicine that should be elective by any rational standard. Yet this adds to the intensity to which citizen and medical interest groups lobby for Medicare, Medicaid, and health insurance coverage. While many of these new developments prove to be beneficial, many do not. Some later prove to be harmful.[14] It is not in the public interest to force the government or insurance to pay for such questionable procedures. This raises Medicare taxes and health insurance premiums, putting extra burdens on both the government and citizens that own health insurance policies.

> **It is not in the public interest to force the government or insurance to pay for questionable procedures. This raises Medicare taxes and health insurance premiums without proven benefit.**

While one of the main solutions to the health care crisis is to reform the way legislation gets passed, a quick solution would be for the U.S. government to adopt standards for what Medicare or health insurance companies are required to cover based upon the standards that Sweden, England, Canada, or Germany use in their socialized systems. Making this switch would eliminate the need for Medicare and health insurance to pay for procedures that socialized countries would consider unnecessary. This would lower health insurance premiums, making insurance affordable to a larger number of people, and it would reduce Medicare expenses. However, it would not cause the downside of socialized medicine, the rationing and delay of service, and the inability of a citizen to choose his or her own medical destiny. Optional treatments and more expensive medicines could be covered by supplemental insurance protection or paid out-of-pocket; they need not place a drain on the entire medical establishment.

There are some other issues that need to be considered in health care reform. One is the practice of defensive medicine. Much wasteful medicine is practiced in order for physicians and specialists to defend themselves from lawsuits. Much of this could be eliminated by passing legislation that only required the number of tests considered necessary in countries practicing socialized medicine. Failing to perform tests and procedures above and beyond this amount would not be subject to a lawsuit; only failing to perform essential tests or to perform such tests improperly would be grounds for a lawsuit. This would also reduce the amount of unnecessary defensive medicine performed at public expense. Again, such tests could be performed if the patient wanted them, but only if the patient paid for them directly or with supplemental insurance coverage.

Eliminate Third-Party Policy Holders

Another healthcare problem in the United States is employer-provided health care plans. These plans cause many unwanted side effects, even though they had short-term benefits after World War II. They evolved due to a unique set of circumstances as a way around government-mandated wage freezes. Because they are a third-party payer, neither the health provider nor the recipient has an incentive to control costs. The provider is motivated to charge extra for his services because he thinks the employer has deep pockets. The recipient is motivated to seek unlimited health care service without regard to cost because someone else is paying for it. The end result is escalating insurance rates for employers, to the point where it is unrealistic to pay for coverage.

Employer-paid health insurance was relatively cheap when it was initiated because, when it began, rates were based on market competition at the time. It also became very popular at a time when most U.S. citizens were employed by large companies. The outsourcing of industrial jobs in the 1960s and 1970s and the outsourcing of clerical jobs after the information revolution left the number of people employed by such companies dramatically reduced. Corporations that still pay such benefits are at a distinct competitive disadvantage and continue to fail as a result. The attempt by government to force employers to provide health insurance only makes the problem worse. It forces more layoffs, outsourcing, and business closings. Many companies have replaced full-time workers with part-time workers to avoid payment of health insurance. Others have turned all their employees into independent contractors, making workers responsible for their own health insurance. The result is a growing number of uninsured and under-insured citizens.

Because employers are a third-party payer, the provider is motivated to charge extra for his services and the recipient is motivated to seek unlimited health care service without regard to cost because someone else is paying.

The government is also a third-party payer. Governments and universities, which both operate with non-market goals, are the last two remaining large sectors to provide the type of third-party insurance that developed after World War II. Such policies are also stressing the budgets of these institutions. Third-party health insurance policy holders are inefficient dinosaurs that have artificially raised health care costs. Government legislation that attempts to enforce this system is counterproductive and socially harmful.

Health Insurance or Health Care?

There is much confusion in political debates and in the media causing people to equate health insurance with health care. Many political lobbies intentionally try to obfuscate this difference as they use the rhetoric of "insurance" to pass legislation for "care." Insurance is what people buy to protect themselves against unforeseen calamities. Care is the day-to-day practice of activities necessary for well-being. Traditional automobile insurance is appropriately called insurance. It pays out for accidents that cause unforeseen damage to a car or for damages to a person or property. Automobile care includes changing oil and worn out or broken parts. Some automobiles carry warranties or the owner can purchase extended warranties that are a form of insurance against premature failure of major automobile components.

One can imagine the escalating costs of automobile insurance if insurance companies were required by law to pay for oil changes, headlights, broken belts, brakes, computerized emissions tests, and other repairs. It would not only be more expensive because of the increased numbers of payouts, but because of the tremendous bureaucracy the processing of all that paperwork would require. Affordable automobile insurance policies do not cover standard auto care. Rather, they do the opposite. They charge a deductible amount, which the policyholder must pay on each claim on damage. This serves as a deterrent to make trivial claims and forces the policyholder to be more responsible in his or her driving habits.

This same principle applies to health costs. Health insurance with a high deductible amount will cover unforeseen health problems like heart attacks, cancer, and hip replacements after a deductible amount has been paid. This type of insurance costs much less than a full-blown health care plan that covers every doctor visit and test. Personal responsibility related to health care can reduce much of the health care cost in the U.S. health care system. Not only do out-of-pocket payments for routine care drive prices down, they also create much less bureaucratic overhead in the health care system. Although computers are now eliminating much of the paper processing for health care that was previously more labor intensive, deductible systems cost less money. High deductible health insurance causes people to think twice about running to the doctor because they are bearing more of the cost themselves.

Personal Health Insurance

Free-market personal health insurance is not only the least expensive form of health care; it is the form that allows individuals the most security and the most freedom. First, it offers security because one's plan stays with a person for life, regardless of where one is employed or if one has to change jobs. Second, it allows the most freedom because one can choose the type of plan one wants to buy and has more control over his or her own health destiny. Employers are also more willing to contribute a fixed amount to an employee's personal health insurance plan than to commit resources to participate in group plans with escalating prices.

Governments can assist citizens in obtaining such plans by exempting the premiums and the out-of-pocket medical expenses from taxes. They can encourage citizens to prepare for unexpected trips to the doctor by allowing individuals to own tax-exempt medical savings accounts. A wise citizen can then, over time, grow his medical savings account to exceed the deductible amount of his health insurance policy, and he will be fully covered, with a satisfaction that his health destiny is under his control.

A priority for reducing U.S. healthcare expenses and making health insurance more affordable would be for governments to provide incentives to employers to convert group plans to personal health insurance policies. This would also eliminate the need to have COBRA insurance that extends employer insurance by law for 18 months if one loses a job. Such insurance is often unaffordable for the unemployed. Combined with the adoption of new standards of coverage based on the experience of countries with socialized medicine, the transformation to personal health insurance and away from health care and group plans would greatly reduce health care costs and enable many more Americans to freely control their own medical destinies.

Patents and Prescriptions

There have been great advances in modern medicine that fight infections and diseases, help prevent heart attacks and strokes, and reduce inflammation and pain. It is important to encourage research and development of good medicines without creating a system that preys on desperation of the sick with false promises. Unfortunately, the U.S. political system has allowed the pharmaceutical companies to become legitimized "snake-oil" salesmen through the persuasion of pharmaceutical industry lobbies. Ironically, it was the scientific medical community that made it illegal for the nineteenth century "snake-oil" salesmen to sell their unregulated bitters and elixirs, often out of the back-end of a horse-drawn wagon, to uneducated and desperate citizens. Yet, today "scientific" companies pitch their patented cures for everything from erectile dysfunction to better heart protection on television and radio advertising. Many of these medicines provide little medical benefit, and many are forced out of the market when patterns of death and other unwanted side effects have been discovered.[15] But by that time, the excessive profits (protected by patents) are long gone.

Patent protection stimulates companies to bring products to market prematurely and to charge excessively for the product while it is under protection. They are motivated to advertise new and unproven drugs heavily while they are under protection because profits can be very high.

Patents provide monopoly status while they are in force. They provide a very strong incentive to research and produce new drugs. But the approval process is lengthy and can be expensive. The existence of patents stimulates companies to bring insufficiently tested products to market prematurely and to charge excessively for the product while it is under patent protection. Companies are also motivated to advertise new drugs heavily while they are under patent protection because profits can be very high. Many of these drugs do not develop a successful track record and are pulled off the market.

Those companies that produce and sell modern medicine are driven by profit, like any company. While many people go to work for these companies out of the hope of helping others by finding cure for diseases, the financial managers and CEOs are driven to increase the value of shares on the stock exchange and other financial factors. It is the role of government to referee this activity. Conflicts of interest and financial incentives exist that must be reduced.

One problem is that pharmaceutical companies want to sell as much medicine as they can. To do this, they advertise their prescription drugs to all consumers. However, the original purpose behind doctor's prescribing drugs is that there are possible harmful side effects, doses should be limited and controlled for some reason, and they should only be prescribed for particular illnesses. In order to protect citizens from possible harmful side effects, a licensed physician is required to make the best decision after his diagnosis. Advertising directly to consumers interferes with this process, as does providing kickbacks or retreats to doctors that prescribe the medicine. Such financial incentives increase sales at the expense of medical objectivity. When these incentives are not properly controlled, the end result is unnecessary medical costs and risks to health.

In 1997, the U.S. Food and Drug Administration (FDA) first allowed radio and television advertising of prescription drugs. Total spending on direct-to-consumer (DTC) advertising in the U.S. increased from about $1 billion in 1996 to $4 billion in 2005.[16] Between 1997 and 2001, DTC advertising spending increased 145 percent, while research and development spending increased 59 percent. Drugs that are promoted directly to consumers are among the best-selling drugs. Between 1999 and 2000, the number of prescriptions dispensed for the most heavily advertised drugs rose 25 percent, but increased only 4 percent for drugs that were not heavily advertised.[17] The FDA action that allowed advertising undermined the designed prescription process.

Pharmaceutical companies are also competing with natural foods and traditional medicines that are inexpensive and sold over the counter. Some of these products have proven health benefits, while others do not. But the drug industry is motivated to label such products as quackery and say that since they are not FDA approved, they should be banned. It is to the advantage of the industry to influence the FDA to ban competing products and approve their own products, even if they are no more proven than competing products. This requires the FDA to be a strong and objective referee who knows the rules, makes sure the rules are fair to all, and treats all players equally.

Adopting standards developed in countries with socialized medicine, without socializing medicine should combine the best of both worlds. However, such standards cannot be easily adopted without changing the way medical legislation is passed and medical oversight is conducted.

The FDA, like many federal regulatory agencies, fails to perform its regulatory task objectively because the personal relationships it has with industry leaders and scientists tend to outweigh the impersonal relationships with the mass consumers it is supposed to protect. As with other regulatory agencies, people in government positions often come from senior positions in the industry, and they will return to even higher positions when they leave their government post. This is a conflict of interest. It is not sufficient to have no income from an industry while serving in the FDA. Perhaps federal regulators should never serve in industry, but follow an entirely different employment track after college graduation. Current regulatory agencies, whether the FDA, the Nuclear Regulatory Agency (NRC), the Federal Aviation Administration (FAA), the Federal Communications Commission (FCC), and others often behave more like extensions of the industry they are supposed to regulate. Sometimes they act more like lobbyists than the protectors of the citizens they are commissioned to serve.

Sales of prescription drugs account for about 11 percent of personal health care spending. Since direct-to-consumer (DTC) advertising was allowed, prescription drugs have been one of the fastest growing components of health spending with double-digit increases (16 percent for 2000-2001).[18] It is an area where medical costs can be greatly reduced with better government oversight and with changes in laws governing the medications government health services and health insurance are required to cover. Adopting standards developed in countries with socialized medicine without socializing medicine should combine the best of both worlds. However, such standards cannot be easily adopted without changes in the way medical legislation is passed and medical oversight is conducted.

Conclusions

Welfare is primarily the responsibility of individuals, families, and communities. It is the role of the cultural sphere—families, schools, and churches—to do their best to make sure that citizens become responsible for themselves, their family members, and their communities. If this is done effectively, there is no necessity for government welfare. The degree to which people and communities fail to become responsible for social welfare determines the degree to which government is asked to step in. Government cannot step in without causing some restrictions on freedom, but there are strategies that government can take that encourage more personal responsibility and others that encourage dependence, less freedom, and ultimately bankruptcy.

Two major challenges in the United States today are Social

Security and Medicare. They were set up to protect elderly and disabled people from becoming destitute or denied medical treatments that could make them well. Most people agree that these are good goals. However, these programs were set up in ways that are inefficient and promote dependency and corruption. As a result, instead of reducing welfare—which would be a measure of success—they are increasing welfare at an unsustainable rate. These two goals of protecting elderly and disabled people from becoming destitute or denied medical treatments can be accomplished at far less cost and in a sustainable manner, if they are structured to push responsibility to lower levels of society and create incentives that encourage individuals and communities to take responsibility.

It would be far more effective to remove welfare entirely from the federal government and allow states to compete to provide the most effective welfare systems. This will bring the greatest amount of government services at the lowest cost, as does competition in religion or the economy. If the federal government remains involved, at least in a transitional phase, its primary goal should be enforcing standards and providing proper incentives to citizens rather than attempting to run programs.

A government that promotes life, liberty, and the pursuit of happiness should create a system by which that is best accomplished. Welfare is a proper concern of government, but neither anarchic freedom nor socialism is capable of accomplishing sustainable human welfare. Since the 1930s, United States federal government has increasingly adopted more socialist policies. Those policies have failed.

The Soviet Union failed in 1991 for many of the same reasons. Consolidated economic and political power, combined with undeliverable promises, created a system that eventually collapsed. It worked against personal incentive and forced a black market economy into existence. The final collapse of the ruble occurred when Soviet social security payments could not be met without devaluation. Suddenly retired people found their savings worthless, and many were forced to beg or sell items in the street.

The U.S. Constitution was established to prevent such developments. The founders knew that the success of their experiment depended upon a responsible people capable of freedom. This meant that people had to create a government and support it, rather than designing a system in which the government supported them. In the area of welfare, personal greed has conflated with compassion in ways that have produced a welfare Leviathan. The Leviathan of Hobbes was a Leviathan of political power. However, consolidated cultural power and economic power can also create their own Leviathans. Each type of Leviathan restricts the ability of people to pursue life, liberty, and happiness. The updates to that Constitution or perhaps an upgrade to a Version 4.0 that better protects against cultural and economic Leviathans is overdue.

Questions for Review and Reflection

1. When did state governments become involved with welfare in the United States? How was welfare handled before then? How did the founding fathers envision welfare to be handled?

2. How is the passage of the federal income tax related to welfare tax payments made by the federal government?

3. Why is it easier to defraud the federal government of welfare payments than state governments?

4. Explain the relationship between government welfare and dependency and why less dependency is created when welfare is provided by churches and other voluntary organizations.

5. In the 1950s Social Security seemed to work well. Why will it soon become unsustainable without reforms?

6. Why are Medicare and Medicaid headed toward bankruptcy faster than Social Security?

7. Why do third-party payers, like employers and governments, cause health care costs to escalate and services to get rationed?

8. What is the difference between "insurance" and "care"? How could personal Social Security insurance and health insurance dramatically reduce the cost of government welfare and health care premiums without the truly needy suffering?

9. Explain why patent protections and the legal advertising of prescription medicines turn pharmaceutical companies into "snake-oil" salesmen.

10. Do you think that the federal government should be involved in health, education, and welfare? If so, in what way should it be involved, as a referee or as a provider? Why?

10

Implementation

When we speak of a city or state, we mean a community of like persons whose end or aim is the best life possible. The best is happiness and this consists of the exercise of all good qualities and their fullest possible use.[1] —Aristotle

Jefferson or Hamilton?

The different political philosophies of Thomas Jefferson and Alexander Hamilton, two of the chief architects of the United States, were never resolved at the founding. The Constitution they created with their peers enabled the people of their day to pursue life, liberty, and happiness. We have called that document "Version 3.0." It created a system of government based on the accumulated knowledge of Western Civilization, especially implementing insights of modern political thought and the analysis of political power.

Thomas Jefferson wanted to create a society where every family was an independent economic and political entity. He advocated an agrarianism in which each family owned a farm or a shop that would provide subsistence. He believed that this type of society, in which everyone took care of themselves and left everyone else free to do the same, was the ideal.

Alexander Hamilton, on the other hand, believed that a society with large scale industry and commerce could create wealth and a standard of living far beyond that of a Jeffersonian democracy. He saw central financial institutions like banks and a stock exchange as essential for raising capital for major social projects that would bring great wealth to the United States.

Thomas Jefferson envisioned a lateral society in which there were many self-contained social units working side-by-side; Hamilton wanted to create a more hierarchal social organism with various social organs that formed specialized functions. Jefferson warned that such political systems inevitably become corrupt. Hamilton argued that it was worth the risk; an organized national society could provide wealth and happiness that far exceeded that of subsistence farmers. Under the presidencies of Jefferson the agrarian and Jackson the populist, democracy was cultivated. Under most other presidencies, the philosophy of Hamilton prevailed. The Jeffersonian view prevailed in the South, while Hamilton's view prevailed in the industrial North. The Supreme Court generally sided with Hamilton and, after the Civil War, the nation was indelibly put on that path.

This book argues that neither view was totally satisfactory. Jefferson's fears of centralization and abuse of power were accurate. However, Hamilton's idea of society as a social organism proved capable of creating far greater prosperity and wealth than individuals functioning as a jack of all trades, living lives of subsistence separately from one another. As with the human body that contains many specialized organs, the entire organism is capable of much more than a single celled animal like an amoeba. However, the Hamiltonian vision came at the expense of democracy and freedom.

Can a Hamiltonian Society have Freedom?

The real political problem for Life, Liberty and the Pursuit of Happiness, V. 4.0 is how to structure a hierarchical social organism in a way that individual cells freely pursue their own well-being within the limits of a healthy organism. Can individual members of society have maximum personal freedom and responsibility without either dropping out of society into a cabin on the frontier, or becoming like cancer cells that attempt to acquire knowledge, power, and money in ways that end up oppressing or destroying others in one's pursuit of life, liberty, and happiness? My answer is yes, but it requires additions to the Constitution as well as the elimination of many viruses that have crept in.

In Chapter Four, it is explained that the separation of powers includes the separation of all social organs that perform different functions. This extends beyond political power to economic power and knowledge power. But the separation of these powers cannot be "walls of separation" that completely isolate the various organs of society from one another. Rather, it is more apt to refer to separation of function of organs and the role each organ plays within the entire social system. In this social organism, government performs a role like the nervous system, providing both peripheral and centralized regulation of various organs, as well as the entire organism. The example of the regulation of traffic on the highway system is used to explain how traffic rules and regulatory mechanisms like signs and stoplights can increase the opportunity for all drivers to freely reach their destinations. Such a system is far superior to either unregulated anarchy or the centrally preprogrammed movement of each individual.

> **The separation of powers cannot be "walls of separation" that isolate the various organs of society from one another. The separation of the function of social organs has to be considered with respect to the well-being of the entire social organism.**

Freedom and Complexity

Another example of a system whose complexity can create greater freedom and pursuit of happiness is a word-processor. Compare the ease of writing on a word-processor to a typewriter. Then, imagine how much easier that is than carving a letter in a stone.

Then, think forward about the opportunities created by improvements that make word processors more complex, like built-in spell checkers, typesetting styles, and multi-national character sets. These developments make it easier for people to communicate their ideas with one another.

However, each new word processing macro created to assist one's pursuit of happiness in writing is a potential opportunity for a software virus to exploit. It can become an opportunity for misuse by the new power it gives to the user. It can also become an opportunity for sabotage by remotely hijacking its power. Such viruses can slow down computers or lock them up. They can hijack a computer and send out messages to the owner's contacts that sabotage the relationship the word processor was purchased to build. The creators of the macros and the users of their word processors have to be constantly vigilant to watch for such viruses and protect against them with anti-virus software and patches when they emerge.

The laws of a government are like the operating system of a computer. They create the flow of the various forms of social power, while software directs the flow of information.

This general principle also applies to legislation. It is common to say "every law is an opportunity for corruption." The laws of a government are like the operating system of a computer. Laws create the flow of the various forms of social power, while software directs the flow of information. The U.S. Constitution did not provide all the necessary checks and balances for the complex society that we have created on the foundation of their political operating system. They gave more freedom and opportunity to people than was previously known. Yet its principles were often lost on those who made new laws, and the new laws were more often forms of viruses rather than improvements that would advance the usefulness of government for its citizens.

Basic Principles of Version 4.0

This book has discussed five basic principles of good governance for life, liberty, and pursuit of happiness version 4.0. They are (1) protection of citizens and society, (2) subsidiarity, (3) separation of powers or functions, (4) transparency, and (5) the right to secede.

The founders believed that one's body, one's material property, and one's intellectual property were to be protected by government. Protection of one's body from arbitrary arrest and imprisonment, while not perfectly implemented, remains a national goal. However, the legal system has been complicated by requirements for rules of evidence, jury selection, and other changes that often have turned court proceedings into expensive legal gladiatorial contests in which the most skilled lawyer, not justice, is too often the winner.[2]

The First Amendment protections of freedom of religion, freedom of speech, freedom of press, and freedom of assembly all serve to guarantee freedom of information and to prevent a government from maintaining control of knowledge. Knowledge and information are a form of power that can be used to harm others. While physical force can immediately put an end to one's physical life or restrict physical movements necessary for the pursuit of happiness, control of information can send people the wrong direction in their pursuit of happiness. While most Americans understand the perverse effects imposing official truth, in the chapters on Congress and taxes and welfare, many examples were given about how inadequate or wrong information led to the passage of legislation that only benefitted minority interests at the expense of the well-being of society and its citizens. This principle has been expanded in the chapter on transparency to include protection from the harm that hiding information gives someone with unjust political or economic power.

While Jefferson understood the dangers inherent in economic monopolies, safeguards against them were not written into the Constitution. Some legislation, like the Sherman and Clayton

Anti-trust acts and the securities and banking regulations introduced in the New Deal, was designed to promote economic freedom and a level playing field. But on the whole, the economic sector has not functioned most efficiently or fairly. Concentrations of economic power have unduly influenced and corrupted not only specific legislation, but also the entire legislative process. This includes the passage of several constitutional amendments that removed protections the founders had put in place, and the creation of a legislative process in which the special interests agree to cooperate in order to gain what they want at the expense of the "forgotten man." These perversions can be combated with subsidiarity, transparency, single issue legislation, and increased separation of commerce and the state, which serves neither as a bystander nor a player, but as a referee.

Subsidiarity, or the principle of giving responsibility to the lowest level possible, is the corollary of freedom. Freedom entails voluntary social responsibility. The absence of this voluntary effort leads to some form of government-enforced social welfare. The farther removed government control is from those it is intended to serve, the less effective it will be. This stems from the fact that rational welfare is not as satisfactory as personal care. Rational welfare may be better than the irresponsible personal behavior that abuses ones neighbor, exploits them, or simply ignores them when they need assistance. However, the further removed the government is from those it is intended to serve and the more concentrated its power, the more inefficient and corrupt it is likely to become.

The separation of powers in Life, Liberty, and the Pursuit of Happiness, Version 4.0 is more than just the separation of three branches of government and the separation of church and state. It is also the separation of state and commerce and of church and commerce. And, within commerce, separation of powers through subsidiarity and competition on a fair playing field are important. Within the sphere of culture, neither science nor religion can claim to represent the entirety of knowledge related to human and social values. Each social organ should be appropriately separated and interrelated by function.

Planning for Competition

One hallmark of a government of Life, Liberty, and the Pursuit of Happiness, Version 4.0 is planning for competition. With the absence of government, the strongest win. There is no social contract, only a "state of nature." However, a government that centrally plans some division of the social pie for each person creates an iron cage that prevents freedom, stifles economic growth, or rejects creative responses to social challenges. Such static societies do not adapt and are forced out of existence by time. The proven principle of creating the best solutions to human pursuits is competition, not just in the market, but also competition in ideas, competition among religions, and competition among governments.

The U.S. founders accepted the competition among the states as a given. However, over time, state power was consolidated into the federal government where a monopoly on political power exists. Citizens and states living under these conditions are both trapped in whatever cage a government monopoly builds. However, competition between states, when refereed by an impartial federal government, holds out much hope for successful reform. The competition among states and local governments for citizens, if refereed fairly, can produce efficiency and excellence in function on par with the efficiency of a competitive economy, or competitive religions and cultural systems. World history shows that cultures adapt and change when new ideas and technologies are able to be introduced. Ideas that work stick around, unless they are eliminated by political force, as in the confiscation of books or the burning of libraries. Societies that prevent competing ideas from emerging become static, ingrown, and often demonic in their persecutions.

Neither a simplistic laissez-faire economy nor communism help the average citizen in the pursuit of life, liberty, and happiness. Allowing each person an opportunity to create a rewarding life for themselves is like unleashing a mature cell from the bone marrow into the bloodstream where it will eventually locate an organ to support in the performance of a beneficial social function.

However, while free societies are a social organism, they are more flexible and adaptable that the genetically programmed cells in the body. Free human beings can find new functions to perform, thus expanding the complexity of the system, whereas the organs of the human body have remained essentially the same for thousands of years.

Implementing Reforms

In this book, I have stated that principles trump particular laws and structures but, throughout the book, a number of reforms based on the principles outlined have been suggested. This book was begun before the economic crash of 2008, yet it was quite simple to analyze the weaknesses and predict the result of the TARP bailout and other attempts by the federal government to solve our problems. It simply furthered consolidation of powers and the collusion of the governmental and economic spheres, the two major reasons for the crash in the first place.

> **To prevent catastrophic upheaval, reforms could be implemented gradually with the takeover of responsibilities by lower level governments being coordinated with the federal government.**

The primary challenge for the United States is to greatly limit and reduce the size of the federal government, its role in social welfare, its power to trump states' rights, its ability to impede the free functioning of the economic sector, and its ability to tax individuals and fund states on a non-apportioned basis.

Current problems arose slowly over a period of 200 years. To prevent catastrophic social upheaval, reforms should be implemented gradually with the takeover of responsibilities by lower level governments being coordinated with the federal government. Some federal programs (Social Security, for example) could be phased out as younger people convert to private insurance and new applicants are enrolled in state programs. Changing from a federal tax system to a state tax system would require a method where current federal non-discretionary spending would be covered by revenues the federal government received from the states.

Passing new amendments would require large popular support. Such measures would need to be overwhelmingly imposed on Congress by large numbers of enlightened citizens. Some measures related to commerce might be accomplished by normal legislation, while others (like the right to secede) would require an amendment that might take a long time to develop. However, the recent proposals for state sovereignty laws might indicate this change in consciousness has already begun.[3]

The list of reforms itemized below are all consistent with the basic principles developed in this book. Some of them depend upon one another. For example, the elimination of some taxes might require the addition of others in forms more favorable to human motivation, subsidiarity, and economic laws. And, certainly the repeal of the Sixteenth Amendment would require a tax structure other than the federal income tax to first be put in place. The elimination of corporate income taxes could be accompanied by taxes on corporate dividends received by individual shareholders. The conversion to private Social Security insurance would need to be accompanied by a phase out and conversion process for people covered by the present federal system. Requiring an up and down vote on all new legislation might be accompanied by a combined vote on existing legislation just being renewed for the new term.

Here are some types of legislation that would help bring the United States into a position more consistent with Life, Liberty, and the Pursuit of Happiness, Version 4.0:

- Repeal the Seventeenth Amendment so that state legislatures appoint U.S. senators.
- Repeal the Sixteenth Amendment.
- Pass an amendment giving states the right to secede under certain conditions.

- Pass an amendment that would eliminate the establishment of commerce or prevent the free exercise thereof.

- Eliminate corporate income taxes.

- Require dividend payouts as a criterion for corporate ratings, with a "B" rating requiring a 4 percent dividend, and an "A" requiring a 6 percent dividend to stockholders.

- Impose a sales tax on corporate mergers and acquisitions that consolidate economic power.

- Have individual states collect all taxes and fund the federal government with apportioned taxes on the states.

- Eliminate personal income taxes on the first $50,000 of income earned from wages, substituting with sales taxes and some progressive taxation on high incomes.

- Divide any federal payments for domestic infrastructure, like highways, in an apportioned manner among the states based on population.

- Outlaw political campaign contributions over $100 per individual and any contributions from organizations.

- Require an up and down vote recorded on each item of new legislation, outlawing the combination of any new legislation into bills.

- Have the individual states pay the salaries and support the offices, staff, and travel of any representative to the federal government.

- Set the salaries of all federal employees through the House of Representatives.

- Place all health, education and welfare programs in the hands of the states and lower governments.

- Require all working citizens to carry personal retirement insurance that pays out at current Social Security levels, or impound taxes for this purpose.

- Import Canadian standards of health care as a federal

guideline as to what Medicare will cover and have Medicare administered at the state level.

- Require no private health insurance policy to cover more than the government minimum, and allow health insurers to negotiate other ranges of coverage with citizens.

- Eliminate lawsuits against physicians that perform the minimum standard required by above plans.

- Allow full tax deductions for medical savings accounts, and allow them to be willed to children.

- Outlaw the public advertising of prescription drugs.

- Eliminate the principle of taxing improvements on property, but charge on land zoning only.

- Deliver any emergency bailout funds to the lowest possible level (e.g., local banks rather than national banks).

Some other possible legislation that was not discussed in this book, but would be consistent with the principles outlined in it, and could be developed elsewhere, are:

- Create a program of government service for two years after high school. These workers would serve as staff in government bureaucracies such as license bureaus, TSA stations, and other relatively low-skilled public service positions. They would replace many bureaucratic positions at minimum wage and receive funding for college after this service. They could alternatively serve as foreign Peace Corps workers or in the military.

- Outlaw political alliances or federations with other countries that do not at least have Life, Liberty, and the Pursuit of Happiness, Version 4.0 implemented (e.g., a representative government, and the right to withdraw from the federation or alliance).

- Do not provide any social benefits with public funds to

individuals who have not established permanent residency in the governed territory.

- States should subsidize any school or university only through tuition credits or payments on behalf of students.
- Create incentives for democratizing the electrical energy grid in the United States, encouraging individuals and cooperatives to supply the national energy grid with local power. Create tax incentives for geothermal power, which provides greater energy self-sufficiency for citizens.
- States should replace all funding for research with large prizes to successful competitive private enterprises after they produce the goal of the research.
- Create additional tax incentives for children to care for aging parents.
- Do not allow individuals incarcerated in prison or on welfare assistance to vote in state elections.

The Endless Possibilities of a Free and Open World

In a predetermined society, the government would decide what people would eat, where they go to school, what they study, where they will work, and what will happen to them when they are no longer useful. This is not the pursuit of life, liberty, and happiness, but the implementation of drudgery. It is like a choreographed Superbowl game in which all the moves of every player are programmed ahead, with the outcome decided. People might be willing to play the game if they get paid enough, but no one will want to watch it.

In a free society, people can decide to compete with others for positions in existing institutions, or they can branch off on their own, like pioneers founding new towns, to create something new. This can allow society to grow and evolve in exciting new and complex ways. If the pioneers succeed, new roads will get built to those towns, more opportunities will arise, and places for more people to live will develop. This complex society is not one of simple horizontal expansion like Jefferson envisioned, but includes the possibilities of cities and complex social organization envisioned by Hamilton.

Such a complex free society requires a political system that, at a minimum, promotes the principles discussed in Part I of this book. They are principles for the growth and well-being of a free society, much like air, food, and water are required to nourish the physical body.

A More Perfect Union

A society based first on these principles and second on particular structures and laws, is a society that can adapt and grow. The U.S. founders did not say the Constitution would create a perfect union; they said it would create a "more perfect union." They worked with the social conditions of their time; it was an upgrade to the Articles of Confederation that weren't functioning well. So too, today's citizens ought to work for a more perfect union. Was there ever a perfect computer operating system? Or a final version of a word processor to which no more bells and whistles could be added? Or the most efficient use of computer memory which could not be improved upon? To proclaim the final and perfect government is to proclaim an end to human creativity and the human pursuit of happiness.

In Part II of this book, suggestions were made to improve the present system. These suggestions were not considered the best, final, or only solution. Rather, Congress, taxes, and welfare were analyzed from the perspectives of the five basic principles, sometimes with suggestions to work with the present hybrid system of state and federal government, while elsewhere suggesting the creation of a more typical federation of states in which individual citizens only relate to states and local governments. Some suggestions are more easily implemented than others, and flexibility is generally a virtue.

Some types of reforms in Washington are urgently needed, as the present course of the United States is unsustainable politically and economically. Without a roadmap consistent with the basic principles of good governance that have been discussed, a Malthusian end is inevitable. Without a healthy and intact social organism, the maggots will feed on the carcass until it is eaten up. Then, the maggots will die. This was the fate of the Roman Empire and many other civilizations. It will likely be the fate of the American Empire unless the health of the social organism is revived.

Congress, taxes, and welfare were discussed because they are the most out-of-control components of society, steering the U.S. into a Malthusian future. The United States has a rich cultural history, an innovative people, and a strong work ethic. All of these things in the operating system of Life, Liberty, and the Pursuit of Happiness V. 3.0 initially flourished and led to unprecedented prosperity in world history. There are plenty of other issues that could be discussed, from energy independence to national defense and foreign policy. It is my hope that the discussion of these three crucial areas will help readers to think about social reforms from the standpoint of basic principles and human incentives.

Ultimately, there is no single way to organize a government that will allow citizens to pursue life, liberty, and happiness, even though there are natural and social laws that must be obeyed. All bridges do not have to be designed the same to provide a way for people to get to the other side. Microsoft Windows, MacOS, and Linux can all be made to support advanced word processing and other desired functions. But all bridges must obey the principles of physics, and all operating systems must be a bridge between the structure of the computer's central processor and the software the computer user wants to use. So it is with governments. In order to function well, they must be set up to interface between the natural and social environment in which they will be placed and provide for the smooth and efficient operation of other functions of the social organism that they serve.

Like a bridge, political systems can be stronger or weaker or more or less elegant. However, they must work with natural and social laws and the nature of the human beings they will serve. This requires a sound understanding of human nature and incentives. In any durable society, the physical needs of human beings must be met in some way. Also, the desire to grow and expand one's territory, wealth, and power should be refereed like a highway system that enables all travelers to freely go from place to place to place on ever-better highways and in ever-more comfortable and efficient cars.

This is the way we should look at the creation of governments. Governments are human creations that should grow and develop with human experience. They need to be protected against various viruses, yet improved in dimensions not envisioned by the preceding generations, and provide the best possible foundation for the generations to come. Our stewardship over the earth requires no less of us than this if we are to pursue our dreams and provide a world in which our children can do the same. In this sense, the creation of good governments, like other collective human endeavors, is an eternal quest.

Each generation has a responsibility to frame its government for the pursuit of life, liberty and happiness, according to the social, technological, and economic possibilities of their age. Our age requires, at a minimum, what is called in this book, "Version 4.0."

Notes

Chapter 1

1. Thomas Jefferson, "Letter to James Madison 1789," *The Writings of Thomas Jefferson, Memorial Edition*, ed. Lipscomb and Bergh, 20 vols. (Washington, DC: 1903-04), vol. 7, p. 310.

2. Thomas Jefferson, "Letter to Judge Spencer Roane, March 9, 1821," Ibid., vol. 15, p. 325.

3. Aristotle, *Politics*, ed.T.A. Sinclair (Middlesex, England: Penguin, 1962), book V, chapter 10.

4. Lord Acton, "Letter to Bishop Mandell Creighton in 1887," (http://www.phrases.org.uk/meanings/288200.html). Retrieved January 23, 2009.

5. Ron Paul, *The Revolution: A Manifesto* (New York: Grand Central Publishing, 2008).

6. Jesse Ventura, *Don't Start the Revolution Without Me!* (Skyhorse Publishing, 2008).

7. Immanuel Kany, *Perpetual Peace*, ed. Lewis White Beck (Indianapolis, IN: Bobbs-Merrill, 1957), p. 18.

8. Cited in, Forrest McDonald, *Novous Ordo Seculorum: The Intellectual Origins of the Constitution* (Lawrence, KS: University of Kansas Press, 1985), p. 188.

9. James Madison, "Speech at the Virginia Convention, June 20, 1788," in W.T. Hutchinson et al., *The Papers of James Madison*, (Chicago and Charlottesville, Virginia, 1962-1991), vol. 11, p. 163.

Chapter 2

1. Augustine, *City of God*, ed. Vernon J. Bourke (New York: Doubleday, 1958), p. 452.

2. Thomas Hobbes, *Leviathan: On the Matter, Forme, and Power of a Commonwealth Ecclesiasticall and Civil*, Introduction by Richard S. Peters, ed. Michael Oakeshott (New York: Collier Books, 1962), p. 13. Original text 1651.

3. Ibid., p. 240.

4. Ibid., p. 252 (emphasis mine).

5. Immanuel Kant, *Groundwork of the Metaphysic of Morals*, trans. H.J. Paton (New York: Harper and Row, 1964), p. 96.

6. John Locke, *Two Treatises of Government* (New York: Mentor, 1965), p. 395.

7. Thomas Jefferson, "Letter to James Madison, Dec 20, 1787," *The Papers of Thomas Jefferson,* ed. Julian P. Boyd (Princeton: Princeton University Press, 1958), vol. 12, p. 440.

8. Montesquieu, *Spirit of the Laws,* XVII, 2. Cited by W.T. Jones, *Masters of Thought,* Vol. II (Boston: Houghton Mifflin, 1949), p. 246.

9. Aristotle, *Ethics,* Book 1, Chap. 4, trans. J.A.K. Thomson (Baltimore, MD: Penguin Classics, 1955), p. 29.

10. Forrest McDonald, *Novus Ordo Seclorum: The Intellectual Origins of the Constitution* (Lawrence, KS: University Press of Kansas, 1985), p. ix-x.

11. Ibid., p. 11.

12. Aristotle, *The Politics,* Book II, Chap. 5, trans. T.A. Sinclair (Baltimore, MD: Penguin Classics, 1962), p. 64.

13. Friedrich A. Hayek, *The Road to Serfdom* (Chicago: University of Chicago Press, 1944), p. 183 and throughout.

14. Robert B. Reich, *Supercapitalism: The Transformation of Business, Democracy, and Everyday Life* (New York: Alfred A. Knopf, 2007).

15. Matthew 7:12. "So whatever you wish that men would do to you, do so to them; for this is the law and the prophets."

16. Kant, *Groundwork of the Metaphysic of Morals,* p. 30.

17. Sidney E. Mead, *The Lively Experiment* (New York: Harper and Row, 1976), p. 44.

18. George Washington, Oct. 1789 letter to the Synod of the Reformed Dutch Church of North America.

19. Reinhold Niebuhr, "The Spirit of Justice," *Christianity and Society,* Summer 1950.

20. Aristotle, *The Politics,* p. 64.

21. "Pew Research Center Surveys, 2002-2005" cited by Robert Whaples, *Modern Economic Issues* (Chantilly, VA: The Teaching Company, 2007), pp. 176-178.

22. Robert Whaples, *Modern Economic Issues* (Chantilly, VA: The Teaching Company, 2007), p. 169.

Chapter 3

1. *Merriam Webster Online Dictionary,* (http://www.merriam-webster.com/dictionary/subsidiarity).

2. "Selected quotes from Jefferson on Consolidation" can be found at http://etext.virginia.edu/jefferson/quotations/jeff1060.htm.

3. Pope Leo XIII, *Rerum Novarum* (Vatican City: May 16, 1891).

4. Pope Pius XI, *Quadresimo Anno* (Vatican City, May 15, 1931), para. 79-80.

5.   "Protocol (No 30) on the application of the principles of subsidiarity and proportionality," the Treaty of Amsterdam, October 2, 1997, *European Navigator,* http://www.ena.lu/protocol-application-principles-subsidiar-ity-proportionality-amsterdam-october-1997-020302471.html. Retrieved, December 18, 2008.

6.   One of the classic discussions of the effect of Protestant beliefs on wealth generation is R.H. Tawney, *Religion and the Rise of Capitalism* (New York: Mentor Books, 1954).

7.   John M. Todd, *Luther: A Life* (New York: Crossroad, 1982), p. 2.

8.   "John Calvin," *New World Encyclopedia* (http://www.newworldency-clopedia.org/entry/John_Calvin). Retrieved December 19, 2008.

9.   "Explanation of the Great Seal's Symbolism," *GreatSeal.com* (http://www.greatseal.com/symbols/explanation.html). Retrieved December 19, 2008.

10.   Jean Bethke Elsthain, "Philosophical Reflections on the Family at Century's End," in *The Family in Global Transition,* ed. Gordon L. Andrerson (St. Paul, MN: Paragon House, 1997), pp. 360-361.

11.   H. Richard Niebuhr, *The Kingdom of God in America* (New York: Harper and Row, 1937).

12.   Conrad Cherry, ed., *God's New Israel: Religious Interpretations of American Destiny* (Chapel Hill, NC: University of North Carolina Press, 1998).

13.   Frederick Jackson Turner, *The Significance of the Frontier in American History* (1893). This was first presented at the World Fair in Chicago to the American Historical Association.

14.   Alexis de Tocqueville, *Democracy in America,* ed. Richard D. Heffner (New York: New American Library, 1956), p. 63.

15.   Ibid., p. 107.

16.   Ibid., p. 60.

17.   Ibid., p. 129.

18.   Morton A. Kaplan, *Law in a Democratic Society* (St. Paul, MN: Professors World Peace Academy, 1993) pp. 78-89.

19.   Thomas Jefferson, "Letter to Joseph C. Cabell," *The Writings of Thomas Jefferson,* Memorial Edition, Lipscomb and Bergh, editors, (Washington, DC, 1903-04), vol 14., p. 421.

20.   The Ponzi scheme works on the "rob-Peter-to-pay-Paul" principle, as money from new investors is used to pay off earlier investors until the whole scheme collapses. "Ponzi schemes," U.S. Securities and Exchange Commission, (http://www.sec.gov/answers/ponzi.htm). Retrieved December 24, 2008.

21.   For an overview of the Social Gospel see, Robert T. Handy, *The Social Gospel in America: Gladden, Ely, and Rauschenbusch* (NY: Oxford University Press, 1966).

22.   Reinhold Niebuhr, *Moral Man and Immoral Society* (New York: Scribners, 1960), pp.xi-xii.

23. See Reinhold Niebuhr, *The Nature and Destiny of Man*, 2 vols. (NY: Scribners, 1943) for his systematic exposition of Niebuhr's teaching on human nature and human destiny.

24. Hans Morgenthau, *Politics Among Nations* (New York: Alfred A. Knopf, 1948), p. 11.

25. Jeffrey D. Sachs, *The End of Proverty: Economic Possibilities for Our Time* (New York: Penguin, 2006).

Chapter 4

1.   Aesop, "The Belly and the Members," *Fables* (Cambridge, MA: Harvard Classics, 1909-14.)

2.   Maintaining "freedom" requires acting within the parameters of natural law. For example, one is free to defy gravity and walk off a cliff, but then one dies and no longer has freedom.

3.   "Population of the Roman Empire," UNRV History (http://www.unrv.com/empire/roman-population.php). Retrieved December 29, 2008.

4.   Paul Halsall, editor, "Tables on Population in Medieval Europe," *Internet Medieval Sourcebook,* (http://www.fordham.edu/halsall/source/pop-in-eur.html). Retrieved December 29, 2008.

5.   "Europe Guide: Maps of Europe," Eupedia (http://www.eupedia.com/images/content/europe_religions_map.jpg). Retrieved December 29, 2008.

6.   Immanuel Kant, *Groundwork of the Metaphysic of Morals,* trans. H.J. Paton (New York: Harper Torchbooks, 1956).

7.   See for example, Gordon L. Anderson, *Philosophy of the United States: Life, Liberty, and the Pursuit of Happiness* (St. Paul, MN: Paragon House, 2004), or Christoph Sprich, "Equality Before the Law and its Role for Transition to Capitalism," *The Journal of Private Enterprise,* vol. 24, no. 1, 2008, pp. 79-94.

8.   "British East India Company," *New World Encyclopedia* (http://www.newworldencyclopedia.org/entry/British_East_India_Company). Retrieved December 29, 2008.

9.   Thom Hartmann, *Unequal Protection: The Rise of Corporate Dominance and the Theft of Human Rights* (Allentown, PA: Rodale Press, 2002).

10.   Thomas Jefferson, "Letter to James Madison," 1787. Papers 12:442.

11.   Aristotle, *The Politics,* Book VI, Ch. 4 (Baltimore, MD: Penguin Classics, 1974), p. 240.

12.   Lipscomb and Bergh, editors, *The Writings of Thomas Jefferson,* (Washington, DC: Memorial Edition, 20 Vols., 1903-04) vol. 7, p. 450.

13.   "History of the Republican Party," Mongomery County Republican Party, (http://www.mcgop.net/History.htm). Retrieved 2/28/2008.

14. Alfred T. Mahan, "The United States Looking Outward," *Atlantic Monthly*, LXVI (December 1890), 816-24.

15. IRS, "Corporation Income Tax Brackets and Rates, 1909-2002," (http://www.irs.gov/pub/irs-soi/02corate.pdf, viewed 2/28/2008).

16. See, Ron Chernow, *The House of Morgan* (New York: Grove Press, 2001), p. 203.

17. "NYSE Euronext Corporate Timeline, (http://www.nyse.com/pdfs/NYSEEuronextTimeline-web.pdf). Retrieved February 28, 2008.

18. Robert B. Reich, *Supercapitalism: The Transformation of Business, Democracy, and Everyday Life* (New York: Alfred A. Knopf, 2007), p. 139.

19. Robert McChesney, et. al., "The Big Six," www.freepress.net/ownership/chart/main. Retrieved April 20, 2009.

20. Greg Palast, *The Best Democracy Money Can Buy* (New York: Penguin Book, 2003).

21. F. A. Hayek, *The Road to Serfdom* (Chicago, IL: University of Chicago Press, 1994, originally 1944), pp. 45, 48.

22. "Reaching across the aisle" is deceptive political rhetoric frequently employed in the 2008 political debates to convince voters that legislation will serve all, even though it serves a minority of each party.

23. The concept of "The Forgotten Man" was developed by sociologist William Graham Sumner, *The Forgotten Man and Other Essays* (New Haven, CT: Yale University Press, 1918). The term was recently revived in Amity Shlaes, *The Forgotten Man: A New History of the Great Depression* (New York: Harper, 2008).

24. Alice Gomstyn, "Bailout Bill Basics: From TARP to Tax Breaks" ABC News, October 2, 2008 (http://abcnews.go.com/Business/Economy/Story?id=5932586&page=1). Retrieved December 31, 2008.

25. Robert B. Reich, *Supercapitalism: The Transformation of Business, Democracy, and Everyday Life* (New York: Alfred A. Knopf, 2007), p. 143.

26. Ibid., p. 214.

Chapter 5

1. Cognitive dissonance is a theory of cognition first proposed by Leon Festinger. It holds that two cognitions are dissonant if they are psychologically inconsistent. Dissonance is unpleasant and people try to reduce it by modifying their ideas or rejecting one and believing the other. See, Elliot Aronson, *The Social Animal* (San Francisco, CA: W.H. Freeman, 1960), pp. 99-157. This same theory was promoted in other terms by Ernst Troeltsch, *The Absoluteness of Christianity and the History of Religions* (Richmond, VA: John Knox Press, 1971), pp. 131-163, originally delivered in Germany in 1901. This is also the

basic premise of Thomas S. Kuhn, *The Structure of Scientific Revolutions* (Chicago: University of Chicago Press, 1966), originally 1962. It was in this book that Kuhn popularized the term "paradigm shift."

    2. Ha-Joon Chang, "The Stiglitz contribution," *bnet*, March 2002. (http://findarticles.com/p/articles/mi_m1093/is_2_45/ai_84152974/pg_1). Retrieved December 31, 2008.

    3. Ibid., p. 8.

    4. William J. Clinton, "Memorandum to Heads of Departments and Agencies, October 4, 1993 (http://www.freedominfo.org/documents/US%20whinitial.pdf). Retrieved December 31, 2008.

    5. Ibid.

    6. George Washington University, The National Security Archive (http://www.gwu.edu/~nsarchiv/NSAEBB/NSAEBB84/Ashcroft%20Memorandum.pdf). Retrieved December 31, 2008.

    7. David Banisar, "Overview of the FOIA," *FreedomInfo.org* (http://www.freedominfo.org/countries/united_states.htm). Retrieved December 31, 2008.

    8. "Declassification, Reclassification, and Redeclassification" powerpoint presentation, *The National Security Archive* (http://www.gwu.edu/~nsarchiv/nsa/foia/guide.html). Retrieved December 31, 2008.

    9. "Torturing Democracy," *PBS*, (http://www.torturingdemocracy.org/). Retrieved December 31, 2008.

    10. Coalition of Journalists for Open Government, Backgrounder: "A Review of the Federal Government's FOIA Act Performance," 2004 (http://www.freedominfo.org/countries/united_states.htm). Retrieved December 31, 2008.

    11. "Declassification, Reclassification, and Redeclassification," *op. cit.*

    12. Kenneth R. Gray, et al., *Corporate Scandals: The Many Faces of Greed* (St. Paul, MN: Paragon House, 2005), pp. 164-165.

    13. Ibid., p. 165.

    14. Adolf A. Berle and Gardiner C. Means, *The Modern Corporation and Private Property* (New York: Transaction Publishers, 1991), originally 1932.

    15. Michael C. Jensen and William H. Meckling, "Theory of the Firm: Managerial Behavior, Agency Costs, and Ownership Structure," *Journal of Financial Economics,* vol. 3, no. 4 (October 1976), 352-353. Cited by Gray et al., *op. cit.*

    16. "Standard and Poor's Dividend Yield since 1871," cited in Gray et al., p. 169-170.

    17. Richard M. Fagley, "The United Nations and Technical Assistance," (New York: National Council of Churches, Department of International Justice and Goodwill, 1949).

    18. Immanuel Kant, *Perpetual Peace,* ed. Lewis White Beck (Indianapolis, IN: Bobbs-Merrill, 1957), pp. 15-17.

19. Saladin Al-Jurf, *Good Governance & Transparency: Their Impact on Development* University of Iowa center for international Finance and Development, (http://www.uiowa.edu/ifdebook/ebook2/contents/part2-V.shtml). Retrieved January 2, 2009.

20. David M. Dickson, "Financial Transparency Sweeps Across Nation; States Shed New Light on Records," *The Washington Times,* August 11, 2008. Cited by W. David Patton, "The Time is Right for Government Transparency," Center of Policy for Public Administration, The University of Utah (http://www.imakenews.com/cppa/e_article001185210.cfm#_edn1). Retrieved January 5, 2009.

21. *Sunshine Week,* American Association of Newpaper Editors (http://www.sunshineweek.org/sunshineweek/orgs). Retrieved January 5, 2009.

22. "Who Guards the Guardians," *The Economist,* September 18, 2003 (http://www.economist.com/science/displaystory.cfm?story_id=2077493). Retrieved January 5, 2009.

Chapter 6

1. Joseph M. Champlin, "Ten Questions About Annulment," *Catholic Update* (http://www.americancatholic.org/newsletters/cu/ac1002.asp). Retrived January 6, 2009.

2. "New York's Ratification," *U.S. Constitution Online* (http://www.usconstitution.net/rat_ny.html). Retrieved January 6, 2009. (Italics mine).

3. "Virginia's Ratification," *U.S. Constitution Online* (http://www.usconstitution.net/rat_va.html). Retrieved January 6, 2009. (Italics mine).

4. "Rhode Island's Ratification," *U.S. Constitution Online* (http://www.usconstitution.net/rat_ri.html). Retrieved January 6, 2009. (Italics mine).

5. Thomas Jefferson, "Letter to James Madison, 20 Dec. 1787," *The Papers of Thomas Jefferson,* ed. Julian P. Boyd (Princeton, NJ: Princeton University Press, 1958), vol. 12, p. 440.

6. Michael C. Dorf, "Does the Constitution Permit the Blue States to Secede?" *FindLaw* (http://writ.news.findlaw.com/dorf/20041124.html). Retrieved January 6, 2009.

7. Walter E. Williams, "DiLorenzo is Right About Lincoln," LewRockwell.com, (http://www.lewrockwell.com/orig2/w-williams1.html). Retrieved January 6, 2009.

8. Thomas Jefferson, "Letter to A. L. C. Destutt de Tracy, 1811", *The Writings of Thomas Jefferson,* ed. Lipscomb and Bergh (Washington, DC: 1903-1904), vol. 13, p. 20. (http://etext.virginia.edu/jefferson/quotations/jeff0500.htm). Retrieved January 6, 2009.

9. Elizabeth Kelley Bauer, *Commentaries on the Constitution 1790-1860* (New York: Columbia University Press, 1952), pp. 61-64.

10   Quoted from Walter. E. Williams, *op. cit.*

11.   Henry Cabot Lodge, *Daniel Webster* (New York: Houghton, Mifflin, 1883. Reprint, New York: AMS Press, 1972). Cited by Daniel Gould in After "Non" and "Nee": Plans B, C, and D for the European Constitution (Institute for International Economics, June 2, 2005). (http://www.iie.com/publications/papers/gould0605.pdf). Retrieved January 6, 2009.

12.   Alexis de Tocqueville, *Democracy in America,* ed. Richard D. Heffner (New York: Mentor, 1956), pp. 66-67.

13.   Thomas Jefferson, "Letter to John Holmes, April 22, 1820," *The Writings of Thomas Jefferson,* vol. 15, p. 250.

14.   C. G. Memminger, "Declaration of the Immediate Causes Which Induce and Justify the Secession of South Carolina from the Federal Union, December 24, 1860," *American Civil War. com* (http://americancivilwar.com/documents/causes_south_carolina.html). Retrieved January 6, 2009.

15.   Harold Holzer, *Lincoln President Elect* (New York: Simon and Schuster, 2008), p. 172 f.

16.   Ibid., p. 107.

17.   James McPherson, *Battle Cry of Freedom: The Civil War Era* (New York: Oxford University Press, 2003), p. 310.

18.   Makubin Thomas Owens, "The Case Against Secession, *The Claremont Institute* (http://www.claremont.org/publications/pubid.171/pub_detail.asp). Retrieved January 6, 2009.

19.   In September 2008, U.S. Treasury Secretary Treasury Henry Paulson requested a bailout of $700 billion from the U.S. government on the argument that some financial institutions were "too big to fail." Whether this is a legitimate argument has been debated for years. See for example, Gary H. Stern and Ron J. Feldman, *Too Big To Fail: The Hazards of Bank Bailouts* (Washington, D.C.: Brookings Institution Press, 2004).

20.   Many resisted the bailout as a subsidy for the mistakes of the wealthy. Former Secretary of Labor Robert Reich argued "If They're Too Big to Fail, They're Too Big Period," (http://robertreich.blogspot.com/2008/10/if-theyre-too-big-to-fail-theyre-too.html). Retrieved January 6, 2009.

21.   Thomas Jefferson, *The Jefferson Cyclopedia,* ed. John P. Foley (New York: Funk and Wagnalls, 1900), p. 978. (Available at http://books.google.com/books?id=ZTIoAAAAYAAJ&pg=PT15&lpg=PT15&dq). Retrieved January 6, 2009.

22.   James Madison, *Report on the Virginia Resolutions* (January 1800), third resolution in *The Founder's Constitution* (Chagago: University of Chicago Press), chap. 8. (http://press-pubs.uchicago.edu/founders/documents/v1ch8s42.html). Retrieved January 9, 2009.

23.   Thomas J. DiLorenzo, *The Real Lincoln: A New Look at Abraham Lincoln, His Agenda, and an Unnecessary War* (New York: Three Rivers Press, 2003), p. 106ff.

24. Ibid., pp. 80-81.

25. Dwight D. Eisenhower, "Farewell Address to the Nation," January 17, 1961. Cited in "Military-Industrial Complex," *New World Encyclopedia* (http://www.newworldencyclopedia.org/entry/Military-industrial_complex?oldid=799558). Retrieved January 6, 2009.

26. Confederate Constitution, Article I, Section 8. Cited in DiLorenzo, op. cit., p. 240.

27. DiLorenzo, op. cit., p. 239.

28. Lord Acton, "Letter to Robert E. Lee, November 4, 1866." Cited by DiLorenzo, op. cit., p. 268.

29. Abraham Lincoln, *The Living Lincoln: The Man and His Times in His Own Words*, ed. Paul M. Angel and Earl Schenk Miers (Fall River Press, 1992), p. 170.

30. Walter Williams, op. cit.

31. "Review of Emancipating Slaves, Enslaving Free Men," *Publisher's Weekly* (Cahners Business Information, 1996).

Chapter 7

1. James Madison, "Federalist No. 62, 1788," *The Federalist Papers by Alexander Hamilton, James Madison, and John Jay* (New York: Bantam Classic, 1982), p. 315.

2. Gordon S. Wood, *The Creation of the American Republic: 1776-1787* (Chapel Hill: University of North Carolina Press, 1998, originally 1969), pp. 230-235.

3. Ibid., p. 244.

4. Forrest McDonald, *Novus Ordo Seculorum: The Intellectual Origins of the Constitution* (Lawrence, KS: University of Kansas Press, 1985), p. 228.

5. John W. Dean, "The Seventeenth Amendment: Should It Be Repealed?" *FindLaw,* Friday September 13, 2002. (http://writ.news.findlaw.com/dean/20020913.html). Retrieved January 7, 2009.

6. Ibid., p. 234.

7. Ibid., p. 237.

8. John W. Dean, op. cit.

9 "Treason of the Senate," *United States Senate* (http://www.senate.gov/artandhistory/history/minute/Treason_of_the_Senate.htm). Retreived January 7, 2009.

10. John W. Dean, op. cit.

11. Robert Whaples, op. cit., p. 49.

12. United States Constitution, Article I, Section 6.

13. David Bent, "James Madison Proposes Bill of Rights," *James Madison Center* (http://www.jmu.edu/madison/center/main_pages/madison_archives/

constit_confed/rights/jmproposal/jmproposal.htm). Retrieved January 7, 2009.

14. James Madison, "Federalist No. 62," op. cit., p. 317.

15. Hernando de Soto, *The Other Path: The Invisible Revolution in the Third World* (New York: Harper and Row, 1989).

16. Robert B. Reich, *Supercapitalism: The Transformation of Business, Democracy, and Everyday Life* (New York: Alfred A. Knopf, 2007), p. 139.

17. Michael M. Uhlmann, "The Supreme Court v. the Constitution of the United States of America," *Claremont Review of Books,* Summer 2006. (http://www.claremont.org/publications/crb/id.1121/article_detail.asp). Retrieved January 7, 2009.

18. Abraham Lincoln, "First Inaugural Address" (http://www.classical-library.org/lincoln/1inaugural.htm). Retrieved January 7, 2009.

19. Alexander M. Bickel, *The Least Dangerous Branch: The Supreme Court at the Bar of Politics* (New Haven, CT: Yale University Press, 1986, first ed. 1962).

20. The opinions on segregated education are primary examples of where the Supreme Court supported it in one decade and opposed it in another. Another problem is when the Court issues a decision on a social question where the citizens are divided nearly evenly, such as *Roe v. Wade.* Decisions on such issues do not stem from the Constitution and only serve to undermine the legitimacy of the government in the eyes of half the society. This is unnecessarily harmful, rather than waiting until an overwhelming majority of society accepts values.

Chapter 8

1. Benjamin Franklin (1789), cited from *Brainy Quote* (http://www.brainyquote.com/quotes/authors/b/benjamin_franklin.html). Retrieved January 9, 2009.

2. U.S. Treasury, "History of the U.S. Tax System" (http://www.treasury.gov/education/fact-sheets/taxes/ustax.shtml). Retrieved January 15, 2009.

3. Ibid.

4. Ibid.

5. Waples, op. cit., p. 139.

6. Ibid., pp. 138-142.

7. See for example, Alfred T. Mahan, "The United States Looking Outward," *Atlantic Monthly,* LXVI (December, 1890), 816-24. Cited in, Gordon L. Anderson, *Philosophy of the United States,* pp. 220-222.

8. The Sixteenth Amendment to the *U.S. Constitution.*

9. Sixty-Third Congress. Sess. I. Ch. 16. 1913 (http://political-resources.com/taxes/cc/IncomeTax1913.pdf). Retrieved January 15, 2009.

10. Thomas Piketty and Emmanuel Saez, "Income Inequality in the United States, 1913–1998," *The Quarterly Journal of Economics,* vol. cxviii, no. 1 (February 2003), p. 8.

11. *Congressional Record,* 61st Congress Session I, p. 1252, May 6, 1913 (http://www.simpleliberty.org/tait/riding_the_camel.htm#en01). Retrieved January 15, 2009.

12. *Congressional Record,* 61st Congress Session I, p. 3841, August 28, 1913. (http://www.simpleliberty.org/tait/riding_the_camel.htm#en01). Retrieved January 15, 2009.

13. Worthington C. Ford, Remarks to U.S. Senate, 1894 (http://www.cato.org/pubs/journal/cj14n3-1.html). Retrieved January 15, 2009.

14. U.S. Treasury, "History of the U.S. Tax System" op. cit.

15. Ibid.

16. Paul Studenski, Herman Edward Krooss, *Financial History of the United States* (Beard Books, 2003) p. 302.

17. Tax History Museum, "1901-1932: The Income Tax Arrives" (http://www.tax.org/Museum/1901-1932.htm). Retrieved January 16, 2009.

18. *Financial History of the United States, op. cit.*, p. 305.

19. Ibid., p. 302.

20. Ibid., p. 357.

21. Ibid.

22. Chris Edwards, "10 Outrageous Facts About the Income Tax," (http://www.cato.org/pub_display.php?pub_id=3063). Retrieved January 15, 2009.

23. Mark W. Everson, "Statement on the FY 2007 Budget," IRS (http://www.irs.ustreas.gov/newsroom/article/0,,id=154282,00.html). Retrieved January 15, 2009.

24. Donna Smith, "Study says most corporations pay no U.S. income taxes," *Reuters,* August 12, 2008, (http://www.reuters.com/article/newsOne/idUSN1249465620080812). Retrieved January 17, 2009.

25. "Magna Carta," *New World Encyclopedia* (http://www.newworldencyclopedia.org/entry/Magna_Carta). Retrieved January 17, 2009.

Chapter 9

1. This is an adaptation of the registered slogan of Lending Tree Financial: "When Banks Compete, You Win.®" (http://www.lendingtree.com). Retrieved January 22, 2009.

2. Gordon L. Anderson, "Social Welfare," *Philosophy of the United States: Life, Liberty, and the Pursuit of Happiness* (St. Paul: Paragon House, 2004), pp. 193-212.

3. These figures are assembled from information available from the GPOAccess website. "Budget of the United States Government: Browse Fiscal

Year 2008," Government Printing Office (http://www.gpoaccess.gov/usbudget/fy08/browse.html#budget). Retrieved January 19, 2009.

4.   David M. Walker, "Medicare: Financial Challenges and Considerations for Reform," (Washington, DC: U.S. Government Accounting Office, April 10, 2003), p. 11. (http://www.gao.gov/new.items/d03577t.pdf). Retrieved January 19, 2009.

5.   "Social Security Reform," (Washington, DC: U.S. Government Accounting Office, 2005.) p. 33. (http://www.gao.gov/new.items/d05193sp.pdf). Retrieved January 19, 2009.

6.   Cori E. Uccello and Ron Gebhardtsbauer, "Medicare and Social Security: Weighing Solvency" (Washington DC: Congressional Briefing, 2006). (http://www.actuary.org/pdf/medicare/solvency_may06.pdf). Retrieved January 19, 2009.

7.   Richard L. Rubenstein, *The Age of Triage: Fear and Hope in an Overcrowded World* (Boston: Beacon Press, 1983).

8.   Ayn Rand, *Atlas Shrugged* (New York: Penguin, 2004, originally 1957).

9.   Stephen Monsma, "Faith-Based Welfare-to-Work Programs Rely Less on Government Funding Than Secular Programs," University of Pennsylvania Center for Research on Religion and Urban Civil Society (http://www.upenn.edu/pennnews/article.php?id=182). Retrieved January 21, 2009.

10. Lisa M. Montiel, "Getting a Piece of the Pie: Federal Grants to Faith-Based Social Service Organizations" (Rockefeller Institute of Government and Pew Charitable Trust Research Project), p. 7. (http://www.religionandsocialpolicy.org/docs/research/federal_grants_report_2-14-06.pdf). Retrieved January 21, 2009.

11. "Social Security Reform," (Washington, DC: U.S. Government Accounting Office, 2005.) p. 12. (http://www.gao.gov/new.items/d05193sp.pdf). Retrieved January 21, 2009.

12. Cori E. Uccello and Ron Gebhardtsbauer, "Medicare and Social Security: Weighing Solvency" (Washington DC: Congressional Briefing, 2006), p. 25. (http://www.actuary.org/pdf/medicare/solvency_may06.pdf). Retrieved January 19, 2009.

13. Dennis Gottfried, *Too Much Medicine: A Doctor's Prescription for Better and More Affordable Health Care* (St. Paul, MN: Paragon House, 2009).

14. Ibid., pp. 86-88.

15. Gottfried, op. cit., pp. 51-80.

16. Allan S. Brett, *Journal Watch General Medicine*, August 15, 2007. (http://general-medicine.jwatch.org/cgi/content/full/2007/815/3). Retrieved January 22, 2009.

17. "Prescription Drugs: FDA Oversight of Direct-to-Consumer Advertising Has Limitations," U.S. Government Accounting Office Report to

Congress, October 2002, p. 3. (http://www.gao.gov/new.items/d03177.pdf).
Retrieved January 22, 2009.

18. "Impact of Direct-to-Consumer Advertising on Prescription Drug
Spending," Kaiser Family Foundation, June 2003, p. 2. (http://www.kff.org/
rxdrugs/upload/Impact-of-Direct-to-Consumer-Advertising-on-Prescription-
Drug-Spending-Summary-of-Findings.pdf). Retrieved January 22, 2009.

Chapter 10

1.   Aristotle, *Politics*, ed. T.A. Sinclair (Middlesex, England: Penguin,
1962), book VII, chapter 8.

2.   John Molloy, *The Fraternity: Lawyers and Judges in Collusion* (St. Paul:
Paragon House, 2004).

3.   For example, Minnesota House File No. 997, 2009-2010 Regular
Session. Short Description: Federal government memorialized to halt its
practice of imposing mandates upon the states for purposes not enumerated by
the Constitution of the United States and affirming Minnesota's sovereignty
under the Tenth Amendment to the Constitution of the United States. (https://
www.revisor.leg.state.mn.us/revisor/pages/search_status/status_detail.php?b=
House&f=HF0997&ssn=0&y=2009). Retrieved February 23, 2009.

Select Bibliography

Anderson, Gordon L., *Philosophy of the United States: Life, Liberty and the Pursuit of Happiness*. St. Paul, MN: Paragon House, 2004.

Aristotle. *The Politics*, trans. by T.A. Sinclair. Middlesex, UK: Penguin Books, 1974.

Chernow, Ron. *The House of Morgan: And American Banking Dynasty and the Rise of Modern Finance*. New York: Grove Press, 1990.

De Tocqueville, Alexis. *Democracy in America*, ed. Richard D. Heffner. New York: Mentor Book, 1956.

DiLorenzo, Thomas J. *The Real Lincoln: A New Look at Abraham Lincoln, His Agenda, and an Unnecessary War*. New York: Three Rivers Press, 2003.

Gottfried, Dennis. *Too Much Medicine: A Doctor's Prescription for Better and More Affordable Health Care*. St. Paul, MN: Paragon House, 2009.

Gray, Kenneth, et. al. *Corporate Scandals: The Many Faces of Greed*. St. Paul, MN: Paragon House, 2005.

Hamilton, Alexander, James Madison, and John Jay. *The Federalist Papers*, ed. Garry Wills. New York: Bantam Books, 1982.

Hartmann, Thom. *Unequal Protection: The Rise of Corporate Dominance and the Theft of Human Rights*. Allentown, PA: Rodale Press, 2002.

Hayek, Friedrich A. *The Road to Serfdom*. Chicago: University of Chicago Press, 1944.

Hobbes, Thomas. *Leviathan: Or the Matter, Forme, and Power of a Commonwealth Ecclesiasticall and Civil*, ed. Michael Oakeshott. New York: Macmillan, 1962.

Holzer, Harold. *Lincoln President-Elect*. New York: Simon and Schuster, 2008.

Jones, W.T. *Masters of Political Thought, volume two: Machiavelli to Bentham.* Boston: Houghton Mifflin, 1949.

Kant, Immanuel. *Groundwork of the Metaphysic of Morals,* trans. H.J. Patton. New York: Harper Torchbooks, 1964.

Kant, Immanuel. *Perpetual Peace,* ed. Lewis White Beck. Indianapolis, Bobbs-Merrill, 1957.

Kaplan, Morton A. *Law in a Democratic Society.* St. Paul, MN: Professors World Peace Academy, 1993.

Locke, John. *Two Treatises of Government.* New York: Mentor, 1965.

McDonald, Forrest. *Novus Ordo Seclorum: The Intellectual Origins of the Constitution.* Lawrence, KS: University of Kansas Press, 1985.

Molloy, John. *The Fraternity: Lawyers and Judges in Collusion.* St Paul, MN: Paragon House, 2004.

Niebuhr, Reinhold. *The Nature and Destiny of Man,* two vols., New York: Scribner's, 1964.

Rawle, William. *A View of the Constitution of the United States of America,* ed. H. Jefferson Powell. Carolina Academic Press; Second ed., 2009. ISBN: 1594605505. (original 1825, rev. 1829)

Reich, Robert B. *Supercapitalism: The Transformation of Business, Democracy, and Everyday Life.* New York: Alfred A. Knopf, 2007.

Shlaes, Amity. *The Forgotten Man: A New History of the Great Depression.* New York: Harper, 2008.

Whaples, Robert. *Modern Economic Issues.* Chantilly, VA: The Teaching Company, 2007.

Wood, Gordon S., *The Creation of the American Republic, 1776-1787.* Chapel Hill, NC: University of North Carolina Press, 1998.

Index

Page references in *italics* refer to illustrations.